A FAIR CHANCE IN
THE RACE OF LIFE

A FAIR CHANCE IN THE RACE OF LIFE

The Role of Gallaudet University
in Deaf History

Brian H. Greenwald
John Vickrey Van Cleve
EDITORS

GALLAUDET UNIVERSITY PRESS
Washington, DC

Gallaudet University Press
Washington, DC 20002
http://gupress.gallaudet.edu

Library of Congress Cataloging-in-Publication Data

A fair chance in the race of life : the role of Gallaudet University in deaf
history / Brian H. Greenwald, John Vickrey Van Cleve, editors.
  p. cm.
Includes bibliographical references and index.
ISBN 978-1-56368-395-4 (alk. paper)
  1. Gallaudet University—History. 2. Deaf—Education
(Higher)—Washington (D.C.)—History. 3. Deaf—Washington
(D.C.)—History. I. Greenwald, Brian H. II. Van Cleve, John V.
HV2561.W18F35   2008
378.1'9827209753—dc22   2008036708

CONTENTS

ACKNOWLEDGMENTS   vii

EDITORS' INTRODUCTION   xi

1   A Fair Chance in the Race of Life: Thoughts on the 150th
Anniversary of the Founding of the Columbia Institution   1
James M. McPherson

2   John Carlin and Deaf Double-Consciousness   12
Christopher Krentz

3   A Legacy of Leadership: Edward Miner Gallaudet
and the Columbia Institution, 1857–1864   22
David de Lorenzo

4   The Thomas Hopkins Gallaudet and Alice Cogswell Statue:
Controversies and Celebrations   33
Michael J. Olson

5   Two Views on Mathematics Education for Deaf Students:
Edward Miner Gallaudet and Amos G. Draper   50
Christopher A. N. Kurz

6   Douglas Craig, 186?-1936   65
Marieta Joyner

7   The Women of Kendall Green: Coeducation at Gallaudet,
1860–1910   85
Lindsey M. Parker

8   The Struggle to Educate Black Deaf Schoolchildren
in Washington, D.C.   113
Sandra Jowers-Barber

9   George Detmold, The Reformer   132
    Ronald E. Sutcliffe

10 Building Kendall Green: Alumni Support for Gallaudet
    University   140
    Noah D. Drezner

11 The Power of Place: The Evolution of Kendall Green   154
    Benjamin Bahan and Hansel Bauman

12 DPN and the Evolution of the Gallaudet Presidency   170
    I. King Jordan

    CONTRIBUTORS   189

    INDEX   195

ACKNOWLEDGMENTS

ARTICLES IN THIS collection are adapted in part from the presentations given at the conference "150 Years on Kendall Green: Celebrating Deaf History and Gallaudet," chaired by Brian Greenwald. The conference marked the celebration of the sesquicentennial anniversary of the beginning of deaf education on Kendall Green. On February 16, 1857, President Franklin Pierce signed into law an act authorizing federal funding for the Columbia Institution for the Instruction of the Deaf and Dumb and Blind located on property in the District of Columbia owned by Amos Kendall–the institution that became Gallaudet University. Over two and half days from April 11 through April 13, 2007, and despite an unscheduled six-hour electrical outage, presenters delivered about thirty papers.

No conference can be completed without the support, guidance, and encouragement of many people. Special thanks go to the conference planning committee for their commitment, diligence, and ingenuity. David Armstrong, Senda Benaissa, Billy Ennis, Gene Mirus, Joseph Murray, and Nicole Sutliffe were knowledgeable and congenial colleagues and committee members. The Schaefer Professorship Committee and the Gallaudet University Graduate School provided some financial support. Wendy Grande, of the Gallaudet University Press Institute, and Deirdre Mullervy, Valencia Simmons, Daniel Wallace, and Ivey Wallace, from Gallaudet University Press, provided staff, resources, and ongoing Web site support. All deserve thanks for their commitment to the conference. Sue Casteel of Gallaudet Interpreting Services and the conference interpreters provided exemplary service and skill. Brian Greenwald's former undergraduate advisee and student, Jeffery Peterson, did an excellent job excavating old photographs and assembling a slideshow. Robert Sirvage graciously volunteered and developed video clips of the Gallaudet presidents. Many graduate students, including Leah Abshire, Scott Reekers,

Sylvie Soulier, and Tiffany Tuccoli, helped attend to the minute details of conference organization and made the conference chair's job easier. Russ Olson, then chair of the Government and History Department, granted Brian Greenwald release time to focus on conference planning. Andre Pellerin assembled a fascinating photograph exhibit of Kendall Green at the Washburn Art Building, and Lindsey M. Parker wrote the captions. David S. Evans contributed in a very special way, writing blog posts for the Gallaudet University Press Institute Web site. His tireless work made it possible for people to enjoy the conference across the country.

Special thanks are also due to all presenters and moderators who came from near and far to participate. Their contributions have made our institution's history more transparent and challenged past interpretations of the people who studied and labored on our campus. The Gallaudet University Department of Theatre Arts contributed in a unique way, presenting Gilbert Eastman's classic performance *Sign Me Alice* for conference participants and the campus. Working with Willy Conley, department chair, and Angela Farrand, who directed the play, was an absolute pleasure.

The Gallaudet University Archives, particularly Ulf Hedberg and Michael J. Olson, contributed directly, graciously allowing students to comb through photographs and loaning paintings for the Washburn exhibit. Even more significantly, the vast majority of the sources for the articles that have been selected for publication are from the Gallaudet Archives. This record is a testament to the importance of preservation and to the value of Gallaudet University's financial and staff commitment to this purpose.

Finally, this conference, like all Gallaudet University Press Institute conferences, was made possible by the financial and administrative support Paul Kelly provided. Over a period of several years, Kelly, Gallaudet University's vice president for administration and finance, allowed Vic Van Cleve and his colleague David Armstrong to use whatever resources they could muster to sponsor a series of conferences and books to engage issues of importance to deaf people and to involve the Gallaudet community in scholarly endeavors.

Brian Greenwald would like to thank his wife, Rebecca, for her patience, support, and guidance through the short dinners and many hours spent away, planning for the conference. He also is grateful that his parents, Richard and Shelley Greenwald, took time out of their busy schedules to attend the conference. No less important, his wife's family, Judy McGregor, Doug McGregor, and Margaret Mattox, traveled to the conference to learn more about Gallaudet and deaf history. It was a lot for them to absorb, and he is grateful they accepted the challenge to learn more about deaf people, whom they have known for all of their lives. Finally, to Cam Czubek: while he's too young to read this book, it is also for future generations of Gallaudet students. Brian Greenwald endeavors to work to leave Gallaudet a better place for you than it was for him.

Vic Van Cleve's greatest debts are to the students he taught at Gallaudet, including the co-editor of this volume and two contributors to it; his colleagues, particularly those involved with the Gallaudet University Press Institute and Gallaudet University Press, David Armstrong, Michael Karchmer, Ivey Pittle Wallace, Dan Wallace, Jill Porco, and Paul Kelly; and his wife Deborah, who tolerated his work on this book, even during his retirement.

EDITORS' INTRODUCTION

GALLAUDET UNIVERSITY, located on Kendall Green in the northeast quadrant of Washington, D.C., is a long-standing, complex, and diverse institution. Simultaneously a world cultural center, a locus of research on deaf culture, history, and language, an experimental elementary and secondary school, and the primary higher education home of nearly every American deaf leader for well over one hundred years, Gallaudet's importance to deaf history cannot be overestimated. Yet surprisingly little has been written about the institution's history, its long domination by hearing presidents, its struggles to find a place within higher education, its easy acquiescence to racism, its relationship with the federal government, or its role in creating, shaping, and nurturing the deaf community. The articles collected in this volume, most based on new research in the Gallaudet University Archives, an unsurpassed repository of primary sources for deaf history, address some of these issues.

The following essays do more that just illuminate Gallaudet's past, however. They confront broad issues, such as the American struggle between social conformity and cultural distinctiveness, the nation's history of racial oppression, and conflicts between minority cohesiveness and gender discrimination, that are important to all students of American history. More specifically "deaf" themes, such as the role of English in deaf education, audism, and the paternalism of hearing educators, have their place as well.

Most of the articles that follow are critical of Gallaudet's past and its past leadership. Michael J. Olson, for example, suggests that the school's first president, Edward Miner Gallaudet, was duplicitous in his dealings with deaf leaders. Lindsey M. Parker finds that both Edward Miner Gallaudet and his deaf male colleagues at Gallaudet were more interested in maintaining gender boundaries than in liberating deaf females. Sandra Jowers-Barber and Marieta Joyner detail the institution's painful history of oppressing deaf African Americans. Ronald E. Sutcliffe accuses Gallaudet's leadership, before the 1950s, of collaborating in the oppression of deaf people and limiting their academic achievement, and Benjamin Bahan and Hansel Bauman argue that Gallaudet administrators have designed and constructed physical spaces on Kendall Green that ignore deaf people's needs.

A few articles are not critical. James M. McPherson, for instance, brilliantly situates Gallaudet's institutional history and nineteenth-century deaf history within the framework of American political and social beliefs and events. Christopher A. N. Kurz and Noah D. Drezner present narratives about the role and value of sign language and English in the curriculum and the school's complicated financial situation, respectively, without drawing conclusions that criticize the institution. David de Lorenzo applauds Edward Miner Gallaudet's accomplishments, recognizing the difficulty of planting the seeds that would grow into today's campus. Christopher Krentz addresses the issue of deaf self-consciousness, and I. King Jordan provides a brief memoir of his presidency, a period that changed Gallaudet forever.

Finally, we believe that criticism and praise, when grounded in historical fact and presented coherently, as they are in all of these studies, are both useful as Gallaudet University moves forward and as the deaf community continues to evaluate, redefine, and reconstruct itself.

1

A Fair Chance in the Race of Life: Thoughts on the 150th Anniversary of the Founding of the Columbia Institution

James M. McPherson

Editors' Introduction

In this essay, historian James M. McPherson weaves the early history of Gallaudet University into the broader context of American history. He begins by arguing that President Abraham Lincoln signed the legislation founding the institution because he believed that all people should have "a fair chance in the race of life." McPherson attributes Lincoln's vision to historical events and ideas, particularly the American and French revolutions, the Second Great Awakening, antebellum reforms, and Jacksonian democracy. McPherson then moves on to discuss the rise of oralism and shows that it, too, was rooted in specific historical conditions, particularly post–Civil War attempts to assimilate immigrants, African Americans, and American Indians. McPherson argues that "the American majority has not always manifested a pluralist toleration for the integrity and value of minority cultures," but he concludes that "creative tension between conformity and pluralism has helped to make the American deaf community the best educated in the world and to make Gallaudet University an institution without parallel anywhere."

ON THE FOURTH OF JULY 1861, President Abraham Lincoln delivered his first message to the United States Congress, which he had called into special session to deal with the Civil War that had begun three months earlier. Explaining what the North was fighting for in this war, Lincoln said: "This is essentially a People's contest. On the side of the Union, it

1

is a struggle for maintaining in the world, that form and substance of government, whose leading object is, to elevate the condition of men—to lift artificial weights from all shoulders—to clear the paths of laudable pursuit for all—to afford all, an unfettered start, and a fair chance, in the race of life."[1]

The artificial weights that Lincoln mentioned referred in part to the weight of slavery on the shoulders of four million African Americans, even though another year would pass before Lincoln made emancipation of the slaves one of the North's war aims. Nevertheless, everyone recognized that the South had seceded and the Confederacy had gone to war to protect slavery from the threat it perceived in the antislavery movement out of which had grown the Republican Party that elected Lincoln president in 1860.

Yet, by lifting artificial weights and giving all people a fair chance in the race of life, Lincoln meant to include more than the question of slavery. The American venture of a republican form of government based on a democratic political system was a fragile experiment in that nineteenth-century world in which most other Western nations were governed by monarchs and based on theories of aristocracy and the inequality of social classes. Americans alive in 1860 had seen two French republics succumb to the elevation of emperors and the restoration of the monarchy. The hopes of European liberals for the formation of democratic governments in 1848 had been crushed by counterrevolutions. And now a democratic form of government in the United States was threatened by a civil war that, if it broke the nation in two, would likewise discredit the very notion of democracy and equal opportunity. "The central idea pervading this struggle," said Lincoln in 1861, "is the necessity of proving that popular government is not an absurdity. We must settle this question now, whether in a free government the minority have the right to break up the government whenever they choose"—as the secessionists were trying to do.[2]

Where did this passion for popular government, for democracy, for giving all a fair chance in the race of life come from? For Americans, one of the principal sources was the Revolution of 1776. Lincoln declared, also in 1861, "I have never had a feeling politically that did not spring from the sentiments embodied in the Declaration of Independence" with its ringing phrases that all men are created equal with inalienable rights of life, liberty, and the pursuit of happiness—that pursuit being another way of describing a fair chance in the race of life.[3] Lincoln was well aware that many Americans did not enjoy equality or a fair chance. He also understood that the author of the words "all men are created equal,"

Thomas Jefferson, and the other signers of the Declaration of Independence, "did not intend to declare all men equal *in all respects*." They did not even "mean to assert the obvious untruth" that all people in 1776 were equal in rights and opportunities. Rather, said Lincoln, "they meant to set up a standard maxim for a free society, which should be constantly looked to, constantly labored for, and even though never perfectly attained, constantly approximated, and thereby constantly spreading and deepening its influence, and augmenting the happiness and value of life to all people of all colors everywhere."[4]

The second great influence that underlay the progressive currents that shaped nineteenth-century movements to lift weights from shoulders was the French Revolution, which drew part of its energy from the example of the American Revolution and part from the intellectual ferment of the Enlightenment in France. That eighteenth-century philosophical movement challenged fixed social hierarchies of feudalism and the ingrained injustices found in dogma and tradition. Enlightenment thinkers urged rational programs and institutions to promote social and political progress. From these currents of thought in France arose, among other things, the best schools in the world for education of the deaf by means of French Sign Language, the direct ancestor of American Sign Language. In 1816 a product of these schools, Laurent Clerc, came to the United States to help a Congregationalist clergyman, Thomas Hopkins Gallaudet, establish a school for the deaf in Hartford, Connecticut—the first of several institutions founded on the same model during the next four decades.[5]

Thomas Hopkins Gallaudet's role in founding what became known as the American School for the Deaf provides a segue for consideration of the third important source of progressive reforms in the first half of the nineteenth century, the Second Great Awakening in the history of American Protestantism. A crucial element in the Second Great Awakening was rejection of the Calvinist doctrine of predestination by many Congregationalist and Presbyterian theologians and clergymen, including Gallaudet. Traditional Calvinism taught that God predestined salvation for only the chosen elect, who had little or no say in the process. Reform Calvinists, plus theologians in other denominations like the Methodists, argued instead that all people had free will to choose the path to salvation by proclaiming their faith in God and in Christ's teachings, renouncing sin, and placing themselves in a state of belief and behavior to receive God's grace.

This was an activist faith that rejected the passiveness of waiting to be chosen by God; to put it in vernacular terms, it was a belief that God helps those who help themselves. This activist faith not only generated evangelical crusades to convert individuals to Christ, it also spawned a host of reform movements against social "sins"—the sin of prostitution, the sin of drunkenness, the sin of holding slaves, the sin of denying an equal chance in the race of life to any group, and many other movements. Most of the reform movements we associate with the antebellum era in the United States—most prominently the abolitionist movement and the women's rights movement—grew out of the ferment of the Second Great Awakening.

The same is true of the movement for education of the deaf. Educators like Thomas Hopkins Gallaudet considered the inability to hear to be a weight on the shoulders of the deaf—not an artificial weight, to be sure, but nevertheless a weight to be lifted or, perhaps more accurately, to be circumvented by teaching deaf people to communicate in sign language and eventually to read and write the English language. Of equal importance, Gallaudet and his fellow evangelical reformers wanted to educate deaf children in order to enable them to open their hearts and minds to the knowledge of the Bible and the teachings of Christ. Just as the Puritan settlers of New England had established a system of public education to enable people to read the word of God, the early educators of the deaf founded schools for the same purpose.

A fourth current of social and political thought that provided an impulse for lifting artificial weights from shoulders was Jacksonian democracy. Emphasizing the political equality of all white males and attacking what they considered institutions of monopoly and privilege such as the Second Bank of the United States, Jacksonians injected a theme of egalitarianism into American politics. In some ways Jacksonianism ran counter to the evangelical reform movements, for many of the white males it empowered were opposed to freedom for slaves and equality for women. But we are talking general currents or impulses of thought, not necessarily of specific reforms, and the egalitarian impulses of Jacksonian democracy contributed to the Lincolnian desire to provide all with a fair chance in the race of life.

To the point of education for the deaf, one of the foremost Jacksonian Democrats was Amos Kendall, whose donation of land and money made possible the funding and growth of the institution that became Gallaudet University. In 1857 Kendall persuaded Congress to charter what was called the Columbia Institution for the Instruction of the Deaf and Dumb and Blind and to appropriate funds for it to begin operations. (Blind students were later transferred to their own school in Maryland.) Under the leadership of its superintendent Edward Miner Gallaudet, the son of

Amos Kendall

Thomas Hopkins, the new school grew and prospered. Edward soon began lobbying Congress to grant his institution a college charter. He succeeded in 1864, when, even though the Civil War was raging, Congress took time to incorporate the Columbia Institution as a college and to authorize it to grant degrees. President Lincoln signed the bill without comment, but had he offered any observations, they likely would have included some words about lifting weights from shoulders and providing a fair chance in the race of life for students in this first institution for higher learning for deaf students in the world. Exactly thirty years after Lincoln signed the bill, the collegiate department of the Columbia Institution was renamed Gallaudet College, in honor of Thomas Hopkins Gallaudet.*

Gallaudet College was not only a pioneer in higher education for deaf people. Its founding as the Columbia Institution in 1857 also established a precedent for direct federal aid to education. This precedent soon spread to other educational efforts. In 1862 Congress passed and President Lincoln signed the Morrill Land-Grant College Act, named for Congressman Justin Morrill of Vermont. This law granted thousands of acres of public land to the states to create what were called agricultural and mechanical colleges to provide opportunities for higher education and advanced technical training to the children of farmers and workers for whom such opportunities had not been previously possible. This, too, at least in part, helped lift some weights from shoulders.

The largest and most visible example of such efforts in the 1860s was the creation of the Freedmen's Bureau to aid the transition to freedom of the four million slaves liberated by the Civil War. Here indeed was a massive lifting of weights, the weight of generations of slavery. Most of the support for the dozens of schools, some of them calling themselves colleges or universities, that were founded to educate freed slaves was provided by Northern missionary and philanthropic societies. But the Freedmen's Bureau, whose funding came from the federal government, furnished significant financial support. One of these schools, Howard University, received a large share of its funding from the government. It became the flagship institution of higher education for African Americans just as Gallaudet had become for deaf Americans. In tandem these two institutions grew and flourished, doing their best to provide two groups of Americans the fairest possible chance in the race of life.[6]

New directions in American development after the Civil War created a cultural climate that impinged both on the deaf community and on Gallaudet College. As a consequence of the nation's trauma and eventual triumph from 1861 to 1865, the war produced an intensified nationalism and an emphasis on creating institutions and sentiments of national loyalty. The first task was to assimilate the former Confederate states back into the Union. The war had been caused by the growing and increasingly bitter differences between the free and slave states over the question of slavery and its expansion. The North and South were sharply

---

*Because the name Gallaudet College—today university—is more familiar to most people, this name will be used from now on, even though it is an anachronism for the period before 1894.

different societies, generating what may be called an irrepressible conflict between two hostile civilizations. After the war, slavery no longer existed, but its remnants in the minds and experiences of both North and South created a significant obstacle to assimilation of these two societies into one.

After a decade of Reconstruction in which the Northern-dominated federal government tried to remake Southern society in the Northern image, and the Southern whites resisted the portion of this effort that mandated equal civil and political rights for freed slaves, the two sides reached a sort of accommodation in the late 1870s. In this settlement the South yielded to Northern ideas of a unified nation, and the North yielded to Southern ideas of racial segregation and white supremacy. By the end of the nineteenth century, the nation was reunited on the basis of white supremacy and the acculturation of both races to the dominant values of capitalism and Christianity. African Americans as well as Southern whites subscribed to these values, even though African Americans were segregated as second-class citizens.[7]

In addition to absorbing ex-Confederates and former slaves into a unified nation after the Civil War, the United States confronted the task of assimilating the millions of immigrants who continued to arrive in growing numbers. That task grew more difficult as the immigrants' principal countries of origin shifted from northern and western Europe to southern and eastern Europe. By the 1890s many old-stock Americans feared that the multiplicity of languages, ethnic groups, religious faiths, and cultural habits would overwhelm American institutions and values. The response of old-stock Americans took two forms: efforts to restrict the number of immigrants, which finally succeeded in the 1920s, and efforts to assimilate them. The latter enterprise manifested itself in several ways: the banning of any language but English in the public schools of many cities and states; the growth of the settlement house movement in cities; the development of outreach programs by churches and synagogues; and a barrage of writings and speeches emphasizing nationalism and Americanism in the national media (newspapers, magazines) and by politicians espousing the same ideals.[8]

What does all of this have to do with the history of Gallaudet and of the deaf community? The post–Civil War generation witnessed the rise of oralism in deaf education. This movement was in some ways a counterpart of the drive for the assimilation of other groups into the dominant American culture—in this case, a culture represented by spoken English. The deaf community, of course, was much smaller than Southerners (either black or white) or various immigrant groups. But a similar impulse caused many hearing Americans—most famously Alexander Graham Bell—to call for the assimilation of deaf people into the American mainstream by teaching them how to lipread and speak. Despite resistance by most deaf adults, who preferred to communicate by means of sign language, and despite the limited success of the oralist drive to teach the deaf to speak, the movement achieved a powerful momentum by the turn of the twentieth century—in tandem with the drive to assimilate and Americanize immigrants.[9]

Historians of immigration have labeled this model of Americanization "Anglo-conformity." Anglo-American culture was held up as the standard to which other ethnic groups were expected to conform. Borrowing from this terminology, we might label oralism as "hearing conformity." Just as some immigrants resisted the pressure for 100 percent Americanism or Anglo-conformity, many deaf educators and institutions resisted the pressures for hearing conformity. Immigrant spokespeople advanced a pluralist model of cultural mix, sometimes labeled—rather misleadingly—a melting-pot model. Likewise some deaf educators and institutions—most notably Edward Miner Gallaudet and Gallaudet College—practiced what President Gallaudet called the combined method, a sort of melting-pot notion of oralism, or articulation, for those who could achieve speech, combined with manualism, or sign language, to sustain the natural means of communication for deaf people among themselves.

The closest analogy between broader cultural developments and the specific experience of the deaf community in post–Civil War America, however, was not the immigrant experience but rather the national policy toward American Indians. Soon after Gallaudet was founded, the government formulated its Indian policy, the consequences of which would carry indirect implications for deaf education.

Prior to the 1870s the United States government officially designated Indian tribes as foreign nations. The government signed treaties with these "nations," and the army fought wars with them. The designation of Indian tribes as nations became increasingly a legal fiction, however, especially as the government herded more and more of these tribes onto reservations. By the 1870s, although warfare against Indians was still going on in Western territories, liberal reformers in the Eastern states prevailed on the government to adopt what they called a "peace policy" toward the Indians. The dominant features of this policy were, first, to cease treating Indian tribes as foreign nations, and second, to begin a process of missionary education on reservations and in boarding schools to assimilate them into mainstream society as American citizens.

To implement this policy, President Ulysses S. Grant appointed members of the Quakers and other religious denominations as Indian agents and commissioners. Religious denominations established schools on the reservations to convert Indians to Christianity and to educate them in the English language. The underlying philosophy of these efforts was that American Indians would never survive and prosper unless they adopted the language, religion, and culture of white Americans. These reformers wanted to break down the Indians' tribal allegiances and prepare them to become American citizens; they wanted to break down the nomadic hunting culture of the Plains Indians and turn them into farmers and workers.

This Indian policy was the counterpart of the efforts to absorb the South and the freed slaves into the American mainstream in the post–Civil War decades, and the similar effort to Americanize immigrants. It was also the counterpart of the oralist movement in deaf education to bring deaf people into the mainstream speaking culture.

It was more than a coincidence that the leading political ally of the reform advocates of this assimilationist Indian policy was Senator Henry L. Dawes of Massachusetts. For more than thirty years, Dawes was also a member of the board of Gallaudet College and one of the college's chief supporters in Congress. Dawes was also the author of legislation enacted in 1887 that was called at the time the Indian Emancipation Act—a label that became ironic as the passage of time revealed its serious defects. This law provided for the dissolution of Indian tribes as legal entities and granted Indian heads of families the opportunity to acquire individual ownership of 160 acres of reservation lands as the first step toward becoming American citizens. For some Indians this policy worked as intended, and they became successful citizens. For many others, however, it was a failure. They lost their land to unscrupulous men and sank deeper into a kind of listless limbo between their once-vital native culture and the mainstream culture to which they either could not or would not assimilate. Finally, in 1934 the government admitted the failure of the Dawes Act and, while ensuring that all Indians remained United States citizens, reinvested the tribes with ownership of remaining reservation land and with considerable legislative authority over tribe members who remained on the reservations. Four decades later, in 1975, Congress passed the Indian Self-Determination Act, which confirmed and amplified the self-government of Indian tribes.[10]

It does not seem too far-fetched to recognize certain parallels between the Indian policy of white reformers and the deaf education policies of hearing people during the same period (the 1870s to the middle decades of the twentieth century). Some deaf people learned to lipread and speak successfully, just as some Indians assimilated to the dominant culture. But many other deaf people could not or would not assimilate to the mainstream hearing society and continued to sustain a separate linguistic community with sign language as the means of communication, just as many Indians retained their tribal allegiance and culture. And just as the government finally recognized Indian tribal authority and institutions in the 1930s and after, in recent decades the combined method of deaf education and the increased recognition of the validity of sign language and other non-oralist means of communication among deaf people has affirmed the cultural validity of the deaf community's indigenous forms of communication.

One other parallel in the endeavors for minority education is relevant here. This parallel concerns schools for African Americans and schools for deaf children. Most of the schools and colleges established for the freed slaves were founded by Northern whites associated with the abolitionist movement and Protestant missionary associations. At first, most of the teachers and all of the administrators in these schools were white. The black beneficiaries accepted white teachers and leadership in the early years of freedpeople's education because qualified black teachers and administrators were not yet available. But as time went on and the schools turned out a new generation of educated black people, the African American community began to demand more black teachers and more authority in these schools.

White administrators started to hire black teachers in the 1870s and 1880s, but the superintendents or presidents of most of these institutions remained white until the twentieth century. The presidents of flagship black universities were still white well into the century. This became an increasingly sore point among students, black faculty, and the African American communities served by these schools. Student demonstrations disrupted Howard University and other institutions. Howard and Atlanta University finally got their first black presidents in 1926 and 1929, respectively; Fisk University did not have a black president until 1946.[11]

One scarcely needs to point out the parallels to schools for the deaf and especially to Gallaudet University. However, developments in deaf education were influenced by broader social and cultural currents in American society. The United States has always been a pluralist nation, but the American majority has not always manifested a pluralist toleration for the integrity and value of minority cultures. There has always been a tension between the majority's desire for the minorities' assimilation to the mainstream culture and the resistance of various minorities to this pressure. At its best, this has been a creative tension in which each side has recognized and learned from the other. The history of deaf education has had its share of tensions and misunderstandings, but the creative tension between conformity and pluralism has helped to make the American deaf community the best educated in the world and to make Gallaudet University an institution without parallel.

Notes

1. Roy P. Basler, ed., *The Collected Works of Abraham Lincoln* (New Brunswick, N.J.: Rutgers University Press, 1953–1955), 4:438.

2. Michael Burlingame and John R. Turner Ettlinger, eds., *Inside Lincoln's White House: The Complete Civil War Diary of John Hay* (Carbondale: Southern Illinois University Press, 1997), diary entry of May 7, 1861.

3. Basler, *Collected Works of Lincoln*, 4:240.

4. Ibid., 2:405–6.

5. Harlan Lane, *When the Mind Hears: A History of the Deaf* (New York: Random House, 1984); John Vickrey Van Cleve and Barry A. Crouch, *A Place of Their Own: Creating the Deaf Community in America* (Washington, D.C.: Gallaudet University Press, 1989), 29–59.

6. Rayford W. Logan, *Howard University: The First Hundred Years, 1867–1967* (New York: New York University Press, 1969).

7. David Blight, *Race and Reunion: The Civil War in American Memory* (Cambridge: Harvard University Press, 2001).

8. John Higham, *Strangers in the Land: Patterns of American Nativism, 1860–1925* (New Brunswick, N.J.: Rutgers University Press, 1955).

9. Richard Winefield, *Never the Twain Shall Meet: Bell, Gallaudet, and the Communications Debate* (Washington, D.C.: Gallaudet University Press, 1987); Douglas C. Baynton, *Forbidden Signs: American Culture and the Campaign Against Sign Language* (Chicago: University of Chicago Press, 1996).

10. Philip Weeks, *Farewell, My Nation: The American Indian and the United States in the Nineteenth Century*, 2nd ed. (Wheeling, Ill.: Harlan Davidson, Inc., 2001), 123–249.

11. James M. McPherson, *The Abolitionist Legacy: From Reconstruction to the NAACP* (Princeton: Princeton University Press, 1975), 262–95.

2

John Carlin and Deaf Double-Consciousness

Christopher Krentz

Editors' Introduction

In 1854, John Carlin called for a national college to expand deaf people's intellectual and professional possibilities and to create an elite deaf class. Fittingly, in 1864, he received the first honorary degree granted by the institution that became Gallaudet University. Yet, as Christopher Krentz shows in this essay, Carlin also belittled "average" deaf people by internalizing mainstream perceptions of deaf persons as below average and incapable of success. Krentz analyzes Carlin's literary works to explain this seeming contradiction. He writes that Carlin suffered from personal experiences with oppression and agonized over the lack of economic and social mobility for deaf people. The result was a deaf "double-consciousness," similar to that of educated African Americans during the late nineteenth century.

Carlin's ongoing struggle between feelings of pride and inferiority elucidates a theme found throughout deaf history. The National Association of the Deaf in the 1920s endorsed marriage limitations between congenitally deaf partners, for example, and passed a resolution to work with medical groups to cure deafness. Furthermore, important segments of the American deaf community resisted William Stokoe's efforts to demonstrate that American Sign Language was a full and complete language, separate from English. Krentz provides a way to understand why "double-consciousness" has persisted, even as historical conditions and attitudes towards deaf people have changed.

It is a peculiar sensation, this double-consciousness, this sense of always looking at one's self through the eyes of others, of measuring one's soul by the tape of a world that looks on in amused contempt and pity. One ever feels his two-ness,—an American, a Negro; two souls, two thoughts, two unreconciled strivings; two warring ideals in one dark body, whose dogged strength alone keeps it from being torn asunder.

—W. E. B. Du Bois

Du Bois's FAMOUS ASSERTION IN *The Souls of Black Folk* (1903) that African Americans have a double-consciousness, a psychic split brought about by living among a white majority that views them with "amused contempt and pity," potentially illuminates the psychology of many oppressed people.[1] According to Du Bois, black Americans internalize dominant condescending views leading to a "peculiar sensation" where feelings of self-esteem battle with feelings of inadequacy. This inner division could describe the mental state of many marginalized or minority groups, from Native Americans to women, who struggle to articulate positive identities in a society that routinely deems them inferior. During the nineteenth century, deaf American authors contended with a double-consciousness of their own. They had to form their individual and collective notions of self through two distinct frames: their association with each other, through fluent sign language and shared experiences, and their interaction with hearing people, who rarely knew sign language, spoke English, and sometimes responded to them with contempt or neglect. As a result, in their writing deaf American authors often both celebrate deaf identity and reinforce assumptions of deaf insufficiency. This double-consciousness shows up especially clearly in the writings of John Carlin (1813–1891), the deaf leader who played a prominent role in the establishment and early days of the National Deaf-Mute College (now Gallaudet University).

Carlin was one of the most accomplished deaf people in mid-nineteenth-century America. Born deaf in 1813 and educated at the Pennsylvania Institution, he went on to a successful career as a painter, writer, sculptor, acquaintance of hearing leaders like Horace Greeley and William Seward, and an orator whose sign language presentations were in demand at deaf events. In 1854 he became one of the first people, if not the first, to issue a written call for a national college for deaf Americans. Ten years later, at the inauguration of the National Deaf-Mute College, he delivered the main address and received the college's first honorary degree in recognition of his accomplishments. Although he used sign language, married a deaf woman, and was a life-long advocate of deaf people, in his written works Carlin displays deep ambivalence toward his deaf identity, oscillating between viewing deaf people as inferior and asserting their equal intelligence and capability. His deaf double-consciousness has consequences for our understanding not just of the educated deaf mindset at the time, but also of the beginnings of the first institution of higher education for deaf people in the world.

Consider his poem "The Mute's Lament," which prominently appeared in the first issue of the *American Annals of the Deaf and Dumb* in 1847. From the opening line, when Carlin describes himself in terms of silence (a metaphor that previous deaf authors seldom employed), we are on notice that he is seeing himself through the majority's eyes, even as he implicitly questions this view. The poem begins:

> I move—a silent exile on this earth;
> As in his dreary cell one doomed for life,
> My tongue is mute, and closed ear heedeth not;
> No gleam of hope this darken'd mind assures
> That the blest power of speech shall e'er be known.
> Murmuring gaily o'er their pebbly beds
> The limpid streamlets as they onward flow
> Through verdant meadows and responding woodlands,
> Vocal with merry tones—*I hear them not.*[2]

Carlin depicts himself as a miserable outcast, reflecting not just the disconnection he felt from the hearing people around him, but also a certain fashionable Byronic alienation. He omits sign language and any hint of the deaf community, presenting himself as a lonely, deaf "I." In these ways he follows the example of the first published deaf poet in the United States, James Nack (1809–1879), who had followed a similar strategy in his poem, "The Minstrel Boy" (1827), a precursor with which Carlin was no doubt familiar.[3] Yet if Nack was affected by hearing models, Carlin was even more so, replicating the dominant ideology that abjects his identity so thoroughly that, according to the poem, little happiness is possible for him on Earth.

In this respect, "The Mute's Lament" is a classic expression of the inferiority complex, for Carlin appears to have thoroughly internalized the majority's attitude that casts him as a subordinate other. Clearly in-

John Carlin

fluenced by hearing poets like Moses Scott (who in 1819 had published a long poem about deaf education, based on a visit to the New York Institution), Carlin applies Scott's images of deaf people being imprisoned in a cell, living in darkness and silence, to himself; while Scott joyfully enumerates all the sounds deaf people cannot perceive, Carlin laments not hearing birds, music, and eloquent orators.[4] What is a bit odd is that Carlin, who was congenitally deaf, never directly experienced the "lyric of the lute divine" and "the cadence soft" of which he writes.[5] These conventional depictions presumably came to him filtered through hearing writers, including one of his favorites, Milton, and their delight in such sounds probably made him feel deficient. The entire poem seems based on hearing epistemology, as the concluding lines, duplicating so many hearing authors' renderings of deaf people becoming hearing in heaven, suggest:

> O, Hope! How sweetly smileth Heavenly Hope
> On the sad, drooping soul and trembling heart. . . .
> ⮞ My ears shall be unsealed, and I shall hear;
> My tongue shall be unbound, and I shall speak,
> And happy with the angels sing forever![6]

In some ways Carlin's attitude makes sense: he undoubtedly had a harder life because he was deaf, and it is customary to anticipate all worldly woes being removed in heaven. In the process, he affirms his commonality with hearing readers who are believers, showing that he is a Christian, too. Yet on closer inspection, his outlook is not unlike the Algerian natives Frantz Fanon describes in *Black Skin, White Masks* (1952) who dream of "magically turning white" due to the privileged position whites have in their society;[7] in both cases, blackness and deafness are positioned as intrinsically inferior. Although earlier deaf authors like Laurent Clerc (1785–1869) and John Burnet (1808–1874) typically emphasized how deaf marginalization was culturally fabricated, how society could be changed to make deaf Americans happy and productive, here Carlin, influenced by Old Testament prophecies of deaf people becoming hearing in heaven (Isa. 35:5) and by hearing sentimental poets like Lydia Huntley Sigourney, adopts an essentialist position, firmly locating the problem in the body: because deaf people are deaf, they are inferior and unhappy. As a young man he yearned to become a "correct writer of verses," studying rhyming and pronunciation dictionaries and asking hearing poets for advice, but Carlin may have emulated hearing models too successfully.[8] As Nigel Gibson glosses Fanon's argument, "the slave who embraces the logos of the master can at best hope for only a pseudo-recognition."[9] In other words, no matter how well deaf people like Carlin accepted the majority's values and how much approbation they received, they could never achieve full recognition as equals since those very values held that deafness is a mark of lower status.

Yet even as he replicates prevailing stereotypes, Carlin manages implicitly to critique them through the poem's central paradox: the so-called "mute" who does not speak is nonetheless expressing himself directly to readers, finding a voice with a pen. If the work on a literal level confirms notions of deaf people's inferiority, just the fact that a deaf poet is writing contradicts some of its mournful images and moves us a step toward ironical satire. For example, while Carlin claims he has a "darken'd mind," he reveals that he is actually perceptive and intelligent, able to produce verse that, in the words of the hearing editor of the *Annals*, "would scarcely do discredit to many a writer of established reputation among us."[10] Carlin's mimicry thus subtly exposes holes in dominant thinking even as it seems to subscribe to it. Through such subversive strategies, Carlin begins to write himself out of abjection and demonstrates that he is a capable deaf adult (even if one who feels inferior), a kind of representation decidedly absent from hearing authors' portrayals. The success of "The Mute's Lament"—it was prominently reprinted in *Harper's* for a national readership in 1884—may well have been due to the tension between the way it reifies hearing assumptions about deaf people and simultaneously undercuts some of them.

If in "The Mute's Lament" Carlin expresses his belief in deaf people's abilities indirectly, he does so more explicitly in an essay he published seven years later, in 1854, although again contradictory feelings about deaf identity appear. Writing in the *Annals*, he issued a call for a national college for deaf Americans, a bold idea at a time when deaf people were at most expected to become teachers of deaf students or manual laborers and no colleges for deaf students existed anywhere in the world. Citing the examples of Clerc, Nack, and Burnet as evidence "that mutes of decided talents can be rendered as good scholars," Carlin shows his awareness and reliance upon the deaf authors who have come before him. He argues against the very notion of deaf inferiority he had seemed to promulgate in "The Mute's Lament," asserting that "there can be found no difference between speaking persons or deaf mutes, of the higher class, in imagination, strength of mind, depth of thought and quickness of perception."[11] Carlin posits the equality of deaf and hearing intellects, even if "higher class" seems elitist, excluding the majority of deaf Americans. Foreshadowing Du Bois's argument for developing a small group of gifted black people he called "the Talented Tenth,"[12] Carlin contends that a college would enable the most promising deaf students, though "few in number," to become achievers as "civil engineers, physicians, surgeons, lawyers and statesmen" who would benefit not only the deaf community, but also the nation as a whole.[13] His appeal, along with the force of a congenitally deaf person producing a learned essay with references to a variety of hearing intellectuals, made a public impression, and his vision became reality only a decade later. Unlike in "The Mute's Lament," here Carlin clearly directs attention to social forces that shape deaf people's "well-being, intelligence, happiness ... and prosperity," showing how much deaf identity depends on cultural conditions apart from the body. But here, too, he mentions deaf people's "misfortune" and lack of "the blessed auditory sense," biological definitions that take us back to the literal thrust of "The Mute's Lament."[14] Carlin's essay and poem move between constructivist and essentialist notions of identity, between assertions of capability, if deaf people only receive opportunities, and the reproduction of hearing values that lead to a certain self-loathing. Taken together, they dramatically reveal deaf double-consciousness at mid-century, suggesting how potent feelings of inferiority and repressed potential coexisted in deaf minds.

Such double-consciousness also appears in an 1854 presentation at the dedication of a monument to Thomas Hopkins Gallaudet, where Carlin portrays deaf people before hearing intervention as scarcely human, but celebrates their adult capability after education. In the first parts of the speech (which he wrote in advance and subsequently published in the *Annals*), Carlin writes that before Gallaudet went to Europe to learn methods of deaf education, "All the deaf mutes of this country were ignorant heathen! Their minds were desolately blank!"[15] Carlin uses hyperbole to provide a stark contrast to the intelligent, respectable deaf people at the assembly, underscoring their fortunate, empowered status and extreme debt to Gallaudet. In Carlin's words, Gallaudet's work brought about "our deliverance from the degradation to which we were unavoidably consigned," hinting that deaf people felt literally and figuratively saved.[16] Such depictions underscore the extreme gratitude that Carlin and other deaf people felt to Gallaudet, but in the process he reinforces the stereotype that uneducated deaf people are subhuman. In the same speech, he celebrated the fact that the monument was erected solely through the contributions of deaf people; no donations from hearing people were allowed. "As there is much reason to believe that this is the first monument in the world that has ever been erected by a community exclusively deaf and dumb, how exquisite is the satisfaction with which we look upon ourselves as its founders!" he wrote, demonstrating his pride not just as a deaf person, but as a deaf American whose national community was achieving what older deaf communities in Europe had not.[17]

If Carlin's comments suggest a certain elitism that privileges educated deaf people while shunning those without an education, we can see this attitude spill over into what today might be called self-hatred during the deaf Commonwealth debate in the late 1850s. Deaf correspondents wrote back and forth in the *Annals* about John Jacobus Flournoy's provocative call for interested deaf people to emigrate west and form a state of their own where they could escape prejudice and manage their own affairs. Carlin, who just a few years earlier had expressed such confidence in the most gifted deaf people's potential in his call for a national college, expressed his latent contempt for average deaf people even more clearly. In a private letter to Clerc that he later agreed to have published, he superciliously belittled deaf competence. "It is a well known fact that the majority of [deaf people] show little decision of purpose in any enterprise whatever," he wrote. "I am content with my being 'lost among the hearing persons,' whose superior knowledge of the English language benefits my mind far more than would the perpetual gestures of the thousands of the *bona fide* residents in GESTURIA."[18] Although he did not speak vocally, had a deaf wife, and interacted with deaf people all of his life, Carlin lived by dominant values so much that he denigrates his own community and language of signs (rarely in deaf writing is there such a negative take on ASL) in favor of hearing people and English. His words seem related to Fanon's observation about the valorization of French among colonized Algerians, which causes them to belittle their own language and cultural traditions in favor of the dominant group's. Once again, we see Carlin struggling with a mixture of pride and loathing toward deaf identity.

In his presentation at the inauguration of the National Deaf-Mute College in 1864, Carlin emphasized that the college, the fulfillment of his dream a decade earlier, marked an exciting time of increased opportunity and possibility, what Carlin called a "bright epoch in deaf-mute history." He offered an optimistic vision of the changes the college might bring about: "Is it likely that college for deaf-mutes will ever produce mute statesmen, lawyers, and ministers of religion, orators, poets, and authors?" he asked. "The answer is: They will, in numbers, like angels' visits, few and far between."[19] He noted that deaf people could be public speakers in the courtroom, the pulpit, and the forum using precisely the method he was using then, by having hearing people read their addresses out loud. Carlin, like several earlier deaf authors, pointed to how changing social conditions would enable deaf people to gain a more equitable and productive place in society.

Despite the hope and buoyant spirits surrounding the inauguration, the promise of the new institution was not immediately realized. In 1869, Carlin, who had scoffed at Flournoy's plan of a deaf commonwealth, disconsolately acknowledged that even deaf college graduates could not secure suitable employment because of bigotry. In an address to the Empire State Association of Deaf-Mutes convention, he wrote,

What is the true obstruction in their way? Prejudice? I am sorry to say that it is. This spirit is common among even the most intelligent—the most benevolent men [—it is] as illogical as it is cruel. . . . Cruel, because it crushes the budding hopes in the applicant's mind . . . but this Prejudice comes rather from ignorance than malice. . . . I presume that the prejudice will cease to exist where the true merits of the case are more properly understood.[20]

Locating prejudice even among the most kind and well-informed business leaders, Carlin confirms the endemic audism against deaf people in hearing society that Flournoy had fervently decried. Unable to imagine a life apart from hearing people, Carlin only dispiritedly holds out the hope for greater understanding in the future since, he writes, deaf people are completely dependent on hearing people for "all things necessary to our livelihood."[21]

John Carlin's writing vividly illustrates the profound feelings of pride and inferiority that even one of the most accomplished deaf people in nineteenth-century America struggled to reconcile. Through his writing, he often asserts the potential of deaf people to be capable, intellectual members of society, and his work on behalf of a national deaf-mute college helped to bring about that institution that would shape the lives of thousands of deaf Americans in the years to come. Yet Carlin, unlike Flournoy and some others, consistently showed a reluctance to challenge hearing oppression. His writing occasionally betrays an elitism that aligns him with the intelligentsia in colonial settings, the *compadre* that is educated and relatively privileged and therefore may be less inclined to struggle for cultural and political independence. He never quite escapes his two consciousnesses: one as a member of a hearing-dominated system, one as a deaf person oppressed by it. As he sought to write his individual and group identity, he revealed how difficult it was to escape this persistent double-consciousness and find a place where deaf people could be truly appreciated and whole.

Notes

1. W. E. B. Du Bois, *The Souls of Black Folk* (1903; New York: W. W. Norton, 1999), 3.

2. John Carlin, "The Mute's Lament," *American Annals of the Deaf and Dumb* 1 (1847): 15–16. This poem and much of the other writing by Carlin discussed in this article has been republished in my collection, *A Mighty Change: An Anthology of Deaf American Writing 1816–1864* (Washington, D.C.: Gallaudet University Press, 2000).

3. Nack published this poem in his collection, *The Legend of the Rocks, and Other Poems* (New York: E. Conrad, 1827), 58–61.

4. See Moses Y. Scott, *The Deaf and Dumb; a Poem* (New York: Elam Bliss, 1819).

5. Carlin, "The Mute's Lament," 15.

6. Ibid., 16.

7. Frantz Fanon, *Black Skin, White Masks* (New York: Grove, 1967), 44.

8. "The Poetry of the Deaf," *Harper's New Monthly Magazine*, 68 (1884): 589.

9. Nigel C. Gibson, *Fanon: The Postcolonial Imagination* (Cambridge: Polity, 2003), 30.

10. *American Annals of the Deaf and Dumb* 1 (1847): 14. The editor also admiringly compared a person born deaf producing respectable poetry with "all the niceties of accent, measure, and rhythm," like Carlin, to a congenitally blind person painting a landscape.

11. John Carlin, "The National College for Mutes," *American Annals of the Deaf and Dumb* 6 (1854): 175–83.

12. W. E. B. Du Bois, "The Talented Tenth," *The Negro Problem: A Series of Articles by Representative Negroes of Today* (New York: J. Pott & Company, 1903), 31–75.

13. Carlin, "The National College for Mutes," 177, 179.

14. Ibid., 180, 183.

15. Luzerne Rae, ed., "Ceremonies at the Completion of the Gallaudet Monument," *American Annals for the Deaf and Dumb* 7 (1854): 33.

16. Ibid., 34.

17. Ibid., 31.

18. John Carlin, letter to Laurent Clerc, *American Annals of the Deaf and Dumb* 10 (1858): 89.

19. John Carlin, "Oration," Inauguration of the College for the Deaf and Dumb, Washington, D.C. (Washington, D.C.: Gideon and Pearson, 1964), 45, 47–48.

20. John Carlin, "Oration" (at the Empire State Association of Deaf-Mutes convention), *The Deaf-Mutes' Friend* 1:9 (September 1969): 265–66.

21. Ibid., 268.

3

A Legacy of Leadership: Edward Miner Gallaudet and the Columbia Institution, 1857–1864

David de Lorenzo

Editors' Introduction

A consistent theme in the history of Gallaudet University is the quality of the institution's presidential leadership from Edward Miner Gallaudet, its first president, through I. King Jordan, its first deaf president. The article below and the ones that follow show that historians can look at the same president and reach very different conclusions. Here David de Lorenzo projects a very positive portrait of Gallaudet, arguing that his leadership was commendable in nearly all respects. Later articles, especially those by Michael J. Olson and Lindsey M. Parker, suggest a sharply contrasting interpretation of Gallaudet's legacy.

IT IS SAID THAT any new business will either succeed or fail in its first three years of existence. This seems relevant to the Columbia Institution, whose start-up was indeed a bumpy road filled with financial challenges, operating ordeals, and political machinations. Edward Miner Gallaudet was a young man, only twenty years old, when he began his new job in Washington, D.C. This paper will focus on the years from 1857, when Gallaudet moved to Washington, to the passage of the Congressional act that established the college in 1864.

More than a simple narrative or snapshot of those early years, this study also reviews Gallaudet's leadership; he, more than any other individual, ensured the permanence of the institution. To understand his story, we must also understand the qualities of leadership itself. However, we must first examine the forces that influenced Gallaudet's life.

Gallaudet was born in 1837, the youngest of eight children. His father, Thomas Hopkins Gallaudet, held a position of great prominence in the Deaf community, as well as being a renowned citizen in their hometown of Hartford, Connecticut. Gallaudet received intensive homeschooling by his father and entered high school at the age of eleven. When his father died he was only fourteen, but Gallaudet immediately acquired a clerical position in the Phoenix Bank of Hartford, with help from family friends. He remained in that position until the age of seventeen, at which point he entered the junior class at Trinity College in Hartford, located a few blocks from his home. He did not stop working though, because his family still needed his financial support. He began teaching at the American School for the Deaf (ASD), the school his father had co-founded with Laurent Clerc and Mason Fitch Cogswell.[1]

Gallaudet's mother, Sophia Fowler Gallaudet, was forty years old when her youngest son was born. She had been a pupil at ASD, was profoundly deaf, and did not speak. As the youngest boy, Gallaudet was pampered by his sisters and was especially close to Sophia (Hunter), whom he hired when she became a widow, and Alice (Trumbull), who was married to one of his closest, lifelong friends. In the family, only his mother was deaf, but he had native fluency in sign language nonetheless.[2]

Hartford was a small city with a population of about ten thousand people during Gallaudet's youth. Because of its proximity to the Connecticut River, which runs through town, business interests, particularly banking and insurance, prospered there.[3] With so few neighbors, his family knew almost everyone in town. His father, an active minister and leader of a school that depended on the kindness of the well-to-do and politically powerful, often socialized with that group. Gallaudet was exposed to the intellectuals, movers, and shakers of Hartford, people like the Beechers and the Morgans.

With this upbringing, it is easy to understand why education was so important to Gallaudet. Although eventually an administrator by day, throughout his life he maintained an active involvement with the arts, writing poetry and two plays. He understood his own energy and potential but at the same time was always driven by a fear of failure.[4] These factors provided the framework for Gallaudet's leadership style.

Leadership Defined

Leadership is offered today as a panacea for almost any social problem, and it was so even in the mid-nineteenth century.[5] Middle managers

Edward Miner Gallaudet

have been known to say their enterprise would thrive if only senior management showed "real leadership." A widely accepted belief is that leadership is a *very good thing* that we need more of. Leadership is not tangible. It exists only in relationships, and in the imagination and perception of the engaged parties. Most images of leadership suggest that leaders get things done and get people to do things. Implicitly, we expect leaders to persuade or inspire and to pursue goals that transcend their narrow self-interest. Leadership is different from management. The distinction often offered is that "managers do things right, and leaders do the right thing."[6] A common view is that management is primarily about structural nuts and bolts: planning, organizing, and controlling. Leadership is seen as a change-oriented process of visioning, networking, and building relationships.

These theories of leadership can be synthesized for the purposes of this discussion of Gallaudet into four general areas: structural (organizational) leadership, human resource leadership, political leadership, and symbolic leadership. Each view will lead to compelling and constructive images of Gallaudet's leadership style. For each, this paper will examine his skills and activities as they are known, and it will conclude that Gallaudet exhibited all four of these leadership qualities throughout his career, though not all at once. His genius was an uncanny ability to change and adapt to the challenges he faced at a given time.

Structural Leadership

Structural leadership focuses on designing and building an effective organization. Such leaders are seen as social architects who are concerned with organizational structures and chain of command. In 1856, when Amos Kendall created the Columbia Institution, he knew nothing about Deaf people and deafness. He was a practical, hard-working man who believed in the power of organizations and governments to effect change for the pubic good. When he saw orphaned children needing assistance in his hometown, his own back yard, Kendall was moved by a sense of charity and philanthropy. He understood his own capacities and limitations, and he immediately sought someone to manage the new school's affairs.[7]

When Kendall offered Gallaudet the opportunity to manage the new Columbia Institution, Gallaudet first discussed the issue of how the school should be organized. His father had endured an untenable management structure at ASD in which the household manager, called the superintendent, had equal power with the principal, who managed the educational aspects of the institution.[8] In this division of power, the faculty and household staff had no coordination except from the board, which saw itself as the manager of day-to-day operations. This meant a lack of central coordination, eliminated any possibility of managing the entire institution as a complete entity, and diminished its ability to defend itself against external forces and influences.

In his discussions with Kendall, they agreed that, in his role as superintendent, Gallaudet would have control over all aspects of managing the institution. Fiscal authority would remain with the board, but all operational expenses would be handled by Gallaudet with funds being funneled, with prior approval of the president, through the treasurer.

Gallaudet was granted full authority to hire staff and faculty, create an educational curriculum, manage the physical plant, and, of course, raise money.[9]

Structural leaders do their homework; think about the relationship of structure, strategy, and environment; and focus on implementation. Although the institution started with a small number of students, Gallaudet devised an organizational structure that could grow as the number of students grew. After making staff selections, he focused immediately on curriculum development and the physical plant. He wrote colleagues at other schools for deaf students with a questionnaire asking about the textbooks they used, how they implemented reading and writing instruction and at what age level (especially for blind students, with whom he had little experience), what building designs they used for housing and instruction, the amount of property they held, and the level and sources of funding.[10] This method of exploration became an essential pattern of evaluation and analysis used throughout his life: Gallaudet's approach was to form an opinion based upon a preponderance of evidence and use that evidence to defend his arguments.[11]

Money is essential to all activities, and it's also the root of many arguments. Gallaudet's first real argument about chain of command and fiscal management arose with William Stickney, who acted as treasurer of the board of directors. A very successful lawyer and banker, Stickney was a member of Calvary Baptist Church and served on the church's building committee along with his father-in-law, no other than Amos Kendall.

Like most of the members of the institution's board, who on average were thirty years older than Gallaudet, Stickney was accustomed to winning arguments. Stickney argued that Gallaudet could not accept donations on behalf of the institution, because that was the treasurer's (his) role. Furthermore, he complained that Gallaudet acted as if he had the authority to approve expenses without prior discussion with the board president. Gallaudet wrote back immediately that he was offended by the tone of the statements in Stickney's letter. He also defended his right as superintendent to accept donations as long as these were properly transferred to the treasurer, which he had done. He also insisted that he could approve expenses for day-to-day items not out of the ordinary, for which the board had prior knowledge, when such expenses came from recognized vendors with whom they had done business before. Stickney wrote back saying he meant no insult but that there were clearly differences of opinion. Gallaudet thanked him for his apology, defending his position again briefly, but politely acknowledged that Stickney had a right to his opinions even though they differed from his own.[12]

Gallaudet understood the importance of winning the argument. He did not want the board involving itself in the day-to-day operations of the institution. He would not be able to perform his duties if he had to review or defend every expense with the board. The board had fiduciary responsibilities to ensure the overall financial health of the institution.

The issue came up again in 1863 with the purchase of two horses, which Kendall felt was overly extravagant.[13] Gallaudet resolved this to Kendall's satisfaction, which put an end to the discussion forevermore. Most importantly, this episode showed an evolving process of trust between himself and the board that eventually led to Kendall's recommendation that Gallaudet be promoted to president of the Columbia Institution when Congress passed the act creating the college program, thereafter referred to as the National Deaf-Mute College.

Human Resource Leadership

Human resource leaders typically advocate openness, listening, participation, and empowerment. They view themselves as facilitators and catalysts who motivate and empower subordinates, colleagues, and associates. The leader's power comes from talent, sensitivity, and service rather than from position or force. This type of leader makes sure that other people's highest-priority needs are being served.

When Gallaudet assumed his role as superintendent in June 1857, the school had nine deaf students and five blind students. His mother acted as matron, and she brought her Hartford housekeeper as the institution's cook. The instructor of the deaf students, whom he hired later that month, James Denison, had been a student at ASD. The instructor of the blind students, Maria M. Eddy, was the only person he did not know personally. He reflected, "these with my three assistants and three servants made a family of twenty-one persons for whose care I was responsible, and I will remember the patriarchal feelings with which I assumed the reins of government."[14]

Gallaudet's view of this enterprise as a family affair is very much the approach he took in his dealings with the parents of the deaf students. As more students matriculated, parents wrote anxious letters for news about their children. Gallaudet always answered immediately and in a manner both supportive and dignified. Given the hectic nature of his schedule in those first years, and the sometimes demanding, almost hysterical worries of some parents, it must have been difficult to be so visible and accessible. He took time, nevertheless, to bring students home on vacations and made time to know the parents and their concerns and issues. His sincerity and honest caring for the students gained him their respect and loyalty.[15]

Gallaudet also empowered his staff. It should be noted that two of the first four staff hired were profoundly deaf. In those first years, Gallaudet spent a significant amount of time on the organization of the institution and on fund raising. Realistically, it would have been difficult, if not impossible, to actively manage the day-to-day business of all the school's functions. It's clear that he let his staff take care of the daily tasks, especially after students from Maryland matriculated in the institution. Surely Gallaudet did not tell his mother what to do. He once remarked that the female staff, given their seniority in comparison with the men, brought dignity and distinction. But he really meant they came with significantly more knowledge, skills, and abilities, and they were vital to him in managing the institution.[16]

Political Leadership

Often, leaders must plunge into a political arena to move their organizations in a desired direction. Political leaders are realists. They avoid letting what they want cloud their judgment about what is possible. They assess the distribution of power and interests by mapping the political terrain, thinking carefully about the key players, their interests, and their power. They look to those whose support they need and discern how to go about getting it, and they analyze who their opponents are and how much power they have. Political leaders focus their attention on building relationships and networks. They recognize the value of personal contacts and face-to-face conversations.

Gallaudet was the consummate political leader. When Kendall offered him a position as head of the Columbia Institution, Gallaudet understood the possibilities that federal financial support presented. If this had been an offer of the superintendency of the Ohio School for the Deaf, for example, he undoubtedly would not have been interested. He had big ideas and a big vision.[17]

The idea of a college for deaf people had been a popular topic and was discussed openly at the time; it certainly was not original to Gallaudet. However, when Kendall mapped out the potential that existed, Gallaudet, the realist, immediately envisioned how such a college could succeed with federal support. Kendall had not been overly excited about Gallaudet's candidacy until they met in person, and Gallaudet excited him with this future vision. Gallaudet was only twenty years old, with little experience in managing anything. However, Kendall was also a visionary; he had been the personal consultant to U.S. presidents and had made large sums of money risking his time and energy on a new, if not quirky, technology, the telegraph.[18]

The personal meeting became Gallaudet's single most effective tool. He employed it at every opportunity. When he needed an increase in the annual support from Congress or additional funds for a building, he walked the halls of the Capitol, pounded on the doors of Congressmen, and flattered them at social gatherings. When he sought Maryland's support to pay the tuition of Maryland students at his institution, he went to Annapolis, the state capital. After several unsuccessful attempts to make an appointment with the appropriate bureaucrat, he waited outside his office, approached him on the street, and got the full support he needed.[19]

Gallaudet accumulated power by networking through planned events and social interactions. In 1858, only eight months after he arrived in Washington, he coordinated an "exhibition" of the students in the old hall of the House of Representatives. He used the opportunity to show Congress what in reality it was supporting. Displaying the "disabled" in such events was traditionally a powerful tool to gain support, and Gallaudet often used it with great success.[20] He attended or hosted an endless stream of soirees, all with the intention of building financial support for the school.

The following year, in 1859, he successfully lobbied Congress to raise the annual per-student support from $150 to $200, add a new annual general appropriation of $3,000, and support any deaf children of members of the armed forces. Obtaining the general appropriation was a vital component; it stabilized the school's fortunes and brought a sense of certainty about its future.[21]

The next year, 1862, was a banner year. While Congress and the nation endured the hardships and reverses of the Civil War, Gallaudet lobbied for a new building and received an even larger appropriation of $9,000. More importantly, Gallaudet finally received this funding with no time limit on annual appropriations. With such support, the school's success was guaranteed. At this early stage, only five years after he began, he saw that the time was ripe to pursue an act of Congress to establish the college, and he laid out his plans publicly in that year's annual report.[22]

Symbolic Leadership

Symbolic leaders lead through both action and word as they interpret and reinterpret experience. What will the future bring? What mission is worthy of our loyalty and investment? Facts, data, and analysis often offer inadequate answers to such questions. Symbolic leaders interpret experience so as to impart meaning and purpose through phrases of beauty and passion. Symbols are used to capture attention, to signal that change is coming.

Gallaudet understood the power of symbols. Even though it was Kendall's request that his mother come with him to act as matron, Gallaudet realized her symbolic importance to fulfilling the vision and mission of the school. To the students, she was a role model, a deaf person risen to a position of power. To outsiders, she stood as a testament of what their fledgling school could accomplish.

Symbolic leaders communicate a vision, a persuasive and hopeful image of the future. Gallaudet's vision of a college for deaf students addressed both the challenges of the time and the hopes and values of its community. He understood that when a people are repressed, as Deaf people had been without access to higher education, they seek meaning and hope. The vision of a college had already existed, but Gallaudet articulated what had been inchoate and transient.[23]

It's impossible to say whether he had great charisma or superlative rhetorical skills, but their existence may be inferred. In this regard, a student of the college noted his style,

> When he appeared before Congress, he spoke in a cultured voice to explain the needs of the school and its need for expansion. . . . Whenever he was asked any questions he would always answer very politely, and should he be the butt of a joke by a congressman who had an abundant sense of humor, he would always laugh with them to prove he was a good fellow. . . . The meeting always ended with Gallaudet in his cutaway suit, shined shoes, immaculate white linen, with graceful gestures bowing right and left until he disappeared through the door.[24]

Without question, he brought a unique blend of poetry, passion, conviction, and courage to articulate his vision.

The best leaders are often the best followers. Gallaudet understood that the work was not about him; he was only a participant in the mission of educating Deaf people. He had a strong will but shunned immodesty. He met and socialized with powerful people but remained silent in his diaries and journals about such interactions, always leaning towards discretion.

At the end of his life, in his history of the college, he stated: "I am deeply conscious that I have not done as well as I ought to have done for the interests of the institution, but I hope it is not presumptuous in me to hope that my services have been of some value to the cause, to promote which the institution was established."[25] Gallaudet was truly a leader for all times and all seasons. He understood his strengths, worked to expand them, and built teams that created what has been described as one of the noblest educational ventures in the history of the United States.

Notes

1. Maxine T. Boatner, *Voice of the Deaf: A Biography of Edward Miner Gallaudet* (Washington, D.C.: Public Affairs Press, 1959), 10–12.

2. Boatner provides some details on Edward Miner Gallaudet's family interactions at various locations in her biography.

3. Susan B. Carter and others, eds., *The Historical Statistics of the United States* (Cambridge: Cambridge University Press, 2006), 44–47.

4. Edward Miner Gallaudet, diary, "Occasionals—E. M. Galluadet, Hartford, Conn." (1852–1884), Manuscript Division, Library of Congress.

5. Most of the management theories provided hereafter were culled from Lee G. Bolman and Terrence E. Deal, *Reframing Organizations* (New York: Jossey-Bass, 1997).

6. Warren Bennis and Bert Nanus, *Leaders: Their Strategies for Taking Charge* (New York: Harper & Row, 1985), 12.

7. For a fuller evaluation of Kendall, see Edward Miner Gallaudet, *History of the College for the Deaf, 1857–1907* (Washington, D.C.: Gallaudet University Press, 1983), 15–18.

8. Boatner, 19–20.

9. Ibid., 25–26.

10. Edward Miner Gallaudet, Letter Press Book, 1857–1858, E. M. Gallaudet President Papers, Gallaudet University Archives.

11. Gallaudet, *History*, 39–56. This approach is outlined by Edward Miner Gallaudet in his description of Kendall's opposition to his plans for the college.

12. Gallaudet, Letter Press Book, January–February 1862.

13. Amos Kendall to Edward Miner Gallaudet, 9 May 1863, Box, 1, Folder 16, Amos Kendall Papers, MSS 41, Gallaudet University Archives.

14. Gallaudet, *History*, 19.

15. Gallaudet's President Papers for this period are filled with letters from parents, especially those from Maryland, writing sometimes on a weekly basis.

16. Gallaudet, *History*, 19.

17. Gallaudet, *History*, 11. Edward Miner Gallaudet states ". . . if he [Kendall] and his associates in the management of the proposed institution would support me in these plans [for a college], I would accept their offer."

18. William Stickney, *Autobiography of Amos Kendall* (Boston: Lee and Shepard, 1872), 527–554.

19. Gallaudet, *History,* 28.

20. Ibid., 21.

21. Ibid., 22–24.

22. Ibid., 31.

23. *Fifth Annual Report of the Columbia Institution for the Deaf and Dumb and the Blind for the Year Ending June 30, 1862,* Gallaudet University Archives. In the report, Gallaudet wrote: "No greater boon could be given them [the Deaf] than a college where those possessing the requisite amount of intellect might press forward their education to a point which would enable them to conduct the education of their fellows in misfortune, and to engage in many pursuits from which they are now . . . necessarily debarred."

24. Undated correspondence of J. Sullivan to Maxine T. Boatner, Gallaudet Family Papers, Gallaudet University Archives.

25. Gallaudet, *History,* 204.

4

The Thomas Hopkins Gallaudet and Alice Cogswell Statue: Controversies and Celebrations

Michael J. Olson

Editors' Introduction

Michael J. Olson's meticulously researched article directly challenges benign interpretations of Edward Miner Gallaudet's presidency. Drawing heavily from primary sources, Olson looks at a previously unexplored controversy that sparked intense debate among American deaf leaders in the late 19th century and raised troublesome questions about Gallaudet's commitment to equality for deaf people. Olson depicts Gallaudet as ironfisted and essentially absolute in his decisions. Gallaudet operated under the guise of hosting an open competition to hire a sculptor to create a statue of his father and Alice Cogswell, but, Olson shows, even before receiving proposals from deaf candidates, he had already commissioned the well-known hearing artist, Daniel Chester French, for the job. Olson's research suggests that audism and paternalism were characteristics of Gallaudet's first president.

I N 1883, AT THE SECOND CONVENTION of the National Association of the Deaf (NAD), held in New York City, C. K. W. Strong, a Deaf member from Washington, D.C., proposed that the NAD sponsor the erection of a bronze statue of Thomas Hopkins Gallaudet on the 100th anniversary of Gallaudet's birth in 1887. The statue would be situated on the grounds of the National Deaf-Mute College—soon to become Gallaudet College—at Kendall Green.[1] The resolution passed, and the NAD formed a committee of fifteen members to manage the project. The next convention was to be held in Washington, D.C., in August 1888, at which time the new statue would be unveiled.[2] No one could have anticipated the controversy this project would entail or the insight that it provides into the Deaf community and the actions of Edward Miner Gallaudet, the college's first president. The controversy created not only friction between some of the nation's prominent Deaf leaders of the time but also involved identity struggles over a hearing sculptor being chosen to create Gallaudet University's iconic statue.

Lars M. Larson, an 1882 graduate of Gallaudet, initiated the first controversy. He made no objection to having the statue erected, but he argued that the statue should not be located in Washington, D.C. He thought that it should be erected in Hartford, Connecticut, where Thomas Hopkins Gallaudet, Laurent Clerc, and Mason Fitch Cogswell founded the first school for the deaf, eventually called the American School for the Deaf.[3] Others countered that the statue should be situated in Washington, D.C., where Deaf people from all over the United States could come to view the statue instead of going to remote Hartford. Some believed that the nation's capital was the most fitting place for such memorials and statues. Also, they argued, Kendall Green, site of the national college, was the ideal place.[4] The Larson controversy lasted for a month but eventually faded away.

A Gallaudet Centennial Commission was formed in November 1883 to collect funds for the statue and to arrange the time and place for holding the celebrations honoring the centennial of Thomas H. Gallaudet's birth. The committee members then appointed agents and subagents for each state and territory of the United States to collect contributions. Their preliminary fund-raising goal was not less than $2,500. It was impossible to know the exact amount needed, since they had not selected an artist to design the statue. The members of the committee chose Theodore A. Froehlich of New York City as their chairman and William H. Weeks to be the commission treasurer.[5] The fund became known as the Gallaudet Centennial Memorial Fund (hereafter, the Memorial Fund). Pennsylvania quickly announced that they had formed a committee to select their own agents to solicit funds, but not before more controversy erupted.[6]

An anguished correspondent wrote in the November 1883 *National Deaf-Mute Leader* that he felt that it was not necessary for Deaf people to contribute money to erect another monument in honor of Thomas H. Gallaudet, as there was already a monument to his memory in Hartford. He suggested dropping the idea and starting a new movement. Instead of raising funds for a Gallaudet memorial, Deaf people would collect money for a monument to be erected in honor of an unnamed person in his native Vermont.[7] The Gallaudet memorial project nevertheless went ahead.

The *Deaf Mutes' Journal* (*DMJ*), a weekly newspaper for the deaf community edited by Edwin A. Hodgson, printed the treasurer's reports of the Memorial Fund. The first report stated that the funds collected between November and December 1883 amounted to $4.25.[8] An editorial in the *DMJ* mentioned that the fund had not increased very rapidly. It stated that there should be more announcements to let the public know where the money was to be sent. The editorial also said that the funds should be held in a savings bank and invested at interest, so that their value would increase.[9]

Lewis A. Palmer wrote a long article describing the slowness of collecting contributions for the Memorial Fund, and he blamed lack of enthusiasm among the fund-raising agents. He pointed out that after President James A. Garfield was assassinated in 1881 and the nation was in mourning, students at Gallaudet College and other Deaf people contributed sufficient funds to purchase a bust of Garfield in a short time. The bust was designed by a well-known sculptor, Daniel Chester French. Palmer went on to say that people had forgotten about Gallaudet, who had died in 1851, thirty years before the assassination of President Garfield. He encouraged Deaf people to come up with more ideas to raise the funds for the Gallaudet statue.[10]

Deaf artist H. P. Arms of Philadelphia was the first person to create a product that could be sold for fund raising. It was a color, six-by-nine-inch alphabet card, called "Souvenir of Silence," and it contained a portrait of Gallaudet with a view of the Hartford School and the National Deaf-Mute College, now Gallaudet University, and a manual alphabet with full colors around the card. The members of the Pennsylvania Association of Deaf-Mutes sold the cards.[11]

In 1885 Edmund Booth, a newspaper owner and editor in Iowa, wrote an article in the *DMJ* encouraging Deaf people to contribute more money to the fund. Booth had been an early pupil of Gallaudet's at the American School and had taught there for a few years after graduating. He wrote in detail about how he knew Gallaudet personally and described Gallaudet's wonderful character and his work with Deaf pupils.[12]

Commission Chairman Froehlich made a plea to the public to contribute more money for the cause, and he spoke about Gallaudet's worth and work for Deaf people. Froehlich and the committee asked people to contribute any amount they could afford, regardless of how much it was, and they encouraged everyone to work together to succeed.[13] Instead, more controversy ensued.

Because of the public pressure on securing a bond for the funds, Weeks, the fund treasurer, resigned. He believed that it was not necessary to have a bond for the funds, and he also thought that the funds were safely secured.[14] His successor, Amos G. Draper, a National Deaf-Mute College professor, came to the rescue by devising a plan to guarantee the funds against possible loss.[15] He prepared his reports and printed his bulletins in the *DMJ* almost every week, listing the contributors by name along with the amount each contributed.[16] During the latter part of 1885, the Memorial Fund project began to boom, as the agents in the different states started to collect contributions vigorously. At the end of 1885, the fund had increased to $651.21, an addition of more than $500 in about two months, compared to a little over $100 in the previous two years.[17]

Meanwhile, American School graduate Thomas Brown of West Henniker, New Hampshire, wrote to Henry Winter Syle, one of the best-known Deaf leaders of the time, with a suggestion. He first told of his experiences meeting Gallaudet and Laurent Clerc. He then mentioned that many Deaf graduates from the Hartford school and other schools for the deaf could not afford to come to Washington to witness the unveiling of the statue. He believed that only a few rich Deaf people would be able to attend the unveiling. He suggested that the best way to overcome this problem was to have a picture of both Gallaudet and Clerc, either photographs or paintings prepared at a modest expense, to be hung in each school for deaf children in the United States.[18]

The most troublesome and long-running controversy about the statue involved selection of the artist who would be commissioned to create it. The opening public statement in what became a major dispute was a brief comment in an article in the *DMJ*, dated January 14, 1886, which simply stated, "It is understood that Dan [Daniel Chester] French, of Massachusetts, the distinguished artist, was engaged to prepare a design for the sculptured group of the founder of mute education."[19] Had the committee selected French as the sculptor for the statue as early as 1886, or had the chairman, Froehlich, made an arrangement with the sculptor without consulting his entire committee?

Froehlich sent many circulars to the committee, state agents and sub-agents, and collectors, announcing that he had requested French to prepare a design for the Gallaudet statue. French visited Washington and consulted with Edward Miner Gallaudet, president of the college and son of Thomas Hopkins Gallaudet, to find a suitable location for the proposed statue. Also, French sent Froehlich a small design in plaster, showing the elder Gallaudet with Alice Cogswell, his first deaf student. Froehlich's circular mentioned having French accept a commission for the statue, and it explained how much money the committee should pay French. It also encouraged all of the agents to solicit more contributions.[20]

French apparently visited the campus on November 18, 1885, to study potential sites for the statue, initiating a rather humorous controversy that eventually resolved itself but that also implies that Edward Miner Gallaudet was less than honest with his Deaf leaders. Gallaudet showed French several portraits of his father and suggested where he would like the statue to be situated; however, French thought the location was too close to a group of buildings and not suitable as a statue background.[21] French wandered around the grounds and suggested "an ideal site" in a treed area in front of Chapel Hall.[22]

Gallaudet cautioned French about an old apple tree near the center of the proposed location, telling him that his daughters were sentimental about that tree. When they were children, they climbed and played house in its branches. Gallaudet warned that they would object to having the tree removed. French told Gallaudet that he should not worry and just wait and see.[23]

A few weeks later, Gallaudet wrote to French.

> A curious thing has happened. There was a terrible storm a few nights ago, and almost half of your precious tree was blown down. I have waited in hopes that my daughters would come to their senses and would agree that the remains of the tree should be demolished, but alas! they still cling to the old broken stump. They will not hear of it. The trouble is I cannot make them understand the importance of the right place for a statue.[24]

French still was not concerned, however, and a few more weeks later Gallaudet wrote to him again.

> What will you say when I tell you that a miracle has happened? Behold! Another storm has come and gone, and the other branch has been torn away, and even my unreasonable offspring do not insist that the bare stump should be left standing. The statue can stand where you and I want it, and where it should stand.[25]

This episode, though ultimately of little inherent importance, suggests that President Gallaudet was more closely involved in the selection of French than some of the Deaf leaders thought. Gallaudet had already

Edward Miner Gallaudet

met with French and had determined the location before yet another controversy brewed among the Deaf leaders. Fund raising and the apparent unilateral decision of President Gallaudet generated further discussion.

Edwin A. Hodgson, editor of the *DMJ*, wrote to Draper about his concerns whether the committee was on the right track for the fund-raising efforts. Hodgson noticed an article in the *Maryland Bulletin*, a publication of the Maryland School for the Deaf, about the arrangement with the sculptor. He asked Draper, "What do you think of it? Is it not rather premature? It may be rather satisfactory to the sculptor, but is it a step onward for us?"[26]

One student from the National Deaf-Mute College wrote a long article on the Gallaudet Memorial, stating that the students were surprised at Froehlich's arrangements with the sculptor. The article suggested that Froehlich had made a bold move to reach this decision without consulting the committee. He wrote that if the chairman indeed acted without the consent of the committee, they should protest against the chairman.[27]

More controversy followed, as the Brooklyn Society of Deaf-Mutes held a meeting and resolved that the contributors would not hand in any contributions to Draper. They complained that he was not a member of the NAD at the time of the second convention in 1883, and that he had not paid his dues at the convention.[28] Angie Fuller, a Deaf poetess and advocate, on the other hand, argued that Draper was deaf and was greatly interested in the work of deaf education; that he held a high position in the community as a member of the faculty of the National Deaf-Mute College; and that he could not afford to be dishonest or any way in abuse the funds.[29]

In the first quarter of 1887, the funds increased comfortably to hit the $6,000 mark.[30] The committee thought that this amount was sufficient to start definite plans and to make arrangements for a binding contract with an artist. In April, the chairman announced a new committee of five that was authorized to make a contract for the statue. They were Froehlich, Job Turner, Dudley Webster George, Draper, and Hodgson. Froehlich also encouraged all interested artists to send in their designs and plans for the proposed statue to the committee, despite the indications several months before that French had already been selected. The announcement was made on April 14, 1887, in the *DMJ*.[31]

Gallaudet, meanwhile, was becoming more involved in the planning of the statute to honor his father. His diary suggests that a decision had been made to choose French well before Froehlich publicly solicited designs and plans. Gallaudet's diary entry for February 24, 1887, recorded that he traveled to New York City and Froehlich visited him. Froehlich gave Gallaudet a promising and positive report on the progress of the Memorial Committee. Froehlich also told Gallaudet that the Fund was "looking to giving Mr. French a Commission the coming Spring."[32]

The apparent conflict in Froehlich's statements, as well as the seeming decision to select a hearing artist without a formal process, began to attract attention in the spring of 1887. Gallaudet wrote in his diary on April 22, 1887, that he was interviewed by a reporter from the *Washington Post* concerning the statue and the controversy engendered by excluding the consideration of deaf artists. Gallaudet recorded that "the deaf are up in arms because the Committee do not give more time to have models prepared by deaf-mute artists."[33] The *Washington Post* reported that Froehlich's request for plans, published on April 14, "has caused some complaint among deaf mute artists. They claim that the time given between the announcement and May 2—a little over two weeks—is not sufficient for those wishing to contest to prepare their plans, and [they] charge that the committee have withheld the announcement until the last minute for the purpose of limiting the number of artists, they having arranged to give the work to a certain person . . . the committee . . . have been requested to postpone the meeting until June, but have refused to do so, and the disappointed artists claim that this action is apparent proof of the favoritism charged."[34]

The committee met at the National Deaf-Mute College on May 3, 1887, ostensibly to review the designs and models and to select the best artist for the project. In addition to the submission by French, at least two Deaf artists, Albert Ballin and J. F. J. Tresch, submitted designs and models. Tresch of New York City presented a design showing Gallaudet seated in a chair with a male pupil in knickerbockers standing beside him. Gallaudet holds a book in one hand while the other hand makes the letter "A" of the American Manual Alphabet. The boy's hand also spells "A."[35] It is possible that Deaf California sculptor Douglas Tilden and other Deaf artists sent in designs as well, but there is no mention of them in the surviving documents. In any case, the committee of five announced that they had selected a model designed by French and awarded the contract to him.[36]

The originality of French's design is open to question. It shows Thomas Hopkins Gallaudet seated on a chair, his arm wrapped around Alice Cogswell and his hand spelling the letter "A," similar to Tresch's design, while Alice stands beside him, holding a book with one hand and spelling "A" with her other hand. French may have copied this from deaf artist John Carlin, who used a similar motif in a bas-relief, carved stone showing three pupils with Gallaudet that was completed about thirty years before. The stone is now mounted on a wall inside the entrance of the main building at the American School in Hartford.

Even putting aside Gallaudet's 1885 discussions with French about a location for the statue, Gallaudet's role in the committee's 1887 decision to select French was significant. He wrote in his diary for May 3, "In the evening I attended a meeting of the Gallaudet Memorial Committee to aid them in deciding about the commission for the Statue. They reached the satisfactory conclusion of giving the commission to Daniel C. French."[37]

Many deaf people reacted strongly and negatively to the committee's announcement that a hearing sculptor had been selected for the memorial. On May 9, Hodgson wrote to Draper to let him know that a mass meeting was going to take place in New York City to protest the decision. He quoted from an article in the New York *World* saying that, "'Mr. Hodgson [was] mentioned as saying no deaf-mute was *capable* of making a statue.' Just think of it! I, who stood up for the deaf-mutes, reflected as the one to make a target of."[38]

The mass meeting occurred, as Hodgson predicted, and deaf people protested against the committee for awarding the contract to a hearing sculptor. They argued that experienced deaf artists would do the job for

Statue of Thomas H. Gallaudet and Alice Cogswell, 1889

only $8,000 to $10,000, including the pedestal, whereas French charged $10,000 for a bronze statue without a pedestal. They also complained that one member of the committee was afraid to give the job to a deaf artist because he thought that a deaf artist could not do the task.[39]

The committee responded by stating they had a difficult choice in selecting the artist, and it took them a long time to make their decision. They had three sessions in one day to decide which artist to accept. The committee believed that French was the best artist, based on his experiences with the many other statues and memorials he had designed.[40] This hardly put the matter to rest.

An announcement in the *DMJ* let the public know that there would be a meeting to discuss the advisability of requesting the committee to suspend all actions in order to give deaf artists more time to submit their designs. It stated that the April 14th announcement gave artists only two weeks to submit plans and models, and that was not sufficient.[41]

Gallaudet continued to play a central role in this controversy. He wrote in his diary for June 2, 1887, "I had a 'season' this morning with Ballin the deaf-mute artist who wanted to make the statue of my father. He wanted me to use my influence to reopen the matter so he could have a chance to prepare a life sized model. I think I succeeded in convincing him that his opportunity has passed by."[42]

French was also aware of the dispute over his selection, though he seems not to have been directly engaged. He received the news of his formal commission to create the statute while he was in Paris, working on other sculptures. However, in July he wrote a letter to a friend in the United States, Charles Moore, saying that there was "a protest from the deaf mutes who think that the statue should not be made by a 'hearing' sculptor. I am glad to be away while the discussion is going on."[43]

In response to the controversy, selection committee member Job Turner, a Virginian and a missionary to deaf people, claimed that the group wished to select a deaf artist, but could not find any. He said that the committee members were afraid to entrust a large sum to an inexperienced deaf artist, and they said that they would gladly award the contract to any deaf artist who had the same skill as a sculptor as French and other hearing artists. Turner also mentioned French's fee, saying that French had originally said that he would ask for $14,000, but he agreed to accept the $10,000 offer because of his respect for Gallaudet. French's uncle, Benjamin B. French, once served on the Board of Directors of the National Deaf-Mute College.[44]

Augustus Saint-Gaudens, a sculptor and friend of French, sent a letter to the Gallaudet Monument Committee, in which he wrote, "You have no doubt been presented by Mr. Ballin the Sculptor with a letter containing an endorsement by me of his proposal. I gave it with great pleasure but at the time of Mr. Ballin's visit I was very much occupied with other matters and I neglected to write all that was on my mind. I must add now that although I consider his proposal a reasonable one I wish it clearly understood that I do not recommend its consideration if that should lead to any action on the part of the Committee prejudicial to

Mr. French's interests such as bringing in a competitor unexpected by Mr. French at the time he made his agreement with you. I do not know Mr. Ballin or his work and in no way must I be understood as endorsing what he may do."[45]

In late June, soon after the announcement of French's selection, deaf sculptor Tresch wrote an angry letter to Draper, asking him to reconsider the decision and saying that he was not satisfied with the committee's actions.[46] Tresch wrote to Draper again a few days later, accusing Draper of making the committee decision to award the contract to French. Tresch lambasted Draper in many ways, and he said that the committee was doing everything wrong. Tresch claimed that French was "a *pet friend* of yours and Gallaudet."[47]

Soon after Tresch's bitter letter to Draper, another member of the committee mistakenly believed the controversy was over. Dudley Webster George wrote to Draper that "the storm in the Brooklyn teakettle seems to have subsided. Bond, Tresch, Ballin et al have ceased to spout."[48] It was not over, however, and a few weeks later Gallaudet wrote in his diary, "I met Froehlich at the 5th Ave Hotel and had a long talk about the Memorial Committee squabbles, this grows pretty tiresome but patience is necessary."[49]

On August 14, 1887, French arrived in New York from Paris and began to work on a couple of designs and on a model of about three feet high.[50] Gallaudet went to New York two days later and met with Froehlich, Carlin, and Hodgson to view the model statue; Gallaudet expressed his satisfaction.[51] Soon after, attendees at the Eleventh Biennial Convention of the Empire State Deaf-Mute Association, held in Syracuse, New York, on August 31 and September 1, 1887, engaged in a contentious debate about whether they should send money to the Gallaudet Centennial Committee. Most opposed sending their money to the committee. They preferred to contribute to another statue committee, the Peet Committee, because they believed that the chairman of the Gallaudet Centennial Committee had committed a breach of trust.[52]

A September 22 *DMJ* article for the first time mentioned California deaf artist Douglas Tilden as a possible sculptor for the Gallaudet statue, although it is not clear whether Tilden, probably the best-known and most accomplished deaf sculptor of his time, actually submitted a plan. The article stated that "Mr. Douglas Tilden, of California, was at the Institution [New York School for the Deaf at Fanwood] on Tuesday. He is the mute who, like Albert Ballin, Tresch and others, was anxious to compete for the contract to erect the bronze statue of the elder Gallaudet, to be unveiled in Washington, in 1888. Mr. Tilden expects to spend a year in this city in the study of sculpture, and then go to Paris."[53]

Daniel Chester French wrote to his friend, Charles Moore, telling of his work on the model of the Gallaudet statue and how he made a study of a little girl's face for the statue of Alice Cogswell. The letter mentioned that a Mrs. Sherman allowed French to have her daughter, Mary, as a study for the model.[54]

The acrimony about French's selection grew worse in the fall of 1887. On October third, Froehlich wrote to Draper informing him that French received a threatening letter from a Mr. Bond. Bond stated that he might file a lawsuit to get an injunction against the committee. French asked Froehlich about what to do with the letter, and Froehlich told him just to ignore it.[55]

Gallaudet and the committee remained staunchly committed to French. Gallaudet visited him in Concord, Massachusetts, on October 31. The next day he saw the model, and he was very pleased with it.[56] In December, the committee visited French's studio in New York City to view the model, and they too were very impressed.[57]

The only controversial issue between French and the committee at this time was the completion date. French thought that he would not able to finish the sculpture before September 1888. The committee originally had wanted the statue to be ready by the middle of June 1888. The committee felt that a contract should force the sculptor to follow the committee's goals for the completion date. Ultimately French's view prevailed, and an agreement was made between the committee and French on January 21, 1888, giving him wide latitude to complete the project sometime between October 1, 1888, and June 1, 1889.[58]

In early 1888, another controversy developed, this time about funding the base of the statue. Gallaudet became concerned when he read an editorial article in the *DMJ* that stated that the college should pay for a pedestal. Gallaudet stated that the board of directors had never been consulted about providing the pedestal. He argued that the costs of design and setting up the pedestal should be covered by funds collected from the people, not from the college.[59]

NAD member C. K. W. Strong of Washington, D.C., further muddied the waters by arguing that the federal government should fund the pedestal. He believed, inaccurately, that Kendall Green was government property. He went on to say that other statues and memorials in Washington were paid for by the government. He encouraged Congress to appropriate funds for the pedestal.[60] Some NAD members opposed Strong's idea, preferring that the construction of the pedestal be paid by deaf people. The controversy continued on and off for about fourteen months, and finally, in March 1889, the committee awarded a contract to Daniel C. French to design the pedestal for the amount of $1,200.[61]

In the early part of June 1888, Froehlich announced a postponement of the convention to June 1889, due to the sculptor's inability to complete the statue in time for the planned 1888 gathering.[62] This was due to errors on the model that Saint-Gaudens discovered and French's wedding in July 1888. While working on the model, French's colleague noticed that Gallaudet's legs were too short. French had not noticed this himself, and he realized that would have to saw out the legs and add a few inches to them.[63]

Finally, in May of 1889, controversy was put aside, and the ground was broken in preparation for the construction of the foundation for the pedestal.[64] The lettering and carving of the inscriptions on the pedestal were done by a Deaf stonecutter named William H. Caldicott, a graduate of Fanwood (New York School for the Deaf).[65] The pedestal was finally placed on June 24, two days before the unveiling ceremony.[66] The next

New England Deaf Group at the unveiling of the statue, 1889

day, the bronze statue was set up during the rain, under the supervision of French.[67]

On June 26, 1889, many Deaf people and friends, including Alexander Graham Bell, came to Kendall Green to witness the unveiling of the statue. Robert McGregor delivered an eloquent address, and Laura C. Redden Searing wrote a beautiful poem. Hodgson, President of the NAD, gave a presentation address, and President Gallaudet made an acceptance speech. Herbert Draper Gallaudet and Marion Wallace Gallaudet, grandchildren of Thomas Hopkins Gallaudet, had the honor of unveiling the statue, and when it was revealed, many people cheered and waved their handkerchiefs in excitement.[68]

Between 1883 and 1889 the Gallaudet Centennial Memorial Fund collected $12,447.77. The total expenses for the Gallaudet statue were $11,968.23, including $11,200.00 paid to French for his services. The remaining balance of $479.54 was given to the National Deaf-Mute College.[69] The college used this money to establish the Gallaudet Memorial Art Fund for the purpose of providing for the perpetual maintenance and preservation of the statue and for the purchase of art works produced by deaf artists.[70]

Notes

1. Chip, "Convention," *Deaf Mutes' Journal*, August 30, 1883, 3.

2. *Washington Star*, "Another Statue Proposed for Washington," *Deaf Mutes' Journal*, September 13, 1883, 2.

3. "New York," *Deaf Mutes' Journal*, October 25, 1883, 2.

4. Dudley Webster George, "Lars M. Larson's Wonderful Opinion," *Deaf Mutes' Journal*, November 1, 1883, 2.

5. Theodore A. Froehlich, "The Gallaudet Centennial Memorial Fund," *Deaf Mutes' Journal*, November 22, 1883, 3.

6. Jerome T. Elwell, "Notice for Agents and Deaf Subscribers in Behalf of the Gallaudet Memorial Fund," *Deaf Mutes' Journal*, December 27, 1883, 2.

7. Catsby, "Too Many Monuments?" *The National Deaf-Mute Leader*, November 19, 1883, 4.

8. William H. Weeks, "The Gallaudet Centennial Memorial Fund," *Deaf Mutes' Journal*, January 3, 1884, 3

9. Editorials, *Deaf Mutes' Journal*, January 10, 1884, and February 28, 1884.

10. L. A. Palmer, "The Gallaudet Statue," *Deaf Mutes' Journal*, January 1, 1885, 2.

11. "Western Pennsylvania," *Deaf Mutes' Journal*, March 26, 1885, 3.

12. Edmund Booth, "The Gallaudet Statue," *Deaf Mutes' Journal*, April 16, 1885, 3.

13. T. A. Froehlich, "The Gallaudet Centennial Memorial Fund," *Deaf Mutes' Journal*, May 28, 1885, 3.

14. E. A. Hodgson, "The Gallaudet Centennial Memorial," *Deaf Mutes' Journal*, October 8, 1885, 2.

15. T. A. Froehlich, "The Gallaudet Centennial Memorial Committee," *Deaf Mutes' Journal,* October 8, 1885, 3.

16. A. G. Draper, "Gallaudet Centennial Memorial Fund," *Deaf Mutes' Journal*, October 22, 1885, 2. "Treasurer's Bulletin, No. 1" listed a Mr. James Jos. Murphy of Delavan, Wisconsin, who made his first contribution of $4.50 on October 19, 1885.

17. A. G. Draper, "Gallaudet Centennial Memorial Fund," *Deaf Mutes' Journal,* December 31, 1885, 3.

18. Thomas Brown to the Rev. Henry Winter Syle, 14 January 1886, Papers of Henry Winter Syle, Box 1, Folder 26, Gallaudet University Archives.

19. Columbia, "Washington, D. C., Notes," *Deaf Mutes' Journal,* January 14, 1886, 4.

20. T. A. Froehlich, "Circular," 25 February, 1886, Collection of Gallaudet Centennial Memorial Fund, Letters—Froehlich, T. A., Box 1, Folder 46, Gallaudet University Archives.

21. Diary of Edward Miner Gallaudet, 18 November 1885, microfilm, Gallaudet University Archives.

22. Margaret French Cresson, *Journey Into Fame; The Life of Daniel Chester French* (Cambridge: Harvard University Press, 1947), 148.

23. Ibid., 148–49.

24. Mary (French) French, *Memories of a Sculptor's Wife* (Boston: Houghton Mifflin, 1928), 172.

25. Ibid.

26. E. A. Hodgson to Amos Draper, 9 March 1886, Collection of Gallaudet Centennial Memorial Fund, Letters-Hodgson, E. A., Box 1, Folder 55, Gallaudet University Archives..

27. Frank Frynell, "College Chronicle," *Deaf Mutes' Journal,* April 8, 1886, 2.

28. George L. Reynolds, "Deaf-Mutes, Read and Meditate," *Deaf Mutes' Journal*, April 8, 1886, 3.

29. Angie Fuller, "A Fine Painting and a Fine Wedding," *Deaf Mutes' Journal,* November 11, 1886, 3.

30. Amos G. Draper, "Gallaudet Centennial Memorial Fund," *Deaf Mutes' Journal*, February 24, 1887, 2.

31. T. A. Froehlich, "Gallaudet Centennial Memorial Fund," *Deaf Mutes' Journal*, April 14, 1887, 3.

32. Diary of Edward Miner Gallaudet, 24 February 1887.

33. Diary of Edward Miner Gallaudet, 22 April 1887.

34. Unidentified reporter, "The Gallaudet Statue. A Charge of Favoritism Denied—The Award to Be Made May 2," *Washington Post,* April 23, 1882.

35. Montague Tigg, "New York," *Deaf Mutes' Journal,* May 5, 1887, 3.

36. Unidentified writer, "College," *Deaf Mutes' Journal,* May 5, 1887, 2.

37. Diary of Edward Miner Gallaudet, 3 May 1887.

38. E. A. Hodgson to Amos Draper, 9 May 1887, Letters—Hodgson , E. A., Box 1, Folder 55, Collection of Gallaudet Centennial Memorial Fund.

39. E. A. Hodgson, ed., "The Gallaudet Statue," *Deaf Mutes' Journal,* May 12, 1887, 2.

40. D. W. George, "The Gallaudet Memorial. Statement of the Sub-Committee," *Deaf Mutes' Journal,* May 12, 1887, 3.

41. W. A. Bond and Thos. Godfrey, "Notice," *Deaf Mutes' Journal,* May 26, 1887, 2; Montague Tigg, "New York, The Mass (?) Meeting," *Deaf Mutes' Journal,* June 2, 1887, 3.

42. Diary of Edward Miner Gallaudet, 2 June 1887.

43. Daniel Chester French to Charles Moore, 2 July 1887, Papers of Charles Moore, General Correspondence, Box 5, Folder 6, Manuscript Division, Library of Congress.

44. Job Turner, "From the Sunny South," *Deaf Mutes' Journal,* June 9, 1887, 4.

45. Augustus Saint-Gaudens to the Gallaudet Monument Committee, 16 June 1887, Letters—Saint-Gaudens, Augustus, Box 1, Folder 84, Collection of Gallaudet Centennial Memorial Fund.

46. J. F. J. Tresch to Amos G. Draper, 27 June 1887, Letters—Tresch, J. F. J., Box 2, Folder 7, Collection of Gallaudet Centennial Memorial Fund.

47. J. F. J. Tresch to Amos G. Draper, 1 July 1887, Letters—Tresch, J. F. J., Box 2, Folder 7, Collection of Gallaudet Centennial Memorial Fund.

48. D. W. George to Amos G. Draper, 7 July 1887, Letters—George, D. W., Box 1, Folder 50, Collection of Gallaudet Centennial Memorial Fund.

49. Diary of Edward Miner Gallaudet, 9 August 1887.

50. Editorial, "Mr. Daniel C. French," *Deaf Mutes' Journal*, August 18, 1887, 2.

51. Diary of Edward Miner Gallaudet, 16 August 1887.

52. N. Y. World, "A Difference Among the Deaf-Mutes," *Deaf Mutes' Journal*, September 1, 1887, 2; "Empire State Convention," *Deaf Mutes' Journal*, September 8, 1887, 3.

53. Aquila, "Fanwood," *Deaf Mutes' Journal*, September 22, 1887, 4.

54. Daniel Chester French to Charles Moore, 3 October 1887, Papers of Charles Moore, General Correspondence, Box 5, Folder 6. Manuscript Division, Library of Congress.

55. T. A. Froehlich to Amos G. Draper, 3 October 1887, Letters—Froehlich, T. A., Box 1, Folder 46, Collection of Gallaudet Centennial Memorial Fund.

56. Diary of Edward Miner Gallaudet, 31 October and 1 November 1887.

57. Editorial, "The Gallaudet Statue," *Deaf Mutes' Journal*, December 1, 1887, 2.

58. Editorial, "The Gallaudet Memorial," *Deaf Mutes' Journal*, January 26, 1888, 2.

59. E. M. Gallaudet, "The Pedestal," *Deaf Mutes' Journal*, January 26, 1888, 2.

60. C. K. W. Strong, "The Pedestal," *Deaf Mutes' Journal*, February 2, 1888, 2.

61. T. A. Froehlich, "Pedestal for the Gallaudet Statue," *Deaf Mutes' Journal*, March 14, 1889, 2.

62. T. F. Fox, "Official Announcement," *Deaf Mutes' Journal*, June 14, 1888, 3.

63. French, *Memories of a Sculptor's Wife*, 154.

64. Van, "College Chronicle," *Deaf Mutes' Journal*, May 16, 1889, 2.

65. Unidentified writer, "Personal," *The Silent Worker* (September 1894): 7; *Deaf Mutes' Journal*, July 25, 1907, 3.

66. Diary of Edward Miner Gallaudet, 24 June 1889.

67. Ibid., 25 June 1889.

68. "The Gallaudet Centennial," *Deaf Mutes' Journal*, June 27, 1889, 1–4.

69. Amos G. Draper, "Gallaudet Centennial Memorial Fund, Final Report of the Treasurer," *Deaf Mutes' Journal*, December 19, 1889, 2.

70. E. M. Gallaudet, "The Gallaudet Memorial Art Fund," *The Silent Worker* (February 1903): 91.

Selected Bibliography

Manuscripts

Collection of the Gallaudet Centennial Memorial Fund, MSS 154, Gallaudet University Archives, Washington, D.C.

Papers of Henry Winter Syle, MSS 65, Gallaudet University Archives, Washington, D.C.

Papers of Charles Moore, Manuscript Division, Library of Congress, Washington, D.C.

Diaries of Edward Miner Gallaudet, Microfilms, Gallaudet University Archives, Washington, D.C.

Books

Cresson, Margaret French. *Journey Into Fame: The Life of Daniel Chester French*. Cambridge: Harvard University Press.

French, Mary (French). *Memories of a Sculptor's Wife*. Boston: Houghton Mifflin Company, 1928.

Richman, Michael. *Daniel Chester French: An American Sculptor*. Washington, D.C.: National Trust for Historical Preservation, 1976.

Newspapers and Periodicals

The Deaf Mutes' Journal, New York.
The National Deaf-Mute Leader, Brooklyn, New York.
The Silent Worker, New Jersey.
The Washington Post, Washington, D.C.

5

Two Views on Mathematics Education for Deaf Students: Edward Miner Gallaudet and Amos G. Draper

Christopher A. N. Kurz

Editors' Introduction

In this article, Christopher A. N. Kurz reviews the history of a disagreement between Edward Miner Gallaudet and one of the best-known deaf teachers at the college, Amos G. Draper. The immediate issue was Draper's desire to reform the mathematics curriculum in order to improve deaf students' mathematics achievement. Gallaudet believed that significant mastery of English needed to precede the study of mathematics. Draper argued that the learning of English and mathematics could proceed simultaneously and that advanced English skills were not necessary to comprehending mathematics. This debate is revealing, as historians know little about pedagogical arguments during Gallaudet's presidency. Kurz's work suggests that there was an underlying conflict in the nineteenth century, long before the idea of bilingual education of deaf children had been articulated, between hearing and deaf approaches to higher education.

O<small>N</small> A<small>PRIL</small> 25, 1876, Amos G. Draper, a deaf professor at the National Deaf-Mute College (now Gallaudet University), delivered an oration on "The Influence of Mathematical Studies upon Personal Character." He gave the speech during the exercises of the college's regular public anniversary in the District of Columbia. In his presentation, Draper noted that,

> As children making their first rude attempts at drawing with only sticks on the sand, so men yet ignorant of science strive to develop regular forms and avoid irregularities and excrescences.

Amos Draper

Children, with eyes and ears opened wide, are filled with admiration by regularity of outline, beauty of color, and harmony of sound. Long before the sciences that mark out present civilization were known, the first children of the earth, the first men, cultivated this kind of knowledge. The intellectual life of our race began, as that of each individual begins, in the appreciation of geometric truths. The earliest Hindoos and Chinese of whom we have any records were familiar with the properties of the right-angled triangle, the discovery of which is commonly attributed to Pythagoras. And still, as civilization advances, and as children grow to manhood, the love of form, color, and harmony remains central among the passions which sway the soul with delight.[1]

During his oration, Draper focused on how a child would learn mathematical principles both indirectly and directly and how knowledge would propel the child's curiosity about the universe. In essence, he believed that each child was a mathematician and that exploration into and understanding of mathematical studies would bring a harmony of personal character and sound mind. The knowledge and understanding of mathematics could become a way of developing character and morals, he believed. The question was how should a deaf child's mathematical studies be molded, propelled, and supported? As superintendent of the Columbia Institution for the Instruction of the Deaf and Dumb and Blind and later president of the National Deaf-Mute College (hereafter, Gallaudet College), Edward Miner Gallaudet faced the same question when he struggled with curriculum development for his institutions. However, Gallaudet and Draper had different views on mathematics education for deaf students, especially for those who planned to go to college.

Whence They Came

Gallaudet, the youngest of eight brothers and sisters, was born on February 5, 1837, to Thomas Hopkins Gallaudet and Sophia Fowler Gallaudet. The fact that he was born after his father retired from teaching at the American School for the Deaf in 1830 did not prevent him from being around deaf people. His father continued to work diligently with Yale College to promote interest among graduates to work with deaf students, and his deaf mother was well liked in the deaf community. After graduating from high school at the age of fourteen in 1851, Gallaudet chose banking for his profession, but he soon found that working in a bank was not challenging enough. He wrote that his "mind began to crave a pabulum of a higher order than the counting of bank bills and the reckoning of discounts."[2] He decided to study theology and teaching at Trinity College, from which he graduated at the age of nineteen. While studying, he also held a part-time teaching position at the American School for the Deaf. In 1857 Amos Kendall invited him to come to Washington, D.C., to become head of the new Columbia Institution for the Deaf and Dumb.[3] He later became president of what became Gallaudet College and remained in the presidency for forty-six years.[4] In addition to his administrative responsibilities, Gallaudet taught courses in moral and political science in the college, and he became acquainted with Draper when the latter was a student.

Draper was born in Shaftsbury, Vermont, on October 24, 1845, to Jonathan and Philena Draper. His father was a manufacturer of augers, hammers, and carpenter's squares.[5] He became deaf when he was around ten.[6] After he attended one of the district public schools for a few years, he worked as an apprentice under his father. At fourteen his father took him to the American School, where he was admitted in March of 1860. The admission record noted: "He can read and write–can articulate distinctly–has studied arithmetic and geography somewhat."[7] He spent two years at the American School, where "he had learned to set type on the Gallaudet Guide," a school newsletter.[8] After Draper left the school in July of 1862, he went to Danville and then Aurora, Illinois, where he worked in newspaper and printing offices, respectively, before deciding to enroll at Gallaudet College in the fall of 1868. Regarding Draper's goal for traveling to Washington, D.C., his friend, James E. Gallaher, wrote: "His object was to see Washington, public men and public life, with the view of fitting himself for further editorial work, and his plan was to stay only one year in college."[9] Draper found the college both challenging and fascinating and graduated in 1872. He then began teaching Latin and mathematics at Gallaudet and remained in the profession for the next forty-five years.

What They Said About Mathematical Studies
for Deaf Students

In his *History of the College for the Deaf*, Gallaudet reminisced about the time when he became head of the world's first college for deaf people: "I was a youngster of twenty-seven, at the head of a little school of deaf and blind children in which no word of Latin, Greek, or any language but English had ever been taught. Arithmetic had not been completed. No higher mathematics had been touched, no science taught."[10] Learning English was the chief goal in schools for deaf children, but Gallaudet saw the importance of establishing a college for deaf scholars to pursue higher knowledge in order to provide them with the tools to gain honorable positions in society.

Colleges at the time focused on liberal arts, and the classics were the heart of their curriculum. The course of study Gallaudet and the faculty developed for their college corresponded "in general to what is known as the Academical Course in American colleges: there have been made, however, such modifications as seemed desirable and necessary to adapt it to the peculiar wants of the deaf and dumb."[11] Like some other colleges of the time, the college for deaf students included a preparatory year before students could enroll in college-level courses.[12] The curriculum Gallaudet and his colleagues first established included the following:

Academic Department
First Year: Analytical Grammar, Higher Arithmetic, Physical Geography, History, Latin
Second Year: Analytical Grammar, Algebra, Natural Philosophy, History, Latin

Collegiate Department
Junior Year: Geometry, Latin, Rhetoric, Chemistry, Mental Science
Senior Year: History of English Language and Literature, Latin, Astronomy, Geology, Political Science, Moral Science[13]

Mastery in arithmetic and algebra up to quadratic equations was crucial to enrollment in the collegiate program. The college's admissions announcement in 1866 stated that "candidates for admission to the Freshman Class are examined in Arithmetic, English Grammar, History, Geography, Physiology, the elements of Natural Philosophy, Algebra to Quadratic Equations, and the principles of Latin Construction in their application to any Latin author."[14] Essentially, future graduates of the college would have knowledge of mathematics up to geometry, which is equivalent to the modern United States high school course for ninth- and tenth-grade levels.

By the end of the 1868 academic year, the course of study in mathematics had changed. Students in the preparatory class studied arithmetic and algebra up to quadratic equations.[15] Freshmen studied algebra and geometry; sophomores studied spherical and solid geometry, conic sections, and trigonometry, including mensuration. The junior and senior classes took no mathematics courses. This curriculum remained unchanged for more than eleven years, with only some modification in 1874 when the preparatory program was divided into two years: the lower preparatory class studied grammar school arithmetic and the advanced class studied algebra up to quadratic equations.[16] There were two major changes in 1879: conic sections was added for the freshman class and surveying for the sophomore class.[17] In 1882, calculus and mechanics were added to the course of study for the junior class.[18] The mechanics of materials was added as an optional course for the senior class in 1907.[19]

Gallaudet's annual report in 1887 gave a description of each year during which a student would study mathematics at the college and concluded: "In all the studies of the mathematical course much original work is required, and it is believed that students who have mastered this course are prepared to undertake the study of the higher branches of mathematics."[20] Six years later, President Gallaudet provided more detailed information about the college's mathematics courses over the previous quarter century. An introductory student would study Wentworth's *Algebra* (through quadratic equations) and problems from Todhunter's *Algebra for Beginners*. A freshman student would work from Wentworth's *Treatise on Algebra* (from quadratics) and Wentworth's *Geometry*. In the next two years, the student would study Olney's or Loomis's *Plane and Spherical Trigonometry* and Loomis's *Analytic Geometry* during the sophomore year and Loomis's *Calculus* and Dana's *Mechanics* during the junior year. For the senior year, no mathematics courses were offered.[21]

It is clear that graduates of the college were expected to leave with knowledge in algebra, geometry, plane and spherical trigonometry, surveying, and mechanics. If the students wished to pursue higher branches of mathematics, they would learn analytical geometry and differential calculus, which were optional.

Gallaudet also provided a glimpse of how mathematics should be taught at the college. He emphasized that two languages were consistently used: sign language and printed English. The students would discuss their mathematical work using sign language and finger-spelled English. They would write their recitations in English. On November 9, 1886, he discussed the relationship between language and teaching mathematics in response to an inquiry by the Royal Commission of the United Kingdom. During the inquiry, the chairman asked him, "You would not give lectures in Mathematics or Logic by signs, would you?" to which he responded, "To a considerable extent; but in the use of the gesture language the interjection of words spelt upon the fingers is very common."[22] Gallaudet suggested that most lectures should be given in signs rather than in the manual alphabet, but he admitted that most technical words would be given by the manual alphabet. The mixture of the signing and the manual alphabet was the practice for most lectures at his college.

Despite Gallaudet's description of the central role of sign language in mathematics instruction and his belief in the importance of mathematics, he subordinated the latter to another goal. In the college's thirtieth annual report, published in 1887, he stated that arithmetic was second in importance to learning English.[23] He also wrote that he believed that the pupils who did not do well in mathematics had been taught by rote and were not taught the principles upon which the rules were based. He further stated that he believed mathematics was no pleasure for students, but was a great bore, trial, and terror. His explained that their problems with mathematics were "not from lack of reasoning power, but from insufficient or defective training in English during their previous instruction." Gallaudet was concerned that English deficiency could be a barrier to mathematical learning. It is possible, he reasoned, that English should be learned first before arithmetic can be taught. In sum, he believed that the learning of English should be the chief aim of every deaf child's education and that it was the foundation and means of knowledge.

In contrast to Gallaudet's rather pessimistic 1887 report, some twenty years later he noted the successes of deaf college graduates in an address he made in England.

> Of its practicability and advantage for those mentally capable of availing themselves of it there can be no doubt, for the College at Washington, liberally sustained by the federal government for nearly thirty years, has [had] within its walls several hundred youth, whose success in the scientific, mathematical, philosophical, linguistic, and other studies offered them, as well as in the practical struggles of life, is a matter of history. Students of this College have become intelligent managers of considerable farms, ranchmen and fruit growers; bank clerks and cashiers; postmasters and recorders of deeds; newspaper reporters, editorial writers, editors-in-chief, publishers and foremen of newspapers; merchants and manufacturers; microscopists, astronomers and practical chemists; draughtsmen and architects; clerks in private and public offices; founders, teachers, principals of schools for the deaf, and professors in the College; one is the official botanist of an important agricultural State; one is a prominent patent lawyer, admitted to practice in the highest courts; several have been ordained as ministers of the gospel and others are at work as lay missionaries.[24]

Some occupations mentioned in his address require mastery of arithmetic. Many graduates found mathematics challenging, yet pleasurable–since they began their learning in the best mode and since they finished the curriculum and went on to hold occupations in which it is used.

In 1876, Joseph Henry of the Smithsonian Institution confirmed Gallaudet's claim about the success of Gallaudet College students when he gave a report based on their work.

> In 1874 a plan was submitted to me for examination, by the president of this institution, of a graduated course, terminating in a collegiate curriculum. In my report upon the proposition I warmly recommend its adoption,

as a means of increasing the enjoyment and extending the sphere of useful-
ness of the class intended to be benefited. I am now happy to say that the
experiment has been successful. The scientific examination papers of last
year were submitted to me for report as to their character; while they involved the solution of questions in mathematics, physics, chemistry, geology, etc., requiring accurate knowledge and profound thought, *the answers
were such as to do honor to the undergraduates of any college in this country.*
    . . . The plan proposed of giving a collegiate course in this institution
has been, as I have said, eminently successful; it has been commended in
foreign journals, and while the graduates have, in several instances, been
employed in scientific calculations, one has received, on account of his
attainments, an honorary degree from Dartmouth College.[25]

Whatever Gallaudet's belief about the affinity of the college's students
for mathematics, there was no doubt that he and Draper disagreed on
its importance. Draper believed that English and arithmetic were equally
important. He thought that both subjects should be studied simultaneously and as early as possible. Furthermore, he believed that mastery of
English was not a prerequisite for mathematical learning. Draper was
very concerned about the mathematical skills of deaf students, calling in
1880 for increased opportunities and time to study arithmetic.[26] Draper
expressed his concern that students should study more arithmetic at deaf
institutions, outlining disappointing statistics showing a declining percentage of students passing the Gallaudet College entrance examination
over a fifteen-year span.

As to the College records, they show that, taking the whole number of
students since the foundation in 1864, only 26, or *twelve-and-a-half per cent.*,
have sustained the entrance examination in arithmetic; of applicants since
the standard has approached its present condition, that is during the last
eight years, only 11, or *seven per cent.*, have endured the same test; while
of 23 who presented themselves at the last examination for admission, not
one was able to answer satisfactorily all the questions asked them.[27]

However, Draper pointed out that the last part of the examination
might be severe, with its emphasis on mathematical problems. Applicants had to answer six problems, as follows:

1. Write the tables of long measure and of cubic measure, and state
   for what each is used.
2. Find the length of a field which has an area of 144 sq. yds, and is
   28 ft. broad?

3. How does a decimal fraction differ from a common fraction?
4. A note of $500 was dated June 10, and bore interest at 5 *per cent;*
   Oct. 3 a payment of $140 was made. What was due on the note
   one year from its date?
5. If 5/8 of a ship cost $9,875, what would 7/8 of it cost? [Solve this
   question first by proportion and then analysis.]
6. What is the square root of the fifth power of 3?[28]

Draper argued that deaf schools should restructure their mathematics
curriculum to involve more instruction in arithmetical terms and more
accuracy in handling problems, such as those on the admittance examination, stressing his belief that deaf children should be taught how to
analyze arithmetical language within questions and perform the operations accordingly. He further reasoned that student's shortcomings were
caused by several deficiencies in their instruction, specifically "that they
had been taught without a text book; that they had never been dwelling
on a subject, but passed rapidly through; that they had long since been
given higher branches; that they had never studied arithmetic at all, or
at least the recollection of it had passed from them."[29] Lastly, Draper
advocated for intensive arithmetic education so that graduates would be
well fitted to assume honorable occupations, or if they wished, to take
up higher education.

Draper's colorful oration on April 25, 1876, titled "The Influence of
Mathematical Studies upon Personal Character," expressed disappoint-
ment in the mathematical performance of the graduates of the College.
He hoped to inspire schools for deaf children to revitalize their mathematics curriculum to prepare their students for advanced studies in
mathematics and, in turn, mold them into well-rounded Americans.
Draper described the importance of mathematics to human civilization
and its contribution to technical progress.

> Mathematics is distinguished among the sciences by the certainty which
> attends its operations and conclusions. The ideas it presents are so distinct,
> its reasonings so evident, that it affords the most certain knowledge with
> which the mind is conversant. The meaning of its definitions, the truth of
> its axioms, and the correctness of the results at which it arrives, are matters
> concerning which there cannot be the slightest doubt or difference of opin-
> ion. While observation and experiment may deceive and confuse, demon-
> stration ends in clear and absolute knowledge.
>
> This exactness of the science has made it a chief instrument of human
> activity. A noble steamship, fresh from the builder's hands, resting lightly
> upon her native waters and ready to speed to other shores, is hailed as a
> triumph. She is but a combination of solidified mathematical theorems. We
> see a still greater triumph when she urges her way out upon the illimitable

ocean, and pursues an undeviating course, day after day and week after week, finally to reach her destined port with unfailing precision. Mathematics again enabled her so to do.

The same instrumentality that empowered mankind to map out the highways of the sea has built those of the land—bridging chasms, tunneling mountains, and striding across rivers. It has fashioned the vehicles that course upon those highways, together with the innumerable machines by which labor is lessened, food and clothing are cheapened, buildings perfected, and conveniences of all kinds multiplied.

Clearly the *utility* of mathematical studies could scarcely be overrated.[30]

In this oration, Draper also discussed the importance of mathematics in forming personal character and claimed that by learning mathematics people could become more disciplined and use reasoning to understand themselves and their place in society and the world. "Mathematical studies," he wrote,

are peculiarly calculated to heighten decision of character. Since in them the mind advances to a final decision by a series of minor decisions, each of them unquestionable because based upon the irrefragable testimony of intuition—since, in fine, it is the very province of our science *to decide*, without the smallest danger of error, it would be strange indeed if a mind impressed and led by such a species of knowledge did not absorb and retain something of the consistency and firmness embodied in its principles.[31]

In Draper's view, therefore, mathematics was keenly important to deaf people. He argued that mathematical studies was strongly related to personal character; that attaining and understanding mathematical knowledge led to sound character and mind; that mathematics was universal and therefore the same for deaf people and hearing people; that mathematics was a means to encourage passionate curiosity about the nature of the world; and that every child was born with mathematical power. Finally, he believed that mathematics was as much a visual language as was sign language. Mathematics, like American Sign Language and English, should be taught as early as possible to deaf children. Draper stressed the importance of arithmetic education for deaf people, equating its value with knowledge of written language. In this case, he called for mathematics in early education where literacy was primarily studied. He thought that deaf graduates possessing advanced mathematical knowledge would contribute significantly to society and to their personal development as they became full-fledged, constructive workers.

Gallaudet and Draper thus held sharply contrasting views on mathematical education. Gallaudet perceived mathematics as subordinate to

English, claiming that basic English skills precluded basic mathematics learning. Draper, however, thought that mathematics and English were equal in importance and could be learned simultaneously.

Furthermore, although both men believed that rote learning, drill, and practice could lead to drudgery in learning mathematics, and both supported the use of sign language and printed English to communicate mathematics, Draper was more progressive in terms of curricular changes. He was more committed than Gallaudet to critiquing and redressing the problems he found in deaf schools and in the college. Draper stressed that appreciation for mathematics could lead to a better understanding of the natural world, and that mathematics was an avenue for moral development. He called for reconstruction of the pre-college mathematics curriculum to increase instruction in vocabulary, analysis of practical problems, automatic performance with operations, and the importance of carefully reading directions.[32]

Whither They Went

Despite their differing views on mathematical studies, Gallaudet and Draper worked together and were close friends for more than forty-five years. Their professional relationship had begun in 1871–72, when Draper served as Gallaudet's private secretary in his last year as a college student. Their affection and respect for each other were mutual. Gallaudet named his youngest son Herbert Draper Gallaudet, and Draper named his son Ernest Gallaudet Draper. Gallaudet and Draper were on the stage for the *Preservation of Sign Language* films during the second decade of the twentieth century. Their lives ended within five weeks of each other in 1917 (Gallaudet, September 26; Draper, November 3). Upon Gallaudet's death, Draper wrote of his dear friend:

> Possessed in his younger years of a very strong and admirable physique,— handsome, stalwart, manly classic in features,—he was perfectly fitted to excel in the sign-language, whether in lecturing, teaching, or dactylology. Nor was his pen less ready; literature overflows with evidences of his talents and industry. The best is yet to be told,— —
>
> > 'That fame is lost which epitaph imparts;
> > Who for his dust a tear would claim
> > On living hearts must write his name.'
>
> This did Edward Miner Gallaudet. He endeared himself to the hearts of all his graduates and students in every generation. Now, as he stands on the threshold of the life to come, clouds of witnesses arise to call him blessed—children, grandchildren, associates, friends,—all.[33]

Similarly, when Draper passed away a few months later, *The Silent Worker*'s obituary was effusive: "Dr. Draper was a deaf man and an early graduate of the Hartford School and of Gallaudet College. For forty-fours he was connected with the latter institution of learning as instructor and professor of Mathematics and Latin, and in this work achieved distinction. Dr. Draper was one of the finest men on the Faculty of Gallaudet—able, upright, courtly and scholarly."[34] His contemporary, James E. Gallaher, described him as "highly esteemed by the faculty and the students, being diligent and always alive to the interests to the college, and . . . always succeeds in interesting his classes. As a lecturer he is entertaining and instructive, and his personal influence among the students has been elevating. He is considered a first-class professor in all respects."[35] Both scholars left behind powerful pedagogical concepts in both their printed words and signs.

Gallaudet and Draper both held high expectations for deaf students to attain mathematical skills and knowledge. The issue was twofold: 1) the order of importance of English and mathematics and 2) the use of language to support the attainment of mathematical knowledge. From a modern perspective of bilingualism, Draper was a progressive thinker in his belief that deaf students should learn English and mathematics as early as possible in their childhood years, simultaneously if possible. He supported the notion that deaf children can learn English as a second language through a natural, dialogic process, in which the focus is on communicating mathematical concepts. The focus is not the language, but the use of it as a medium to learn mathematics. Gallaudet, on the contrary, believed that deaf students needed to acquire English first before studying mathematics. Two possible rationales for his subordinate view of learning mathematics are that deaf children should build a basic foundation of English to enable them to succeed in mathematics effectively, including the ability to read mathematical textbooks, and that learning mathematics may delay deaf students' acquisition of English as a second language. Both scholars, however, supported the use of sign language as a mode of communication to exchange thoughts in the mathematics classroom.

Notes

1. Amos G. Draper, "Oration, 'The Influence of Mathematical Studies upon Personal Character,'" *Nineteenth Annual Report of the Columbia Institution for the Deaf and Dumb for the Year Ending June 30 1876* (Washington, D.C.: Government Printing Office, 1876), 9.

2. Edward M. Gallaudet, *History of the College for the Deaf, 1857–1907* (Washington D.C.: Gallaudet College Press, 1983), 4.

3. Edward F. Fay, "Edward Miner Gallaudet," *American Annals of the Deaf* 62, no. 5 (1917).

4. Columbia Institution for the Deaf and Dumb was later transformed into a two-school system, which included Kendall School and the National Deaf-Mute College. The National Deaf-Mute College was later renamed Gallaudet College and is now Gallaudet University.

5. James E. Gallaher, *Representative Deaf Persons of the United States of America containing Portraits and Character Sketches of Prominent Deaf Persons who are Engaged in the Higher Pursuits of Life* (Chicago: The Author, 1898).

6. Register of Student Admissions, American School for the Deaf Archives. In his biography of Amos G. Draper, *Representative Deaf Persons of the United States of America*, James E. Gallaher wrote, "He became deaf when nine years of age from severe exposure while skating." Further investigation on symptoms of Typhus fever showed no mention of deafness.

7. Ibid.

8. Gallaher, *Representative Deaf Persons*, 65.

9. Ibid, 67.

10. Edward M. Gallaudet, *History of the College for the Deaf, 1857–1907* (Washington D.C.: Gallaudet College Press, 1983), 36. His manuscript was first entitled *The Story of the Origin and Growth of the College for the Deaf at Washington, D.C., now Called Gallaudet College, in Honor of Thomas H. Gallaudet, Begun by Edward M. Gallaudet in the Winter of 1895–6.* Edward M. Gallaudet assumed the position of president of the college when it was first opened in 1864, when he was twenty-seven.

11. Announcement of the National Deaf-Mute College, Washington, D.C. 1871–72 (Washington, D.C.: Gibson Brothers, Printers, 1872), 14.

12. Edward A. Krug, *The Shaping of The American High School: 1880–1920* (Madison, Wisc.: The University of Wisconsin Press, 1969). Krug provides an intensive study on the evolution of high school curricula in the United States.

13. Gallaudet, *History of the College for the Deaf*, 42.

14. Announcement of the National Deaf-Mute College, Washington, D.C., 1866 (Washington, D.C.: Joseph L. Pearson, Printer, 1866), 19.

15. *The Eleventh Annual Report of the Columbia Institution for the Deaf and Dumb for the Year Ending June 30, 1868* (Washington, D.C.: Columbia Institution, 1868), 9.

16. The preparatory program was designed for students who desired to enter the College, but did not prepare fully elsewhere, especially at those institutions that did not offer high classes. High classes existed in few of the institutions of the country at the time.

17. Announcement of the National Deaf-Mute College, Kendall Green, Washington, D.C. 1879–80 (Washington, D.C.: Gibson Brothers, Printers, 1880).

18. Announcement of the National Deaf-Mute College, Kendall Green, Washington, D.C., 1882–83 (Washington, D.C.: Gibson Brothers, Printers, 1883).

19. *Gallaudet College (FOR THE DEAF) Kendall Green, Washington, D.C. 1907* (Washington, D.C.: H.L. McQueen, Printer and Publisher, 1907).

20. Edward M. Gallaudet, *Thirtieth Annual Report of the Columbia Institution for the Deaf and Dumb to the Secretary of the Interior* (Washington, D.C.: Government Printing Office, 1887), 7–9.

21. Edward M. Gallaudet, *The Columbia Institution for the Instruction of the Deaf and Dumb, 1857–1893* (Washington, D.C.: National Deaf-Mute College, 1893), 16–17. Calculus and mechanics were added to the course of study for the junior class for the year 1882–83.

22. Joseph C. Gordon, ed., *The Education of Deaf Children, Evidence of E.M. Gallaudet and*

A.G. Bell presented to the Royal Commission of the United Kingdom on the condition of the blind, the deaf and dumb, etc with accompanying papers, postscripts, and an index (Washington, D.C.: Volta Bureau, 1892).

23. Gallaudet, *Thirtieth Annual Report of the Columbia Institution.*

24. Edward M. Gallaudet, *The Combined System of Educating the Deaf* (Washington, D.C.: Gibson Bros., 1891): 20–21. The author revised and corrected his address, which was delivered upon invitation before the second congress held under the auspices of the British Deaf and Dumb Association in the Mission Hall of the Glasgow Deaf and Dumb Mission August 5–7, 1891.

25. Edward M. Gallaudet, *History of the College*, 122–3. Joseph G. Parkinson, class of 1869, received this degree in 1873. He later became a patent lawyer in Chicago.

26. Amos G. Draper, "The Discontinuance of the 'Lower Preparatory' Class," *American Annals for the Deaf and Dumb* 25, no. 4 (1880): 251–54. In an article, Draper mentioned that the issue was raised of the importance of teaching arithmetic to the deaf-mutes at the Northampton Conference of Principals in May of the same year. The concern contradicted Professor Henry's report findings.

27. Ibid., 253.

28. Ibid., 252.

29. Ibid., 253.

30. Draper, "Oration, 'The Influence of Mathematical Studies upon Personal Character,'" *Nineteenth Annual Report of the Columbia Institution for the Deaf and Dumb*, 9–10.

31. Ibid., 10.

32. See Donald T. Rogers, "In Search of Progressivism," *Reviews in American History* 10 (1982): 127, for the use of the term, "progressive."

33. Amos G. Draper, "Edward M. Gallaudet," *The Silent Worker* 30, no. 1 (October 1917): 9.

34. The Silent Worker, "Dr. Amos G. Draper," *The Silent Worker* 30, no. 4 (January 1918): 61.

35. James E. Gallaher, *Representative Deaf Persons.*

Selected Bibliography

Announcement of the National Deaf-Mute College, Washington, D.C., 1866. Washington, D.C.: Joseph L. Pearson, Printer, 1866.

Announcement of the National Deaf-Mute College, Washington, D.C. 1871–72. Washington, D.C.: Gibson Brothers, Printers, 1872.

Announcement of the National Deaf-Mute College, Kendall Green, Washington, D.C. 1879–80. Washington, D.C.: Gibson Brothers, Printers, 1880.

Announcement of the National Deaf-Mute College, Kendall Green, Washington, D.C., 1882–83. Washington, D.C.: Gibson Brothers, Printers, 1883.

Draper, Amos G. "Oration, 'The Influence of Mathematical Studies upon Personal Character.'" In *Nineteenth Annual Report of the Columbia Institution for the Deaf and Dumb for the Year Ending June 30 1876.* Washington, D.C.: Government Printing Office, 1876: 9–12.

———. "The Discontinuance of the 'Lower Preparatory' Class." *American Annals of the Deaf and Dumb* 25, no. 4 (1880): 251–254.

———. "Some Results of College Work." Report of the Gallaudet College. Washington, D.C.: Government Printing Office, 1890.

———. "Edward M. Gallaudet." *The Silent Worker* 30, no. 1 (October 1871): 9.

Gallaher, James E. *Representative Deaf Persons of the United States of America containing Por-*

traits and Character Sketches of Prominent Deaf Persons who are Engaged in the Higher Pursuits of Life. Chicago: The Author, 1898.

Gallaudet College (FOR THE DEAF) Kendall Green, Washington, D.C. 1907. Washington, D.C.: H.L. McQueen, Printer and Publisher, 1907.

Gallaudet, Edward M. *Eighth Annual Report of the Columbia Institution for the Deaf and Dumb.* Washington, D.C.: n.p., 1865.

_____. "The American Asylum." Edited by J. Hammond Trumbull. *The Memorial History of Hartford County, Connecticut, 1633–1884.* Boston: Edward L. Osgood Publisher, 1886: 425–430.

_____. *Life of Thomas Hopkin Gallaudet, Founder of Deaf-Mute Instruction in America.* New York: Henry Holt & Co., 1888.

_____. *The Combined System of Educating the Deaf.* Washington, D.C.: Gibson Bros., 1891.

_____. *The Columbia Institution for the Instruction of the Deaf and Dumb, 1857–1893.* Washington, D.C.: National Deaf-Mute College, 1893.

Krug, Edward A. *The Shaping of The American High School: 1880–1920.* Madison, Wisc.: The University of Wisconsin Press, 1969.

Register of Student Admissions, American School for the Deaf Archives.

The Silent Worker. "Dr. Amos G. Draper," *The Silent Worker* 30, no. 4 (January 1918): 61.

Urban, Wayne and Jennings Wagoner Jr., *American Education: A History.* New York: Mc-Graw-Hill, 1996.

6

Douglas Craig, 186?–1936

Marieta Joyner

Editors' Introduction

The Gallaudet campus was racially integrated from the school's founding in 1857 until 1905 when five decades of segregation began. In the following essay, Marieta Joyner focuses on the history of one deaf African American, Douglas Craig, who attended Kendall School while it was still integrated and then worked for Gallaudet long after educational integration ended. Joyner's essay adds to the scant literature on the history of deaf black Americans generally, and it adds specifically to the literature on Gallaudet and minorities. Near the end of the paper, Joyner also subtly approaches the question of racist attitudes on Kendall Green by examining the issue of skin color, carefully contrasting the employment roles of dark-skinned Craig with his contemporary colleague, light-skinned deaf African American William J. Rich.

Douglas, your presence haunts the great staircase [of Gallaudet] and the stories of your great strength lives on forever—you are a legend.

—Felix Kowaloewski, Class of 1937

THE CHILD WAS approximately nine years old, but he did not know his age, could not speak or hear, and could not find his way home. That was the dilemma for an African American boy found on the streets of Washington, D.C., in 1870. New Hampshire Senator Aaron Harrison Cragin just happened to drive by in his buggy that cold wintry night. After convincing the boy to get into the carriage, Senator Cragin took him to the Columbia Institution for the Instruction of the Deaf and Dumb and Blind, later renamed Gallaudet College.[1] Edward Miner Gallaudet was president then of the world's only school and college specifically designed to accommodate deaf and hard of hearing students. Since the boy's birth date was unknown, for the next 65 years, the date that he was officially signed over to Gallaudet, January 31, 1871, became his birthday. Because he did not know his name, he was given the name Douglas Craig.

Freedman Village and Alley People

The 1870 United States census lists Douglas Craig as living at a house operated by the National Association for the Relief of Destitute Colored Women and Children (NARDCWC).[2] It is not known how long he had lived at the house or who took him there. The home was established in 1863 by an act of Congress as a shelter to support aged or indigent African American women and children, who were to be provided with clothing and Christian instruction.[3] Many individuals in the house came from the Freedman's Village that was established to handle the overflow of freed slaves after legislation of April 16, 1862, manumitted slaves in the District of Columbia.[4] Under the direction of the government and the American Missionary Association, the Freedman's Village housed the refugees, trained them in skilled labor, and educated the children.

The Freedman's Village soon became a showplace for government officials to direct foreign visitors and other dignitaries to see the progress of former slaves.[5] There were so many people in the village, however, that the Army had to expand and build an industrial school, several "normal" schools for children, a hospital, a home for the aged, and churches. Although the buildings were originally intended to be temporary, moving people out soon became a serious problem. Destitute women and children such as Douglas Craig were particularly noticeable. One historian wrote that the creation of Freedman's Village's had less to do with eventually helping Blacks integrate into the free society than with maintaining segregation.[6]

Craig may have come from one of the notorious alleys where former slaves gathered. After the Civil War, the nation's capital was a major center for the Black population, both in absolute numbers and in terms of their proportions of the city's total population. Many of them dwelled in alleys. Although the early history of alley house construction remains unknown, one theory is that they were built as slave quarters, but after slavery ended free people migrated from the countryside and moved into them. These new alley dwellers were considered a "separate class," or simply the "other Americans" in the nation's capital. It is also likely that landowners, builders, and others saw potential profit and developed low-cost housing in the alleys. In any event, the socialization process for children in the alleys was limited, and external institutions often could not and did not assist them.[7] There was tremendous concern about children such as Craig, and they were taken to charitable groups to be cared for. Yet the condition of the homes the groups managed was poor, and the inhabitants were poverty stricken.

In their 1867 annual report, the secretary of NARDCWC, Eliza Heacock, confirmed the challenges the organization faced. The report indicated that there were a total of eighty-five people in the house. Eleven children and two women died between 1866 and 1867, and twenty-four children were sent to other homes.[8] Indeed, the long-term goal of the NARDCWC staff was to find permanent placement for homeless women and children who were displaced by the war, but since Craig was deaf, placing him was a daunting task. Heacock's report described the general health of the "inmates" as good, yet it stated that there were childhood diseases in the house; and one child had been badly burned. With the crowding, sickness, and confusion at the home, it is easy to understand why Craig ran away.

Senator Aaron Harrison Cragin

When Senator Cragin picked up Craig from the streets of Washington, D.C., he soon realized that the child was deaf and could not speak. He took him to the Columbia Institution, which was 5.1 miles from NARDCWC. Compassion and justice for African Americans were not new sentiments for Senator Cragin. In an August 4, 1856, speech he argued passionately in support of Senator Charles Sumner of Massachusetts, the leading Senate opponent of slavery, whom Congressman Preston Brooks of South Carolina had beaten brutally with a cane.[9] It is likely that Cragin's act demonstrated empathy beyond just picking up a small "colored" child hovering in the cold, and it was unusual for the time. The predominant attitude of white people toward Blacks in Washington, D.C., was becoming increasingly hostile due to the large numbers of freed slaves who poured into the city during and after the Civil War.[10]

Senator Cragin was well aware of the deaf school and knew it was the only place in Washington, D.C., where Craig could be educated and become part of a community. The school's president, Edward Miner Gallaudet, had a personal and professional relationship with James W. Patterson, the other senator from New Hampshire. Patterson was Gallaudet's primary advocate on Capitol Hill and helped him obtain funding for the school. In fact, Patterson was a member of a key committee that was responsible for making recommendations and ultimately approving funds for institutions such as the Columbia Institution. Patterson was also a trained meteorologist from Dartmouth College (1854–1865), and he taught astronomy part-time at the college for deaf students.[11] How this relationship affected the acceptance of Craig to the Columbia Institution is unknown. What is known is that funds were distributed by the Department of Interior to the institution to support Craig, and the legal transfer of Craig from the Charity Home to Gallaudet was also handled by the Interior Department.[12]

Craig's Name

Roy Stewart, an 1899 graduate of Gallaudet College, knew Craig well and wrote stories about his interaction with individuals on the campus. According to Stewart, John Wight, family supervisor for the Columbia Institution, created Craig's name. He chose the first name in honor of Fredrick Douglass, who in 1870, when Douglas Craig was found, had just become owner and editor of the *New National Era,* a weekly newspaper in Washington, D.C. The last name was derived from, and in honor of, Senator Cragin.[13]

The exact date when Senator Cragin found Craig is unknown, but it is likely that Craig stayed at the Columbia Institution as an unofficial resident before his formal transfer to the school. Whatever the situation, the official documents from the Department of Interior giving Gallaudet legal guardianship of the child were not signed until January 31, 1871. Secretary Heacock represented the home during the legal transfer at the Department of Interior. The following statement was notarized and signed in 1871.

> District of Columbia Washington D. C.
> I Eliza Heacock do affirm that I am Matron for the Home for the National Association for the Relief of Destitute Colored Women and Children in the District of Columbia and that I have been such Matron for the six months . . . I know a colored boy Douglas Craig who is a deaf mute. He was in the home when I became Matron and he has been there every since. He is about ten years old and has no relatives that are known to us or any person connected with the home. From such evidence that as I have, I believe that he probably belongs to the District of Columbia. Eliza Heacock

subscribed before me the 30th Day of January In 1871 N. Callan, Notary Public[14]

The next day Edward M. Gallaudet signed the following statement on behalf of the Columbia Institution.

Sir,
I have the honor to forward the application of Douglas Craig, through Mrs. S. C. Pomeray [President of NARDWCC] for admission to this Institution. The Certificate of N. Collan a Notary Public for the Court of Washington with the Washington January 31, 1871 original evidence on which it was granted, are herewith transmitted. I am satisfied that the said Douglas Craig is a proper person to be received and instructed in this Institution, and therefore recommend that an order for his admission be issued.
Very respectfully,
Yours obedient servant,
E. M. Gallaudet President Columbia Institute
To the Hon. Columbus Delano Secretary of the Interior[15]

After January 31, 1871, Douglas was an official resident of the Columbia Institution for the Instruction of the Deaf and Dumb and Blind.

Living Quarters

The few African American students who were accepted to the school between 1857 and 1905, when the school became formally segregated, had separate sleeping rooms and dining tables from white students, but they took classes in an integrated setting. Unlike other African American students who had families and often went home, Craig's permanent home was the school. He was not given a dormitory room. Instead, his living quarters were over the stable where the horses' buggy was kept and where later the college's automobile was housed and maintained. Eventually his room became private space that he extended, often without permission, so he could store his collection of what some viewed as "junk," old tin bathtubs, bed springs, clothes, and stove-pipe hats that other people had given to him. In addition to Craig's space, another part of the garage was later turned into a quiet work place for President Gallaudet to write a book on international law.

Although primarily a student his first eight years on campus, Douglas was viewed much like an African American servant. Washington's Black servants and white employers lived side by side in what was described as an "intertwined" way. Servants were kept close at hand yet out of sight. In some homes, the butler had a closet near the door where he could wait out of sight until someone came to the house. Servants also often lived in what was called "a servant wing" or a free-standing structure in back of the house.[16]

Schooling At Kendall

Douglas's precise status for several years while he was at the Columbia Institution is somewhat unclear. An Interior Department document shows that he was expected to be a student until 1885. Yet he was only listed as being an official student at the Kendall School from 1871 to 1879, and personnel records state that he became an employee of the school in 1875, with no indication of whether he was full-time or part-time. The Book of Honors, a monthly honor roll of students who preserved unbroken records of faithful performance of duty, whether in school, at work, or in their general department, showed Craig on the list several times between 1872 and 1879.[17]

There was never any official explanation of why Craig ceased being a student in 1879, but students around the campus were told that Douglas had all the training that he could get. According to Stewart, after three or four years of schooling—which meant that Douglas was about twelve years old—business manager John Wight decided that Douglas was larger than most of his classmates and had to be removed from the classroom setting.[18] There were other options to educate Douglas if race was the issue. The Maryland School for "colored" deaf students at Overlea, for example, accepted African Americans from Washington, D.C. However, if Craig were to be transferred to Maryland, at least some of the federal funds from the Department of the Interior that Gallaudet was receiving would have been transferred as well. Because of Douglas's residential status at Kendall School, transferring funds and losing his free labor would not have been to the school's advantage and may have created a complex issue. In this respect, Craig's situation differed markedly from African American students who did not live on campus.

There was sometimes "grumbling" about Craig's mischievous behavior on campus. One incident involved a female student who was an American Indian. Someone told Craig that female Indians were different from other women, or at least different from white women. Craig's curiosity about the girl led to inappropriate behavior, or what some students described jokingly as his "anthropological research" of her. Of course there was no reprimand for the boys joking, yet Craig was severely punished. In fact, teasing about the incident continued for several years and was often used as a way to get reactions from Craig. If Craig was hanging out in the reading room and students wanted him to move on, all they had to do was sign "Indian girl." Former student Oscar Guire described one such incident.

> Douglas turned his head and caught a prepster sophomore named Schneider signing 'Indian Girl.' This action caused Douglas to freeze in his tracks and [he] stared at Schneider for minutes. This was a true test of Douglas' anger as everyone in the room stopped reading, writing and waited to see what would happen next. Schneider was afraid to leave the room but Douglas finally left. After that day, the word Indian Girl was never mentioned again.[19]

Welcoming Students to the Campus

There are many stories about Craig's interaction with staff, faculty, and students but none more memorable than his collecting one dollar from students who arrived on campus needing help with their heavy trunks. Craig would lift the heavy trunks and take them to the students' rooms. Then he would ask the student for one dollar, which most students gave without hesitating. Craig marked the dollar so that he could give the same one back to each student when he or she went off to camp during the school year. While students were always happy to receive the dollar back, the welcoming was later privately discussed as being "aggravating." But once students got to know Craig, most loved his humbleness and sense of humor, because he was harmless.

Whatcoat Black Deaf Mission and Religious Services

Religion has been a powerful, deeply felt, and influential force in African American communities, and it was very much a part of Craig's life. He attended service at the Shiloh Baptist Church near the Gallaudet campus. Since he interacted with, and proposed to, many of the female African American cooks in the kitchen, it is likely that he joined them on Sundays for service. He was later married less than two miles from the school in the Saint Calvary Episcopal Church, probably because his wife was associated with that church. In 1895 the Reverend Daniel Moylan established a church specifically to hold services for deaf people in Baltimore. It is the oldest known operational church of its kind in the Methodist congregation.[20] It was a place where lasting friendships developed among deaf people, many of whom were very much a part of the vibrant

and organized community in Baltimore near the Overlea School for African American deaf students. When Craig found time for pleasure, he
went to Maryland.

In 1905 a group called the Whatcoat Black Deaf Mission organized
within the Christ United Methodist Church in Baltimore, and it may
have influenced Douglas. The Whatcoat Black Deaf Mission's goal was
to create a network and foster social interaction between deaf people. A
former member of the group recounts,

> We all arrived at Overlea School for the Deaf and Blind when we were
> between 6 and 12 years old. We learned their language skills, starting with
> how to finger-spell our names. We all had one thing in common and that
> was "fear" when we were left at the residential school. But we all found
> Whatcoat and our place was in the basement. Blacks and Whites were
> forbidden from worshipping together. Whites were up stairs and Blacks
> were down stairs. We worshipped at 10 A.M. and they worshipped in the
> afternoon. The place needed painting which I helped do. A farmer donated
> a furnace and the place was beautiful. We did shows with skits and perfor-
> mances every Saturday night.[21]

It is very likely that Craig attended the Whatcoat performances and took
ideas back to Gallaudet where he had his own stage and generated lots
of laughs.

He was a "community icon" at Gallaudet and was viewed though
various prisms. During one graduation season a "mock convocation"
was held to award Craig a humorous degree called "M. M.," conferred
on him by the college boys. The original meaning of the M. M. degree is
unknown because the meaning changed over the years. One meaning
was "Master of Mail," because Craig frequently rode his bicycle to Union
Station to pick up the campus mail and deliver it within the school. Craig
was trusted on the campus, and therefore he became another type of
mailman, delivering many "cupid' notes from one student to another.
M. M. also designated "Master of Mechanics," because Craig was considered a "jack of all trades" and could fix almost anything, including the
campus tower clock. It is not clear whether he had any training to do
repairs or whether he was simply creative and kept things "ticking."
When he was introduced as "Professor Craig, M. M.," he "mouthed gib-
berish and used exaggerated gestures" of appreciation for being honored.[22]

A New Hat

Most stories about Douglas Craig include one about the new hat. Jonathan Hall, the son of second Gallaudet President Percival Hall, offered
this version:

Douglas Craig, bicycling

Douglas interacted with everyone including the president. After all it was Edward Gallaudet who Senator Cragin negotiated with regarding taking Douglas into the school. There was a comfort level that Douglas had with President Gallaudet, yet he knew his boundaries. Since he often considered himself the campus 'greeter' of guests arriving on campus he took pride in the way he dressed. One day Douglas entered the president's office and asked for money for a new hat and was given a lecture on thrift. In the meantime, he was holding his old hat in his hand. He held it up, then put it on the desk of the lecturer and asked, "Will you wear this hat? You can have it." Gallaudet replied, "All right. I will give you money for a new hat."[23]

Financial Ventures

Although Craig had what he called his private secretary, a trusted student, to help him write letters and handle his business, he managed to get himself into several difficult situations regarding money. It was not unusual for Gallaudet to receive a letter informing him that Craig had borrowed money and not paid it back. This letter from attorney Jas S. McDonogh of Washington, D.C., written to President Gallaudet January 22, 1904, is an example.

> Sup. Gallaudet Inst.
> Dear Sir,
>   One of your employees Douglas Craig is indebted to a client of mine, Mr. A. H. Hutterly for $15.30 which is long past due and unpaid. He has often promised but always failed to pay. I do not like to report him but I think that it is a rule in your institution that all employees shall pay their honest debt and this is one. We are willing to make the terms so that he can easily pay it if he is willing and if you will call this to his attention I am sure that he will settle soon. Thanking you in advance for any favor. I am.
> Yours very truly
> Jas S. McDonogh[24]

Although there is no documentation of how the funds were collected from Craig, Superintendent W. G. Fowler responded to the letter for President Gallaudet by sending a payment, acknowledged by McDonogh on February 16, 1894. Ten years later, on April 7, 1904, McDonogh again wrote President Gallaudet.

> Dear Sir,
>   Please accept my thanks for your favor of enclosing check for $5.00 on a/c of Douglas Craig. This is 4 years interest due on this a/c which he should also pay if you can make him so it is $3.60. Please again accept my thanks.
> Jas S. McDonogh.[25]

Another deal went sour when Craig was persuaded to enter a real estate scheme and purchased lots in a subdivision in the eastern section of Washington, only to find that the seller did not have a good title. In the end, Douglas lost several hundred dollars that he had faithfully paid towards the purchase of what he thought was his property.[26] At one point, Craig tried to start his own business of raising pet rabbits to sell, but wild animals always killed the babies and that venture failed.

Marriage

Craig spent much of his adult life searching for a wife. Race apparently was not an issue. He often told white students that he would "take their girlfriend." One student wrote, "When Douglas was told that White people did not marry Black people, he pointed out how a team of one Black and one white horse were married in 'holy wedlock.'"[27] After proposing to every African American cook at Gallaudet, dressing in fancy clothing on weekends, and making sure he always wore his signature vest, Douglas finally met a deaf woman named Katie Jones who would marry him. The date was set for April 21, 1920, and everyone who received an invitation knew it would be a "class act." The wording was printed in an eloquent script on fancy paper. The wedding was held at the Calvary Episcopal Church, Eleventh and G Streets, NE, Washington, D.C. It was indeed an elegant event, and most faculty and staff from Gallaudet attended. Brides usually get most of the attention at weddings, but Douglas was the man of the hour and the day. He wore a dark suit, white tie, his signature vest, and white gloves. Percival Hall interpreted for the hearing people in the audience.[28]

After a reception, the couple went to Baltimore for a honeymoon, but it only lasted for one day. Their plans were cut short when Douglas's wallet, containing about $300, was either lost or stolen. The entire Gallaudet community was concerned, and individuals did all they could to try and retrieve the money. Tracing the route that the couple said they took, Hall wrote a letter to the Chief of Police of Baltimore and to the Washington Railway and Electric Company, which operated between Washington and Baltimore, asking for their help in finding the money.[29]

This incident suggests the problems Craig had functioning outside the campus. Vacations or time off from work proved to be problematic. In fact, he did not know what a vacation was when he was encouraged to take one. Once he made plans and took a trip to Norfolk, Virginia. While there he saw several men loading packages on a dock and agreed to work. He considered that a vacation and came back to the campus with the money he earned and said that he had a good vacation.

After the wedding and honeymoon Douglas and Katie Craig moved off campus but remained close by; in fact, they could see the campus from the Camp Meade Cottage housing unit where they lived. A year later, when Gallaudet alumni held a reunion at the college, many who had fond memories of the wedding decided to give Douglas and Katie a chance to use some of the wedding gifts they received. The crew bought ice cream and cake and paid the couple a visit. The Craigs were gracious hosts and fun was had by all.

Married life was not what Craig expected, however. He was used to his own space in the stable and barn and soon realized that living on campus was better than living in an apartment in a poverty stricken area

Douglas Craig and his wife Katie

of Washington, D.C., where the roof in the house leaked, and the landlord refused to do repairs. Before marriage, he had never washed his
own laundry or had to worry about where the next meal would come
from, because all of those things were done for him. As mentioned earlier, Craig had never learned to manage money, either. After several mis-
haps, including losing his money on the honeymoon, being robbed often,
and frequently borrowing money that he could not pay back, he was
given an allowance from his own money by the payroll department at
Gallaudet. Payroll also deducted funds from his salary for some services
and personal items, such as shoe repairs, glasses, and so on.[30]

After the excitement of the marriage waned, Craig spoke to President Hall about being unhappy. Later, a letter dated October 29, 1924, from Katie Craig indicated that they were having financial difficulties. She asked if Hall could "please give [her] husband more money each month." She stressed that she had to "work nights" for them to survive. Katie requested that President Hall give her mother, who was probably a hearing person, the answer to the letter.[31] He responded the same day.

> My Dear Mrs. Craig,
> Your husband, Douglas Craig has just had a raise of $5.00 per month. This is all we can pay to our lawn hands at the present time. If he wishes to make an arrangement to take his meals at home we can make a change in the rate of his pay. Any such arrangements should be made between him and me and not by other members of the family.
> Very truly yours
> Percival Hall President[32]

The second cry for help from Craig and his wife to Hall came five months later, March 10, 1925, regarding their apartment and living space. Apparently the apartment was in such poor condition that when it rained the walls became wet. Hall wrote to the landlord for the Craigs, asking him or her to "repair the leak in the roof." He also reminded the owner that Craig was "deaf and could not use the phone to communicate with him and if the situation was not resolved soon, Douglas and his wife would be in further discomfort."[33]

When Katie became ill, Craig's life changed again. On November 23, 1928, Katie Jones Craig died after a short illness. Her death was announced in the *Buff and Blue*, and notes of sympathy were sent to Craig from many alumni around the country. After Katie's death, Craig moved back to the Gallaudet campus. Although he had been living off campus for eight years, it seemed as if he never left, for he had been working there all along. Kendall Green was home for him, and he continued the routine that he had before moving; but he was older and not well.

Honoring Douglas Craig

By 1935, Craig was quite frail and no longer worked or lived on campus, but in a special ceremony he raised the campus flag one last time. One of Craig's tasks during his long employment at Gallaudet had been to raise the American flag to the top of the chapel tower. The 1935 graduating class purchased a new flag for the university and decided that it was only fitting to bring Craig back to raise the new flag. He arrived on

Douglas Craig

campus in a cab and sat in a special arm chair, because of weakness, but he hoisted the flag to great applause.

Many faculty, students, and alumni noticed Craig's frailty during the flag raising ceremony and decided it was time to pay tribute to him for his legacy at the college. The once energetic, happy "Old Craig" was quite ill, so this was the time to acknowledge his over sixty years of work.

On January 14, 1936, President Hall received a letter from Florence

Bridges Crammatte, one of the organizers of an Alumni Association banquet to be held on Edward Miner Gallaudet's birthday, February 5th, requesting President Hall's assistance in getting stories, anecdotes, and incidents "whether happy or sad" about Craig's life at the college.[34] Since Gallaudet was instrumental in bringing Douglas to the campus in 1871, both men would be honored at the banquet. There were many stories submitted and compiled in an essay about Douglas written by Roy Stewart. Stewart's documentation of the stories about Craig became part of the Gallaudet Archives, and many others were written referencing Stewart's original stories.

Death of Douglas Craig

On February 11, 1936, six days after the banquet honoring Edward Miner Gallaudet and Douglas Craig, President Hall wrote to Katherine Gallaudet, daughter of Edward, informing her that Craig had died at the Freedman "Colored" Hospital in Washington, D.C. (later named Howard University Hospital), and a "proper and impressive funeral was held for him in the campus Chapel."[35] The announcement was also made to Gallaudet alumni. Condolences were sent from around the country. Toivo Lindhoom of the *Deaf American* wrote, "Craig was liked, respected and trusted by perhaps all students of Gallaudet."[36] The *North Dakota Banner* noted that "it was a day of sadness at Kendall Green. Douglas was an integral part of the institution."[37] Gallaudet's *Buff and Blue* newspaper's heading read: "Kendall Green Pays Last Respect to Douglas Craig." The paper described Craig as having "a body of steel, a big heart and a jolly disposition. Perhaps the only deaf Darkie whom any Gallaudet [student who] graduated would call his bosom pal and be proud of it."[38]

Many beautiful floral arrangements covered the pulpit of the chapel where the funeral service for Craig was held on Thursday, February 13, 1936, at 2 P.M. The Reverend H. L. Tracey officiated and was assisted by the Reverend Harrison of the Shiloh Baptist Church. President Hall paid high tribute to Craig, noting that "for so many years he had been a good and faithful worker on the Green." Other hearing and deaf members of the Shiloh Baptist Church attended and sang hymns, including, "Abide With Me." Ernest G. Draper, D.C.'s assistant secretary of commerce and at that time a member of the Gallaudet College Board of Directors, attended. Members of the Washington, D.C., chapter of the alumni association, students, faculty, staff, fellow workers, and "colored" friends filled the chapel to capacity. Richard Thompson, his wife, and their daughter were also at the funeral. Craig moved off campus to the Thompsons' home once he became too frail and weak to take care of himself. Gallaudet College continued to pay his salary until his death.[39]

Douglas Craig was buried next to Katie Craig in the Columbia Harmony Cemetery, once located at Ninth Street and Rhode Island Avenue, NE, and later moved to the new National Harmony Memorial Park (NHMP) in Landover, Maryland. Established by a group of free and inspired African Americans in the early nineteenth century, Harmony became the premiere black cemetery in the city, and along with the Craigs numerous African Americans who were important to local and nation history were interred there.

William Rich

During Craig's lifetime, the Gallaudet campus employed other African American men in addition to Craig. One employee whose job was similar to Craig's was William J. Rich. A District resident, born in 1868, his mother brought him to the school in 1874, three years after Craig was enrolled. They became lifelong friends. It is not known whether Rich lived on campus when he was a student, but he graduated from Kendall School in 1885, which is when Douglas should have graduated as well.

Craig and Rich looked very different.[40] Although they were about the same height and age, Craig was a dark-skinned man, and Rich was a mulatto. The mulatto status was an advantage for Rich, as he was immediately hired after graduation as a janitor and waiter in the girl's dining hall. Craig was not always very visible, but Rich was head waiter at all receptions held at President Gallaudet's home. Rich was a quiet and private man who had a life outside of the campus. Eventually he married a hearing woman. They had three children who were quite successful. One son, Vernon, graduated from Howard University; William, Jr., received a master's degree from New York University; and Celestine graduated from Dunbar High School in Washington.

Although Craig and Rich were the best of friends, they had occasional disagreements. At one point, Craig reported Rich to President Gallaudet as being a "rascal." It was rumored that Rich had invaded Craig's space. Whatever the issue, it was resolved quickly. Whenever Rich left the campus Craig would wave good-bye and sign "pray for me."[41] Craig often had holiday dinners off campus with some of the kitchen help or with Rich and his family.

There were two big events held for Rich. One took place in June 1937, one year after Craig's death. President Hall organized a special dinner to honor Rich for his fifty years of service. Another was in 1944 for his 76th birthday. When the idea of the surprise birthday party was announced, faculty and staff eagerly agreed to participate in the planning. The party was a picnic for Rich, but he was led to believe that the party was for President Hall so he gladly donated one dollar to help the cause. At the party, Rich was acknowledged for his unfailing courtesy and kindness.[42] Rich died at his home in Washington, D.C., on July 27, 1945, at the age of seventy-seven.[43]

Street Naming and Douglas Craig

In 1969, thirty-three years after Douglas Craig's death, Edward C. Merrill, Jr., from the University of Tennessee's College of Education, became the fourth president of Gallaudet, then in its 105th year. One of Merrill's legacies was a street-naming project on campus. A committee formed in 1978 to choose people who were worthy of having a street named for them. The committee set three major criteria: first, the person could not have any other memorials; second, the person had to be retired or deceased; and third, the individual had to have some significant connection with the college, deafness, or deaf people. A ballot of forty-one names and biographical information was sent to faculty, employees, students, and those attending the 1979 Gallaudet College Alumni Association reunion. Each person was asked to vote for eight individuals on the list. By 1981 the process was complete, and several streets and buildings were named, one in honor of Craig. The committee decided that for "his meritorious, achievement in the field of services" to the university a street would be named Craig Street.[44]

Integration at the Kendall School

Like all great institutions, Gallaudet has had its moments of shame and its moments of honor. While the school can proudly acknowledge many honors, one shame cannot be ignored–injustice and segregation. From the time the school was formally established in 1857 until 1905, the school admitted some African American students, such as Douglas Craig and William Rich. The total number of Black students was so small, however, that according to President Gallaudet they were of no "particular difficulty." By 1905 the total number of Blacks attending the school reached an all time high of about fourteen students.[45]

There were three components to the problem of Blacks students attending the school by 1905. One, white parents of the deaf students started to complain about the mixing of races on the campus. Two, there were complaints about the way Blacks were being treated on the campus. Three, some white teachers embraced and kissed the younger deaf students as they entered the school each morning, a practice that was viewed as being problematic with Black students.[46] In fact, the parents of the white students were so concerned about integration that they pressured members of Congress to pass an appropriation act to assure that the school would become, and remain, segregated.

By 1905, white parents had accomplished their goal. The annual report for the Columbia Institution included a subheading that read "Education of Colored Deaf-Mutes."

> March 3, 1905. The directors of said (Columbia) institute are hereby authorized to provide for the education of colored deaf-mute children properly belonging to the District of Columbia in the Maryland school for Colored Deaf-Mutes, or some other suitable school, at a cost not exceeding the per capita expenses of educating the State pupils in such school.[47]

Kendall School and Gallaudet College would remain segregated for nearly fifty years.

Douglas Craig did not live to see an integrated Kendall School. However, sixteen years after his death, deaf students of the District of Columbia received a pre–*Brown v. Board of Education* victory in the *Miller v. District of Columbia Board of Education* suit filed in 1952. The case reversed a forty-seven-year policy that segregated the only school in the District of Columbia created to educate deaf children. The school that removed Craig from the classroom in 1879 for unknown and unconfirmed reasons again became integrated.

Eventually, a picture of Douglas Craig, wearing one of his signature vests, was hung in the lobby at the Kendall School, where he symbolically greeted children as he did in the nineteenth century. Douglas Craig was a legend and very much a part of the history of the Columbia Institution, Kendall School, and Gallaudet College.

Notes

1. Kenneth Lane, "You Are a Legend, Douglas Craig, M. M.," *Blue, Buff and Blue* 1 59, no. 3 (November 1949).

2. United States 1870 Census, http://www.heritagequestonline.com.

3. *Annual Report of the National Association for the Relief of Destitute Colored Women and Children* (Washington, D.C.: McGill & Witherow, Printers, 1864), 2.

4. Joseph P. Reidy, "Emancipation at Arlington: Freeman's Village 1863," history and restoration, National Park Service, http://www.nps.gov/archive/arho/tour/history/arlingtoninbetween3.html

5. Ira Berlin, and others, *Slaves No More: Three Essays on Emancipation and the Civil War* (Cambridge: Cambridge University Press, 1992), 133.

6. Reidy, "Emancipation."

7. James Borchert, *Alley Life in Washington, Family Community, Religion, and Folklife in the City, 1850–1970* (Champaign: University of Illinois Press, 1982), 23–25.

8. Annual Report: National Association for the Relief of Destitute Colored Women and Children (Washington, D.C.: Boston Rockwell & Rollins, Printers, 1867), 785–800; *Slavery and Antislavery Pamphlets from the Libraries of Salmon P. Chase & John P. Hale* (Ann Arbor, Mich.: University Microfilms, 1974). Microfilm of Pamphlet Collection at Dartmouth College Library.

9. Aaron Harrison Cragin, "Jefferson Against Douglas Speech," delivered in the House of Representatives, 4 August 1856 (Philadelphia: Philadelphia Rare Books & Manuscript Company).

10. Constance Mclaughlin Green, *Washington: A History of the Capital, 1800–1950* (Princeton: Princeton University Press, 1962), 279.

11. Edward Miner Gallaudet, *History of College for the Deaf 1857–1907*, ed. Lance J. Fischer and David L. de Lorenzo (Washington, D.C.: Gallaudet College Press, 1983), 8.

12. United States Interior Department, "Affidavit to the Secretary of the Interior of Washington D.C., re: Douglas Craig," 31 January 1871, C .I. D. D. Admissions 13 February 1868 to 15 January 1885, 142A, National Archives.

13. Roy J. Stewart, "Douglas Craig, M. M.," *Buff and Blue 1* 59, no. 3 (November 1949): 10; Green, 83. Fredrick Douglass became a life member of the NARDCWC for various reasons but mostly because he believed for Blacks to become an integral part of the American nation, "they must make their own way."

14. Eliza Hancock, "Affidavit to the Secretary of the Interior of Washington D.C., re: Douglas Craig," 31 January 1871, C.I. D. D. Admissions 13 February 1868 to 15 January 1885, 142A, National Archives.

15. Ibid.

16. Sarah Luria, "Early Cities of the Americas National Domesticity in the Early Republic: Washington D.C.," *Common-Place* 3, no. 4 (July 2003), http://www.common-place.org/vol-03/no-04/washington/.

17. *Columbia Institution Book of Honor* (April 1877, 1878, 1879), Gallaudet University Archives.

18. Stewart, 2.

19. Oscar Guire, "Douglas Craig," *The Deaf American* 22, no. 8 (April 1970).

20. Mary Cahill, "Baltimore Church Preserving Faith Stories of Black Deaf History," 17 February 2004, *Deaf Today*, http://www.deaftoday.com/news/2004/02/baltimore_churc.html.

21. Melissa Lauber, "Seniors Offer Remembrances of Whatcoat Mission," 25 February 2004, United Methodist News Service, http://www.christdeafchurch.org.

22. Guire, "Douglas Craig."

23. Jonathan Hall (son of Percival Hall), interview by author, 2004.

24. Papers of Dr. Edward Miner Gallaudet, Box 42, Folder 11, Letter 211, Gallaudet University Archives.

25. Ibid.

26. Stewart, "Douglas Craig," 14.

27. Ken Lane to B. M. Schowe, 19 April 1949, Gallaudet University Archives.

28. "Marriages," *Buff and Blue* 27, no. 8 (May 1920): 350, Gallaudet University Archives.

29. Pervical Hall to the Police Department regarding Douglas Craig missing money, Papers of Perival Hall, Gallaudet University Archives.

30. "Repairs and Mending," Payroll Department, Boxes 48, 50, Gallaudet University Archives.

31. Papers of Percival Hall, Box 42, Folder 21, Gallaudet University Archives.

32. Ibid.

33. Papers of President Hall, Box 42, Folder 12, Gallaudet University Archives.

34. Papers of President Hall, Box 73, Folder 13, Gallaudet University Archives.

35. Letter from President Hall Regarding the Death of Douglas Craig, 20 February 1936, "G" Misc., Box 73, Folder 24: 1935–1936, Gallaudet University Archives; telegram from Katherine Gallaudet, 12 February 1936, Gallaudet University Archives.

36. Toivo Lindholm, "Humor Among The Deaf," *The Deaf American* (December 1967): 15.

37. "Douglas Craig, M. M.," *North Dakota Banner* repr. from *Once a Month*, (March–April, 1936).

38. "Kendall Green Pays Last Respect to Douglas Craig," *Buff and Blue,* February 27, 1936.

39. "Kendall Green Pays Last Respect to Douglas Craig," *Buff and Blue,* February 27, 1936.

40. Registration card of William J. Rich as a student at the Kendal School 1874 to 1885, Gallaudet University Archives.

41. Stewart, "Douglas Craig."

42. "Picnic Honoring William Rich," *Just Once a Month* 27, no. 1 (1944): 2, Gallaudet University Archives.

43. "William Rich," *Just Once a Month* (October 1945), Gallaudet University Archives.

44. Mike Kaika, "What's in a Name: Campus Landmarks and Building Honor a Variety of Persons," *Gallaudet Today* 12, no. 1 (Fall 1981): 24.

45. Edward Miner Gallaudet, *History,* 201–2.

46. "Class of 1952 video and transcript," VHS, 43 min., Gallaudet University Archives.

47. *Annual Report for 1905 of the Columbia Institution*, 11, Gallaudet University Archives.

7

The Women of Kendall Green: Coeducation at Gallaudet, 1860–1910

Lindsey M. Parker

Editors' Introduction

Lindsey M. Parker presents one of the most carefully argued and one of the most critical essays yet published about Gallaudet's institutional history and, along with Michael J. Olson's, one of the most critical of Edward Miner Gallaudet's leadership. Even more importantly, it suggests interpretations that challenge common assumptions about the history of the American deaf community. Parker traces the history of women students at Gallaudet College—their initial acceptance, then rejection, eventual readmittance, and subsequent struggle to gain equality with male students—and observes that gender seemed to mark educational expectations and social boundaries more strongly than deafness. Her conclusion suggests that deafness, or the shared use of sign language, has not been the strongly unifying force in American deaf history that many scholars have depicted.

COEDUCATION IN AMERICA was a source of controversy during the nineteenth and twentieth centuries, delineating distinct boundaries between those who viewed women's familial roles as incompatible with classroom education, particularly higher education, and those who saw gender equality in education as an inalienable right. While this issue has been extensively vetted in the context of mainstream studies of American history, coeducation specifically and, more generally, gender inequality have been relatively neglected lenses through which to view the field of Deaf history.

Deaf women pioneers produced the momentum that would ultimately tear down the barriers to women's acceptance at Gallaudet College. Their concerns were rejected initially, but the college later capitu-
lated under pressure from a broader women's rights movement. The
early stages of acceptance reveal great similarities among women in
higher education, both Deaf and hearing, arguably more so than between
male and female cohorts at Gallaudet. These women banded together to
establish a presence that would ultimately extend beyond the walls of
higher education and into their own communities.

The History of Coeducation and the Founding
of Gallaudet College

The nineteenth century marked a new emphasis on education. The societal transition from a barter-based economy to one relying upon the exchange of cash increased the demand for literacy and mathematic skills
and created a greater need for higher education institutions.[1] However,
a majority of the institutions created to meet this demand were for elite,
white, male, upper-class citizens. The women's rights movement seized
this issue, and coeducation proved to be a driving force in nineteenth-
century demands. Coeducation was a highly controversial topic from its
commencement in the mid-1800s to well into the late twentieth century.
Opponents cited countless reasons for banning women from higher education in the company of men, including the assertion that women's
brains were five ounces smaller than their male counterparts and the
widely referenced myth that advanced scholarship would "damage a
woman's ability to bear children." Harvard Medical School professor,
Dr. Edward Clarke, was an influential advocate of this latter theory. He
argued in his 1873 book, *Sex in Education* that, "women needed to save
their limited energy for childbearing. If they used it all up studying, they
would damage their female apparatus."[2]

Female activists capitalized on the idea of private spheres and motherhood to advocate for the higher education of women. In rebuttal to those
opposing coeducation—who argued that women belonged in the private
sphere of their home, rearing children—women's rights activists responded with what women's historians today refer to as "republican
motherhood," or an argument based on the stance that women's domes-
tic roles would improve with higher learning.[3] As the concept of republican motherhood spread and gained acceptance in mainstream society,
coeducation started to take root. Oberlin College in Ohio holds the dis-

tinction of being the first coeducational institution, admitting women in 1833. By 1880, three in five women in higher education attended coeducational colleges.[4]

Women were not the only minority group yearning for higher educational opportunities in the mid-nineteenth century. The Deaf community echoed the same need for a college education. John Carlin, a graduate of the Pennsylvania School for the Deaf who was also a teacher and an artist, argued in favor of a college for deaf students in an 1854 article featured in the *American Annals of the Deaf.*

> Universities, Colleges, Free Academies and High Schools have been built. For whom? For speaking persons of fine minds. For what? For their intellectual culture to the utmost degree. Why should not *one* college be reared in fair proportions to elevate the condition of our most promising deaf mutes and semi mutes, seeing that they have a just claim to the superior education enjoyed by the former?[5]

The events leading to the establishment of the first such college began in 1857, when Amos Kendall, philanthropist and former postmaster general, decided to establish a school for deaf and blind students, inspired by five deaf orphans for whom he was legal guardian.[6] Kendall appointed twenty-year-old Edward Miner Gallaudet as the superintendent of the primary school, known today as Kendall Demonstration Elementary School, because of Gallaudet's famous lineage in the field of deaf education. Gallaudet's father, Thomas Hopkins Gallaudet, established the first residential school for the deaf in the United States, the American School for the Deaf (ASD), while his Deaf mother, Sophia Fowler Gallaudet (one of the first pupils of ASD and a Deaf cultural icon), accompanied him as matron on his new endeavor. However, unlike his father, Gallaudet's vision was not limited to the establishment of a residential institution; he hoped to build a college.

Kendall's endowment of land and Congressional funding provided the new superintendent with the means to establish a college for deaf students. In 1864, President Abraham Lincoln signed legislation authorizing the granting of collegiate degrees by the Columbia Institution for the Instruction of the Deaf and Dumb and Blind, renamed Gallaudet College in 1894 in honor of Thomas Hopkins Gallaudet.[7] Carlin, being an early advocate for higher education in the Deaf community, was one of the main speakers at the inauguration of the college and received the first honorary degree.[8]

It did not appear at the outset that the Deaf community would face the same controversies over the issue of coeducation at Gallaudet College as at mainstream schools. Upon the college's founding in 1864, no official statement was made in favor of or in denial of women's admittance. Two Deaf women, Emma Sparks and Annie Szymanoskie, were among the seven students in the inaugural preparatory class.[9] However, President Gallaudet closed the doors to women in 1871, and they remained shut for sixteen years.

Little is known about these first two Gallaudet women beyond what is stated in their admittance records: Emma Sparks was from Maryland and became deaf when ten years old, while Annie Szymanoskie was orphaned at a young age after becoming deaf from scarlet fever at the age of two. Szymanoskie was one of the five orphans Kendall adopted and a pupil of the first class to attend the Kendall School. President Gallaudet described her as "an extremely intelligent girl with a pleasant personality and an occasional stubborn streak." Despite this compliment, neither woman continued past her introductory year, possibly for financial reasons.[10] However, historians John Van Cleve and Barry Crouch believe that "Gallaudet realized that many would not have the means to pay this sum [college fees], and from the beginning the college attempted to find a way to support all deaf pupils who had the desire and the ability, but not the money, to pursue college study."[11]

Although Sparks and Szymanoskie did not continue their college education, the following year two more women took their places. Adelaide Smith, deaf at eighteen months from scarlet fever, followed in her predecessors' footsteps and did not remain at the college past her preparatory year. Lydia Kennedy, a classmate of Smith's at the Pennsylvania School for the Deaf, surpassed her cohort and entered as a first-year student in the fall of 1866.[12] However, consistent with all of the female students before her, she left the college the following year. The 1867 annual report mentions that Kennedy left the college in pursuit of a teaching position at the Missouri School for the Deaf in Fulton.[13]

Lydia Mitchell, a Kendall School alumna, was the last of the women of the era to enter Gallaudet College. She began her studies in 1868 and had the longest tenure at the institution, continuing into the fall of 1871. In a letter addressed to President Gallaudet in September 1871, before the start of the fall term, she inquired about the availability of housing for her on campus, "I do not suppose you have as yet taken pains to seek a place for me?" She explained her desire to continue her education at the institution, "But what I wish to ask you is how soon you think I may be admitted—I should like very much to get an occupation this fall as soon possible, for I feel that I am spending my time in idleness at home." Wanting to continue her education, but unsure if she had a place to live at the college, she concluded her letter to the president with, "I will leave it all to you, trusting you can judge better what will be best for me."[14] Mitchell did not return to Gallaudet College that fall. The only documentation of her discontinuance at the institution can be found in the faculty minutes, stating that "she leaves college with [a] certificate [in] June 1871."[15]

Ambiguous school records and the absence of known diaries of the female students leave one to speculate why the female students initially had such a short tenure at the college. Many were noted as bright and intelligent, and there is every reason to believe that the women's initial acceptance to Gallaudet College was well deserved. President Gallaudet ensured strict admission standards,

> Applicants for admission had to be recommended by the principals of the schools from which they graduated. Gallaudet personally reviewed and decided upon on all the applications during the nineteenth century. After acceptance, each student was given a battery of examinations.[16]

Still, the majority of the women did not continue past their first year, and none advanced past her sophomore year. In contrast with the female students, twelve of the seventeen male preparatory students in the 1868 incoming class advanced to the freshman class. The male attrition rate declined the following year, as eleven students went on to attend their sophomore year.[17]

If the female students were prepared academically, their failure to succeed at the Deaf college must have some other explanation. Mitchell's correspondence with Gallaudet about the insufficient accommodations may provide a possible answer, as it alludes to an unwelcome environment condoned by the faculty and male students. The few female students were housed with the elementary school children in Old Fowler Hall, the original Kendall School building, while their male cohorts had their own residence within Rose Cottage. Rose Cottage was the original building on the Kendall estate and former primary school house. Often referred to as the "cradle of Gallaudet," this historic building was replaced by the Kendall School building, which is now part of the east wing of College Hall.[18]

No female students were admitted to the institution for the next seventeen years after Mitchell's withdrawal in 1871, even though a considerable number applied. President Gallaudet used the excuse of lack of accommodations to keep his college an exclusively male domain.[19] Over the next sixteen years, the issue of coeducation continued to be highly contested within both the Deaf community and within mainstream society.

The Road to Acceptance

The matter of coeducation at the college for deaf students lay dormant in the Deaf community for only a couple of years after Lydia Mitchell's departure. Surprisingly, the all-male literary society reignited the fire, debating the issue at one of its meetings in 1873. The proceedings from the debate were featured in the *Silent World*, a periodical dedicated to Deaf community issues, in an article titled, "Should Ladies Be Admitted into Our College?" The literary society argued favorably for the admission of women. One student claimed that,

> The presence of ladies in our college would certainly be beneficial to us in many respects, and especially in refining our manners. Were we to associate with ladies in our college daily, and occasionally have social gatherings, our manners would be very much improved, and we would go into society without embarrassment after graduating college.[20]

The men's argument embodied gendered stereotypes, but it may have looked to persuade more conservative readers to accept coeducation, leaving room for speculation that an all-male deaf college campus may have ulterior motives in its desire for female attendance outside of "refining manners." Regardless of the arguments and true intentions, the writer's recognition of the obstacles facing Deaf women took a more sincere tone, "Many ladies desire to pursue a collegiate course of study, but men have placed a barrier to their progress, and are now unwilling to remove it."[21] Although the male students of the college recognized the benefits of coeducation, their administrators did not; the male students' views failed to have any effect on the admission policies at the time.

Two years after the literary society debate, Laura Sheridan of Indiana wrote a poignant article, "The Higher-Education of Deaf-Mute Women," in the October 1875 issue of the *American Annals of the Deaf. The Annals* was the first publication dedicated to deaf education and was (and remains) the official journal for the Council of American Instructors of the Deaf (CAID) and the Conference of Educational Administrators of Schools and Programs for the Deaf (CEASD).[22] Sheridan, known as a "pioneer in the Deaf world," was also the first woman to present a paper to the CAID in 1882 and was a leader in the Chicago Methodist community, serving as an interpreter to Deaf minister Philip Hasenstab.[23] In her article, Sheridan recognized the lack of reaction from the Deaf community to the literary society's article in the *Silent World*, and asked, "What have we heard of the question [of coeducation] in the *Silent World*? Nothing. Are deaf-mute women different in nature, mind, function, and influence from their hearing sisters? No."[24]

Sheridan was no different than her "hearing sisters" in her argument for coeducation. She capitalized on the "republican motherhood" theory that many mainstream female activists used in the latter half of the nineteenth century. "A high state of culture is as necessary for woman as for man—for the beings who must be the mothers of our greatest men and mould [sic] the impressible years of childhood for those who cast the ballot," she wrote.[25] Sheridan's article also questioned whether the college was satisfying its mission.

> Has the National Deaf-Mute College, whose proposed object is 'to give competent deaf-mutes and others, who by reason of deafness cannot be educated elsewhere, a thorough education in the studies usually pursued in American Colleges,' opened its doors to women?

The emotionally charged article concluded with her own concession of "longings and ambitions" for a higher education, an unattainable goal that would "haunt her memory with a sadness inexpressible."[26]

Female students continued to submit applications for admittance into Gallaudet College despite the lack of public response from the college administration and the Deaf community to both the literary society's article and Sheridan's piece. Other scholars have written that President Gallaudet created a circular argument in the consideration of female applicants. While using the excuse that there were not enough applicants to justify the construction of accommodations for the students, denying them entrance into the college ensured that a low number of females would apply. "Women would hardly apply in large numbers to a school that only admitted men," one observer noted.[27] However, from 1871 when the last enrolled female exited the institution, to 1886, the time when the college officially acknowledged its coeducational status, at least seven female students inquired about the possibility of attending the college.[28]

In the fall of 1880, after the college rejected seven female applicants due to alleged inadequate accommodations, Gallaudet announced that Congress had appropriated over eight thousand dollars to construct a state of the art gymnasium on campus. The construction of "Ole Jim," as the gymnasium is called today, focused Deaf community debate on coeducation. Articles surrounding this issue flooded Deaf newspapers, such as the *Deaf Mutes' Journal*, from August 1880 to April 1881. The coeducational supporters, both men and women, questioned why Congressional funds would be used for the "physical development" of male students, when the money could have provided a physical space to enable a college education for female students.[29] Female leaders in the community, such as Angeline Fuller, a Deaf poetess and female activist from the Illinois School for the Deaf, were outspoken in their opposition to the construction of the gymnasium. Fuller blamed the male students for what she considered the misappropriation of funding, and she criticized their self-indulgence for wanting a gymnasium over supporting their cohorts' educational efforts. In an editorial featured in the *Deaf Mutes' Journal*, she warned deaf women not to marry the *gluttonous* college men.[30]

Fuller was one of the first and foremost supporters of the idea of establishing a Deaf women's college separate from Gallaudet. She pledged five dollars (which equates to roughly eighty dollars in today's terms) of her own money toward this endeavor and began collecting pledges from other supporters, such as the esteemed deaf writer, Laura Redding Searing. This idea was short lived; without Congressional funding, the sixty dollars raised in donations was not enough to establish a separate college for female students.[31]

As the bantering over the gymnasium continued, there was no official response from President Gallaudet or his administration in the pages of the *Deaf Mutes' Journal*. When the construction of the gymnasium concluded in 1881, complete with state-of-the-art amenities such as an indoor pool and bowling alley, so did the public debates within the Deaf community about higher education for women.[32] Women continued to show interest, however, by submitting letters to President Gallaudet requesting admittance into the college.

The issue reentered the public forum at the July 1886 meeting of the CAID. Georgia Elliott, a pupil of the Illinois School for the Deaf, read a letter promoting female attendance at the college. Elliott echoed many of Sheridan's points from eleven years before, using sentiments of republican motherhood in her argument. "Girls need a higher education as much as boys," Elliott wrote. "Their influence upon society as women, as mothers, as sisters, is very great, and a thorough education will better fit them for all their duties."[33] While Elliott's letter did not reverberate throughout the Deaf community newspapers, it did bring to light a topic that President Gallaudet had actively discouraged for the past twelve years.

Ole Jim

The late nineteenth century marked a burgeoning time for female solidarity, and it was an era of female political reform, resulting in the formation of clubs, organizations, and social movements.[34] College-educated women of the era formed the Western Association of Collegiate Alumnae (WACA). One of the main goals of the organization was the promotion of higher education for women. Amelia Platter, spokeswoman for the committee on higher education, contacted President Gallaudet in August of 1886 in this regard. She opened her letter with,

> I was appointed a committee of one to ask you, on behalf of that organization, and also in behalf of the unfortunate deaf-mute ladies of our country, to take such steps, and to use your influence to the end that the institution over which you preside and have control, be opened to the admission of lady as well as gentlemen students.[35]

While acknowledging a difference between deaf and hearing people, "the unfortunate deaf-mute ladies," the organization's members did not discriminate against their fellow "sisters" in regard to hearing status.

The social uplift of women through higher education took precedence over disability, as gender transcended the boundaries of hearing status.

Platter did her research on the history and founding of Gallaudet College and carefully organized her argument accordingly.

> The National Deaf-Mute College is a public institution. It has been built and supported almost entirely by the government. Since the college was inaugurated in 1864, Congress has appropriated to it $304,660.64 and seventeen acres of ground, besides building four dwelling houses for the college officers and providing improvements and extensions. It is certainly simple justice that our institution supported by the *people's* money should admit *all* who need and desire its instruction.[36]

The crux of her argument hinged on the public funding of the institution, driving home the point that Gallaudet College should follow the wants of American citizens, including deaf women.

Platter's letter on behalf of the WACA may have been the driving force behind President Gallaudet's change of heart in 1886. It was influential enough to be referred to in his 1886 annual report, "[The WACA] urges with much force that deaf women ought to be permitted to share in the advantages afforded by the bounty of Congress for the higher education of deaf young men of the country."[37] Later Gallaudet shared his opposition to coeducation in his history of the college.

> The admission of young women to the college was agreed to by me with a good deal of reluctance and considerable apprehension that the college education of the sexes together might lead to unsatisfactory results. I had never been warmly in favor of co-education.[38]

It was probably disconcerting to him that a well-known organization, external to the Deaf community, had questioned the institution's Congressional funding and insisted upon the right of women to attend the college. Less than five months after Platter's letter, the politically astute president of Gallaudet College began to probe superintendents of residential schools about the possibility of opening the college to women. His letter of inquiry requested the opinion of the superintendents and the recommendation of qualified female students, if any were available.[39]

The range of responses to Gallaudet's letter varied greatly. The superintendent of the Wisconsin School, John W. Swiler, "heartily approved of the coeducational movement," and felt that "the spirit of the age and intelligence of the period would justify such a movement."[40] Job Williams, superintendent of the American School for the Deaf, did not view coeducation in the same light.

> I would say that there is no young lady connected with our school, who would be at all likely to apply for admission to the college next academic year. I have an idea that if the doors of the College are opened for the admission of young ladies, there will be much less desire to enter than there has been while the doors were closed.[41]

While Williams' hypothesis proved to be false—when the doors opened, women did apply—some superintendents in 1886 stated that they did not have any female students to recommend for the upcoming academic year.

The *Deaf Mutes' Journal* was one of the first newspapers to publish the announcement that women would be permitted to attend Gallaudet College, declaring that "the Board of Directors of the Institution, having considered at two previous meetings, decided unanimously on Saturday of last, to try the experiment of admitting young women to the college." The article attempted to close the chapter on the highly contested debate of coeducation within the Deaf community, stating, "No comment is necessary. The young ladies are to be congratulated in having secured so quietly and easily a privilege which other colleges have been slow to bestow."[42] However, the author's perspective on the effortless admittance process is a bit skewed, as the Deaf community had debated coeducation for fifteen years.

Due to the lack of adequate accommodations for women on campus, Gallaudet decided that the incoming female students would reside in House One, the President's residence. The Gallaudet family relocated to Hartford, Connecticut, and President Gallaudet was granted absence "ad libitum" for the two-year trial period that he had determined would be necessary to evaluate coeducation.[43] The six female students lived on the third floor of the president's house with their matron Ellen Gordon.

The two-year experimentation period began in the fall of 1887. As a class of 1893 alumna described it, "when the time was ripe they took their places by the sides of their brothers and prepared to enter a life of better endeavor and higher thought."[44] Six women moved into House One to embark upon the world of higher education. The inaugural class of ladies included Alto Lowman of the Maryland School for the Deaf; Georgia Elliott, valedictorian of her class at the Illinois School of the Deaf; Ella Florence Black from the Indiana School for the Deaf; Anna Luella Kurtz, also from the Indiana School from the Deaf; Hattie A. Leffler of the Pennsylvania School for the Deaf; and Margaret Ellen Rudd of the Nebraska School for the Deaf.[45] All had been highly recommended by their former superintendents, and all had exhibited their intellects by passing the entrance exams on a par with their male peers.

Although these women gained acceptance into Gallaudet College, their presence at the institution was far from welcome. The experiences that the sextet endured may explain why only one member of their class, Alto Lowman, graduated.

The Female Experience

While the female students had earned admittance to Gallaudet College in the fall of 1887, they had yet to earn the respect of their peers and the faculty. In September 1887, the faculty members devoted the first three meetings of the academic year to the "regulations" for the female students.[46] However, no specific regulations for the women were documented during these meetings. Although the women were admitted under the same "terms and conditions as have been applied to young men," as President Gallaudet reported to the superintendents of the residential schools the previous spring, the women did not receive this same equality in regard to campus life.[47]

Still, in 1889 the college administration decided to make coeducation permanent at the college. The administration did not make a formal announcement about this decision. The annual report simply no longer referred to coeducation as an experiment.[48] The *Deaf Mutes' Journal*'s "Washington correspondent" noted, however, that "from the fact that the two years of experiment have expired and the college is still open to the admission of young women, we infer that the trial has been satisfactory to the board and co-education is an established fact in the National College."[49]

The faculty members did not make any concessions to make the women students feel more at "home." In fact, they were actually more rigid in the regulations placed on female students. Five years after the experimentation period was announced over, female students were still being treated as outsiders. Consistent with Victorian era values, the women were not allowed to leave campus without a chaperon. According to Agatha Tiegel Hanson, a member of the class of 1893, "To go in groups for hikes, to visit public buildings, to go skating or to the theatre, a chaperon was always required. If the girls were unsuccessful in finding someone who had the leisure and the will to go with them, they had to forego the contemplated diversion."[50] While it is understandable given

Alto Lowman

the time period that young females were not to leave campus unchaperoned, "babysitters" for on-campus activities seem more onerous, but faculty minutes clearly documented that female students were not allowed to attend on campus extracurricular activities without a matron or faculty member escort.

While some of the male students began to adjust to the female presence on campus, and even welcomed it, the faculty and administrators sought to keep a division between the sexes, especially in regards to extracurricular activities, such as the literary society. Commonly referred to as "The Lit," the organization was established in the early 1870s "for the improvement of signs, oratory, and readiness in debate."[51] When chaperoned, female students were permitted to attend the literary meet-

Female students in 1888

ings in the lyceum located on the third floor of College Hall; however, their involvement was restricted to the degree where they "sat meekly back and watched brother-students hold forth in lectures, debates, dialogues and declamations on the platform."[52] In 1889 an officer of the literary society requested that female students "might be allowed to join the same [as male students]." However, the faculty minutes reveal that female involvement in the organization was "voted to not be so allowed." Almost exactly a year to the day later, a female student formally requested permission to join the organization via a letter to the professors and administrators. Again, the faculty "voted that the request be not granted, but that [the females] be advised to associate among themselves for literary improvement."[53] While the faculty and administration gave no reasons for their decision, it is apparent that they sought to segregate the student body and were thus responsible for deepening the gender divide by passing on myriad opportunities to create parity between the sexes, relegating the female students to second-class status.

Male faculty fostered the gender chasm. Agatha Tiegal Hanson recalled that in her experience, "we were conscious of being under constant and critical observation, as though the faculty and male students were holding a silent court on us and our ability to make good."[54] May Martin, an 1895 graduate, had similar recollections. At an alumni gathering at the turn of the century she recognized one unnamed professor in particular "who was loudest in opposition" to the female students' attendance.[55] Hanson openly expressed her contempt for the situation forced on the females: "I resented this being on trial, both at Gallaudet and at the world at large."[56] Not only were the women's actions monitored, but their academic records were also under close observation. However, contemporaneously with the expiration of the experimentation period and numerous high ranking scores on their examinations, the women began to gain some respect at least in the realm of academics and test scores.[57]

The male students at Gallaudet College in the 1880s also contributed to the difficult situation the females faced. The inaugural year of coeducation at the college included not only criticism but also physical hazing of the female students. A *Buff and Blue* (the college newspaper) article recalls a time when the women were regarded as "freaks" on campus— "when the girls went to and from recitations in the college halls, all the [male] students would line up in rows and thus compel them to run a daily gauntlet of masculine curiosity."[58] The females reported experiencing "fear and trembling when faced with that mockery crowd of boys in halls." One woman who survived her first years at the college passed on these words of advice to an incoming 1890 freshman, "Don't take any aprons to college! The boys make fun of a girl who wore aprons to recitations, no matter how pretty and dainty said aprons might be."[59]

Harassing the women not only divided relationships between male and female students but also caused hardship for the men who stood up for their cohorts. There was one group of male students who were persistently "frank and outspoken" in their opposition to the female students, while a smaller coalition of men denounced the others' actions, calling them "persecution of a number of weak and defenceless [sic] creatures who were in College 'on trial.'" The opposition between the two groups of males grew, forcing individuals to choose sides, and resulting in the annulment of many friendships and prohibiting potential ones.[60]

Even though the sextet did garner some support from their male peers during their first year at the college, only three women advanced from the preparatory class to the freshman class the following year: Georgia Elliott, Alto Lowman, and Margaret Ellen Rudd.[61] However, the female students would gain more support with the influx of five more women in the preparatory class. The women of Gallaudet College did not retaliate against the hazing and "harsh treatment by their fellow students."[62] Instead, they continued to prove their worth academically and waited for the experimentation period to expire before establishing a place for themselves at the college.

Making a Place of Their Own

The experience of exclusion at the academic and social levels in higher education during the late nineteenth century was not unique to Kendall Green. Marginalization from campus organizations and athletics was a common experience for female students attending previously all-male institutions.[63] In 1877, a graduate of the University of Michigan, Olive San Louie Anderson, described her coeducation experience as follows: "A freshman year in college is full of trials for a boy; but, for a girl, who enters an institution where boys have held undisputed sway for generations, everyday brings persecutions which he never feels."[64]

Gallaudet College was unique among other educational institutions in that all of its students had one thing in common—their deafness. This one unifying factor may have even transcended gender or race. Christopher Krentz has written that "for many deaf people, the deaf community functioned as a second family, a group where one was understood and accepted, where one felt happy, normal, and at home."[65] John Vickrey Van Cleve and Barry A. Crouch effectively argue in *A Place of Their Own* that the nineteenth-century Deaf community formed a subculture, focused on organizations and residential schools, within American society. Van Cleve and Crouch apply this same argument to Gallaudet College, describing the college as a "place" for the Deaf community. However, due to gender divisions within the nineteenth-century college community, further analysis reveals that Gallaudet, despite the alleged uniqueness of its mission and the unifying characteristic of deafness, was similar to other institutions of higher learning that were physically and socially a place exclusively for white males.[66]

The female students were astutely aware of their "place" within the elite Deaf institution. In the fall of 1887, theoretically and physically, the women did not have a place, as intangible walls barricaded them from complete inclusion within the college. Throughout the coeducation experimental period, the women were treated as "outsiders." While some of their male counterparts viewed their dormancy in the first few years at the institution as a form of weakness and dependence, the women began to take action.[67] Taking extracurricular activities into their own hands, the women started their own organization in response to their exclusion from the male-only literary society. The O.W.L.S. (an acronym whose definition is still a tightly held secret) was established in 1892, marking one of the first attempts by the women to make a place for themselves at the institution.

One challenge women faced was that they did not have a physical place for their meetings, although male students had a designated "reading room" on campus. Occasionally, the females were permitted to use the library at the Kendall School, the primary school on campus, for a pseudo "sitting" room. The gesture of giving the women their own sitting room within the primary school reinforced the perception the campus community had of women—they were denigrated to the status of children with whom they shared space. Furthermore, the women had access to only secondhand newspapers given to them after their male peers were finished reading them. The O.W.L.S. rejected the meeting space within Kendall School and borrowed Professor Samuel Porter's private library to hold their tri-weekly meetings.[68] The retired professor of philosophy and mental science had resided on Kendall Green for over thirty years.[69] His empathy for the female students' situation may have evolved from his prominent family background. His father, Noah Porter, was a former president of Yale University and his sister, Sarah, was an educator as well, establishing a seminary for women.[70]

The O.W.L.S. quickly developed larger aspirations for their organization than their male cohorts had for their literary society. These aspirations included dramatic and social aspects. The women soon realized that although society allowed for women to share their intellectual ideas and opinions, their "voices" were only being heard among themselves, behind closed-door meetings. After a few private meetings, the O.W.L.S. began to hold open forums to discuss literature and to demonstrate their theatrical interests. By the beginning of the twentieth century, the O.W.L.S. organization had evolved to serve a dual purpose, not only for literary discussions, but as an active response to women's marginalized place at the college.

The leaders of the O.W.L.S. began to exhibit their agency on campus in other ways under the leadership of Agatha Tiegel, the organization's first president and a member of the second class of women to attend Gallaudet, and May Martin, treasurer and secretary, from the fourth class of women.[71] Recognizing the need for a school publication, Tiegel, Martin, and the O.W.L.S. were influential in the founding of the *Buff and Blue* newspaper in 1892. Although the concept of a college publication had been discussed in previous years, because of monetary and leadership reasons, the idea was rejected.[72] President Gallaudet knew too well of the bleak history of independent papers established for the Deaf community, many of which were abandoned, and he wanted to avoid such "humiliation."[73] Therefore, he appeared to have a predisposition against embarking on a new publication. With the persistence of a group of female students along with some of their male cohorts, however, President Gallaudet granted permission for the newspaper under a conditional agreement that the students would recruit over one hundred and fifty subscribers before the first publication, to ensure the newspaper's success.[74] Although Martin has been credited for the innovation of the newspaper, her leadership role stopped there.

Historically, the women's role within the Deaf community has been one of support and spectatorship for their male leaders.[75] Perhaps Martin declined the coveted position of editor-in-chief in an effort to make sure President Gallaudet did not close it down because of female leadership, or perhaps she did so to build male alliances.[76] Although a male student assumed the role of *Buff and Blue* editor-in-chief, the female students continued to influence the publication. Tiegel gained a spot on the editorial team, while Martin contributed numerous articles. For the next eighteen years, article contributions and editorial assistant positions were the extent of involvement for the women. It was not until 1910 that a woman, Alice Nicholson, would hold the position of editor-in-chief of the college newspaper at Gallaudet. It would be another seventeen years until the position was granted again to a female student, Alice McVan, in 1927.[77]

Continuing their initiatives on campus, the female students established Gallaudet College's first basketball team in 1896. Nine years later their male counterparts set up their own team. It is not surprising that the female students founded the first basketball team, as they seemed to explore areas of social interest that the male students had not already occupied. Although the team's schedule consisted of only three games, all against the same organization, Sanatory Gymnasium, the females maintained an undefeated record for three consecutive seasons.[78]

The women of the O.W.L.S. used their 1896 public forum in Chapel Hall as another outlet to publicize the institution's treatment of them as inferior. While most literary meetings included recitations of essays or comparative literature dialogues, this group of women decided to make a more prominent expression. The highlight of the event was a performance piece entitled "Our Side." From a male student's perspective, the *Buff and Blue* recounted the female student's performance.

> The tableau represented Miss Block, '96, at the top of an immense ladder, erected on the stage, about to grasp a ponderous diploma. Then in order

Group photo of the O.W.L.S.

were Misses Kershner, '97, Stemples, '98, Watts, '99, and Phelps, E. Taylor, and B. Taylor, I.C. From the whole, we can imagine what it meant. As the last three [women] were at the foot of the ladder stretching out their hands to the suspended diploma at the top."[79]

Actions speak louder than words. In this case, without a single sign, the women clearly depicted their experiences of inequality and oppression at the institution. The ladder represented the hierarchy of education, while the female students standing underneath the woman at the top of ladder were indicative of her only source of support at the college.

This dramatic performance was well ahead of its time, and it was a precursor to a 1915 drawing by suffragist Blanche Ames. Ames's drawing also depicts a woman climbing the ladder of progress. From the bottom up, each step represents advancement for women: education, property, professions, business, votes for women, and true democracy (fig. 1). Rather than a ponderous diploma inhibiting the growth of women, Ames's work depicts two flying devil-pigs labeled "injustice" and "prejudice" attacking a woman as she reaches toward the next step to equality.

Conscious of the societal and institutional limitations on their actions, the female students carefully chose venues in which to express their discontentment with the patriarchal institution. "Presentation Day" at Gal-

Figure 1. Blanche Ames's depiction of women's ascent toward equality (Boston *Transcript*, November 1915).

laudet College (similar to today's commencement ceremony) was held annually at the beginning of May. The celebration included orations and dissertations presented by students of the graduating class. With a large, captive audience consisting of congressmen, parents, alumni, and leaders of the Deaf community, the female students astutely chose this ceremony as another one of their outlets. In 1893, Agatha Tiegel became the first woman to graduate from the college with a bachelor's degree. Tiegel's presentation was entitled "The Intellect of Women," and it openly challenged the inherent belief that female students were intellectually inferior to their male cohorts.[80] Tiegel began with a powerful statement.

> The apparent inferiority of woman's intellect is to be attributed to many restrictive circumstances. We are so accustomed to behold her in a stage of development so far below her powers that we do not apprehend the full evil of these circumstances.[81]

Tiegel's oration sought to dispel the myth that women could not be successful college graduates. She concluded her address by stating, "there yet remains a large fund of prejudice to overcome, of false sentiment to combat, of narrow-minded opposition to triumph over."[82] While Tiegel never specifically mentions Gallaudet College in her speech, she made abundantly clear the unsatisfactory circumstances that female students endured while attending the college and highlighted the gendered division on campus.

Two years later, May Martin, valedictorian of her graduating class, titled her oration based on Oliver Wendell Holmes's poem, "The Chambered Nautilus." She too addressed an audience with great weight, as the keynote speaker of the graduation ceremony was the Honorable William L. Wilson, postmaster general.[83] At first glance, this topic seems to have little to do with coeducation at the institution; however, her address was saturated with metaphors. Her description of the life of a nautilus, a shell growing at the bottom of the sea, parallels that of the coeds due to the similarities in societal status and living environment.

> We are filled with reverential admiration when we observe the pains which nature has taken to beautify even when the unseen portions of a shell habitant at the bottom of the sea. Its dim, dreaming life reminds us of the low scale in the order of creation upon which the Nautilus is placed. Yet there is still a prophecy of something higher. Living amid the darkness and dreams did not hinder.[84]

Martin capitalized on the metaphor of the sea as the social environment that vastly limited women's ability to exhibit their intelligence, strength, and skills. The female students were the beautiful shells, unnoticed, "chambered" beneath a sea of patriarchy.

In the same tradition, Laura McDill, a graduate of the Iowa School for the Deaf, presented her oration "It Is Fate" to the influential audience at the 1896 Presentation Day ceremonies. Her definition of fate was something that is "never heard or seen, but stands behind us and casts its dread shadow over all." Although McDill conceded that fate may determine opportunity in life, she also noted, "nothing can work me damage but myself; the harm that I sustain I carry about with me, and never am I a real sufferer but by my own fault."[85] Her experience at Gallaudet reflected a similar sentiment to her graduation address. Fate may have determined her second-class status at Gallaudet College; however, she sought to change the injustice through her involvement in extracurricular activities and efforts to make a place for women at the college.

Emma Kershner, captain of the 1896 women's basketball team, cast member in the "Our Side" performance a year prior, and graduate of the Pennsylvania School for the Deaf, opened her poignant 1897 oration, "What the World Owes to Woman," with the following,

> The problem of woman's position or 'sphere,'—or her duties, responsibilities, rights, and influence, as woman,—has been, and is still a matter of debate. There has existed in the mind of men a tone of feeling toward women as toward slaves.[86]

This was the last documented address of the century to encompass the underlying and explicit messages of a woman's place, or lack thereof, at Gallaudet College. Kershner's address summarized a history of patriarchy and discrimination toward women, highlighting famously powerful women such as Queen Victoria, Queen Elizabeth, and Mary Lyon, founder of Mt. Holyoke College. Kershner used this venue to exemplify the influence of women throughout history, even though in present day, she argued, her gender was still viewed as subordinate.

Throughout the late 1890s, the women continued to make a theoretical place for themselves within the institution. In 1895, May Martin became the first female faculty member at Gallaudet College. She received a letter at her home in New York from Edward Miner Gallaudet several months after her graduation from the college, inviting her to teach English at the college and at Kendall School.[87] Not only was her field of instruction gendered, but being female also made her a prime candidate and motherly figure for the elementary students. The only other instructor to hold a dual position at both the college and the primary school was Arthur Bryant, the art and drawing teacher, who also happened to be the lowest paid instructor at Gallaudet College, just under Martin.[88] After teaching at the college for just four years, Martin's salary increased to five hundred dollars per year. Her male counterparts made on average more than double her salary, even though some began working at the college after she had.[89] Martin's position at the institution was significant for the future of women on campus, providing a female ally at the faculty level. However, Martin's tenure was short lived; she resigned from the college in 1900, after receiving her master's degree, to marry Henry Stafford, a fellow Gallaudet College alumnus. Stafford was a clerk and bookkeeper for an iron mining company in Minnesota, where the couple resided after their marriage.[90]

By the turn of the century, the female students were successful in attaining one of their goals, etching a permanent place for themselves within campus society. However, the women still lacked a tangible residence of their own. During their first two years at Gallaudet College, they lived in House One with President Gallaudet. In 1889, the women were moved to the main building of the primary department, more commonly known as Old Fowler Hall, and forced to share corridors with girls from Kendall school. Meanwhile, the male students had their own dormitory called Dawes House. At the turn of the century, the female students were relocated again. This time they were moved across campus to faculty row, residing in what is now referred to as Denison House.[91] The constant relocating of the female students as well as pairing them with primary school students exemplifies the administrators' perception of the women as inferior and childlike. Excuses, such as deficient funding and lack of necessity, inhibited the female students from achieving their goal of a permanent residence until the reconstruction of Fowler Hall in 1915.

Conclusion

The shared characteristic of deafness inspired the creation of a separate college for Deaf students in 1864, but it did not tear down the boundaries of gender within academe. The treatment of women as second-class citizens in higher education characterized the hearing community in the nineteenth and twentieth centuries, and it characterized the Deaf community. Even gaining admittance to Gallaudet College was a struggle for women, and Deaf and hearing women worked together to pressure the college to accept women. Once the doors finally were open to them,

Deaf women's experiences at Gallaudet College resembled those of their hearing female counterparts. Treated as outsiders within their own community, the Deaf women sought to establish their own identity and carve their own niche. The pseudo-equality of women in higher education institutions, coupled with resistance met by their presence, led to the coalescence of female students in efforts to make a place for themselves on campus.

The similarities uniting hearing women with their Deaf kin in the experience of higher education in the United States suggest broad conclusions. One is that the bond of womanhood transcended that of being deaf in the realm of higher education, as hearing and Deaf women rallied to provide the latter with access to Gallaudet College. For the hearing women in the WACA, the status of a woman's hearing was not as important as her second-class citizenship if denied higher education. A second conclusion is that the bond of maleness transcended deafness in higher education. Deaf community males, from President Gallaudet through at least a significant part of the college's student body, resisted the admittance of women into their enclave. After women were admitted, they were denied equality with male students. A gendered lens of Gallaudet College history reveals tensions and complicates the previous image cast of the Deaf world as unified and homogenous, suggesting the powerful signifier of gender within the context of higher education in the late nineteenth century. Therefore, this paper suggests that historians need to reexamine their interpretations of general Deaf culture and ask to what extent boundaries were defined more by larger social constructions, such as gender, than by being Deaf or use of a common language alone.

Notes

1. Margaret Nash, *Women's Education in the United States, 1780–1840* (New York: Palgrave Macmillan, 2005), 2.

2. Nancy Cott, *No Small Courage: A History of Women in the United States* (Oxford: Oxford University Press, 2000), 314.

3. Linda Kerber and Jane Sherron De Hart, *Women's America: Refocusing the Past* (New York and Oxford: Oxford University Press, 1995), 90.

4. Leslie Miller-Bernal and Susan L. Poulson, *Going Coed* (Nashville: Vanderbilt University Press, 2004), 3, 5.

5. Christopher Krentz, *A Mighty Change* (Washington, D.C.: Gallaudet University Press, 2000), 100.

6. John Vickrey Van Cleve and Barry A. Crouch, *A Place of Their Own* (Washington, D.C: Gallaudet University Press, 1989), 80.

7. Ibid.

8. Krentz, *Mighty Change*, 92.

9. Edward Miner Gallaudet, *History of the College for the Deaf: 1857–1907*, ed. Lance J. Fischer and David L. de Lorenzo (Washington, D.C.: Gallaudet College Press, 1983), 57.

10. Nancy Carolyn Jones, *Don't Bring Your Aprons to College!* (master's thesis, University of Maryland, 1983), 18, 19.

11. Van Cleve and Crouch, *A Place of Their Own*, 85.

12. Jones, *Don't Bring Your Aprons*, 19.

13. *Annual Report of the Columbia Institution for the Deaf and Dumb, 1867*, Gallaudet University Archives.

14. Lydia Mitchell to Edward Gallaudet, 11 September 1871, Gallaudet University Archives.

15. "Faculty Minutes: 1867–1887," vol. 1, Gallaudet University Archives, 487.

16. Van Cleve and Crouch, *A Place of Their Own*, 84–85.

17. *Annual Report of the Columbia Institution for the Deaf and Dumb, 1868, 1869*, Gallaudet University Archives.

18. *History of KDES*, pamphlet, Gallaudet University Archives.

19. Jones, *Don't Bring Your Aprons*, 20.

20. J.C.W., "Should Ladies Be Admitted to Our College?" *Silent World*, (February 1, 1873), 9.

21. Ibid.

22. For more information on CAID and CEASD's contribution to AAD, refer to Lindsey Parker, "American Annals of the Deaf," *Encyclopedia of American Disability History* (Facts on File, forthcoming).

23. Kent Olney, "The Chicago Mission for the Deaf," in *The Deaf History Reader*, ed. John Vickrey Van Cleve (Washington, D.C.: Gallaudet University Press, 2007), 174–208.

24. Laura Sheridan, "The Higher-Education of Deaf-mute Women," *American Annals of the Deaf*, 20 (October 1875), 248.

25. Ibid.

26. Ibid.

27. Jones, *Don't Bring Your Aprons*, 27.

28. Edward Miner Gallaudet Presidential Papers, Gallaudet University Archives.

29. *Annual Report of the Columbia Institution for the Deaf and Dumb, 1880*, Gallaudet University Archives, 13, 30.

30. Jones, *Don't Bring Your Aprons*, 29. Fuller had played a central role in gaining female membership to the CAID in 1870.

31. Ibid., 33

32. Ibid., 13.

33. Georgia Elliott to the 1886 Convention of American Instructors of the Deaf in California, repr. in the *Annual Report of the Columbia Institution for the Deaf and Dumb, 1886*, Gallaudet University Archives, 177.

34. Sara Evans, *Born for Liberty: A History of Women in America* (New York: The Free Press, 1989), 145.

35. Amelia Platter to Edward Gallaudet, 4 August 1886, Gallaudet University Archives.

36. Ibid.

37. Edward Miner Gallaudet, "Annual Report of the Columbia Institution for the Deaf and Dumb, 1886," in *American Annals for the Deaf* 32:65.

38. Gallaudet, *History of the College*, 166.

39. Edward Gallaudet to superintendents, 8 December 1886, Gallaudet University Archives.

40. John W. Swiler to Edward Gallaudet, 18 December 1886, Gallaudet University Archives.

41. Job Williams to Edward Gallaudet, 10 December 1886, Gallaudet University Archives.

42. *Deaf Mutes' Journal*, February 10, 1887, Gallaudet University Archives.

43. *Annual Report of the Columbia Institution, 1886*, Gallaudet University Archives. "Ad libitum" translates into "at one's pleasure."

44. Agatha Tiegel, "Co-education at Gallaudet College," *The National Exponent* (1895).

45. Jones, *Don't Bring Your Apron*, 61–65.

46. Faculty Minutes, vol. 2 (September 1887), Gallaudet University Archives.

47. Edward Miner Gallaudet to Superintendents, in *American Annals of the Deaf*, 32 (1887): 128.

48. W.B., "Kendall Items," *Deaf Mutes' Journal*, October 3, 1889, 2.

49. Ibid.

50. Hanson (1937), 6.

51. Tom L. Anderson, "The Value of Literary Societies," *Iowa Hawkeye* (1937), 10–11.

52. Hanson (1937), 6.

53. Faculty Minutes, vol. 2, (October 22, 1889 and October 14, 1890), 71.

54. Hanson (1937), 6.

55. May Martin, "GCAA Minutes and Proceedings, 1889–99," Gallaudet University Archives, 45.

56. Hanson (1937), 6.

57. Jones, *Don't Bring Your Aprons*, 86.

58. *Buff and Blue* 3, no. 4 (March 5, 1895), Gallaudet University Archives, 49.

59. GCAA Minutes and Proceedings, 1889–99, Gallaudet University Archives, 45.

60. V., "Twenty Years After," *Buff and Blue* (1905), Gallaudet University Archives, 108–110.

61. *Annual Report of the Columbia Institution for the Deaf and Dumb, 1887, 1888*, Gallaudet University Archives.

62. Jones, *Don't Bring Your Aprons*, 77.

63. Miller-Bernal, *Going Coed*, 7.

64. Anderson, "Literary Societies," 70.

65. Krentz, *A Mighty Change*, xvii.

66. Van Cleve and Crouch, *A Place of Their Own*.

67. Jones, *Don't Bring Your Aprons*, 107.

68. Hanson, (1937), 6; Hanson (1912).

69. "Samuel Porter," biographical file, Gallaudet University Archives.

70. "Noah Porter," *http://virtualology.com/apnoahporter/*.

71. "Agatha Tiegel Hanson," biographical file, Gallaudet University Archives; "NYSD school reports, 1889," Gallaudet University Archives.

72. *Buff and Blue Centennial Issue*, (1992): 8–11.

73. Hanson (1937), 6–8.

74. *Buff and Blue Centennial Issue*.

75. Sara Robinson, "The Extended Family," in *Women and Deafness: Double Visions*, ed. Brenda Jo Brueggemann and Susan Burch (Washington, D.C.: Gallaudet University Press, 2006), 40–56.

76. J.B.H. "May Martin," *Silent Worker* (December 1908).

77. *Buff and Blue Centennial Issue*, 12.

78. Gallaudet University Archives Timeline, http://archives.gallaudet.edu/Timeline.htm (January 16, 2007); *The Gallaudet Almanac* (Washington, D.C.: Gallaudet College Alumni Association, 1974).

79. *Buff and Blue,* (March 1896).

80. James Fernandes and Jane F. Kelleher, "Signs of Eloquence," in *The Deaf Way: Perspectives from the International Conference on Deaf Culture,* ed. Carol Erting and others, (Washington, D.C.: Gallaudet University Press, 1994), 179.

81. Agatha Tiegel, "The Intellect of Women," (April 1893), biographical file, Gallaudet University Archives.

82. Ibid.

83. *Annual Report of Gallaudet College, 1895,* Gallaudet University Archives.

84. May Martin, reprinted in *Buff and Blue* (June 1895): 95–96.

85. Laura McDill, reprinted in *Buff and Blue* (June 1896): 87–88.

86. Emma Kershner, reprinted in *Buff and Blue* (June 1897): 158–60.

87. *Annual Report of Gallaudet College, 1900,* Gallaudet University Archives.

88. *Annual Report of Gallaudet College, 1895,* Gallaudet University Archives; Gallaudet College Payroll Report, 1903, National Archives.

89. *Annual Report of Gallaudet College, 1899,* Gallaudet University Archives.

90. J.B.H., *Silent Worker,* December 1908, 48; "Henry Stafford," 1893, Gallaudet Alumni Cards, Gallaudet University Archives.

91. *History of KDES,* Gallaudet University Archives.

Selected Bibliography

Anderson, Olive San Louie. *An American Girl and Her Four Years in a Boy's College.* Edited by Elisabeth Israels Perry and Jennifer Ann Price. Ann Arbor: University of Michigan Press, 2006.

Antler, Joyce. "After College, What?" *A History of Women in the United States. Vol. 12, Education.* Edited by Nancy Cott. Munich: K.G. Saur, 1993.

Bailey, Thomas A. and David M. Kennedy, *American Pageant: A History of the Republic.* Lexington: D.C. Health and Company, 1994.

Barreca, Gina. *Babes in Boyland: A Personal History of Co-education in the Ivy League.* Hanover and London: University Press of New England, 2005.

Burch, Susan. *Signs of Resistance.* New York: New York University Press, 2002.

Carleton, David. *Student's Guide to Landmark Congressional Laws on Education.* Westport: Greenwood Press, 2002.

Cott, Nancy. *No Small Courage: A History of Women in the United States.* Oxford: Oxford University Press, 2000.

Evans, Sara. *Born for Liberty: A History of Women in America.* New York: The Free Press, 1989.

Famous Americans. "Noah Porter." http://famousamericans.net/noahporter.

Fernandes, James and Jane F. Kelleher. "Signs of Eloquence." In *The Deaf Way: Perspectives from the International Conference on Deaf Culture,* edited by Carol Erting et al., 179. Washington, D.C.: Gallaudet University Press, 1994.

Gallaudet, Edward Miner. *History of the College of the Deaf 1857–1907.* Edited by Lance J. Fischer and David L. de Lorenzo. Washington, D.C.: Gallaudet College Press, 1983.

Gallaudet Almanac. Washington, D.C.: Gallaudet College Alumni Association, 1974.

Gallaudet University Archives Timeline. http://archives.gallaudet.edu/Timeline.htm.

Gannon, Jack. *Deaf Heritage.* Silver Spring: National Association for the Deaf, 1981.

Holcomb, Marjoriebell Stakley and Sharon Wood. *Deaf Women: A Parade Through the Decades.* Berkeley: Dawn Sign Press, 1989.

Howe, Florence. *Myths of Coeducation.* Bloomington: Indiana University Press, 1984.

Jones, Nancy Carolyn. *Don't Bring Your Aprons to College!* Master's thesis, University of Maryland, 1983.

Kerber, Linda and Jane Sherron De Hart. *Women's America: Refocusing the Past.* New York and Oxford: Oxford University Press, 1995.

Krentz, Christopher. *A Mighty Change.* Washington, D.C.: Gallaudet University Press, 2000.

Lee, Jessica. "Family Matters: Female Dynamics within Deaf Schools." In *Women and Deafness: Double Visions.* Edited by Brenda Jo Brueggemann and Susan Burch. Washington, D.C.: Gallaudet University Press, 2006, 5–20.

Lundt, Christine, Susan L. Poulson, and Leslie Miller-Bernal. "To Coeducation and Back Again: Gender and Organization at the University of Rochester." In *Going Coed.* Edited by Miller-Bernal and Poulson. Nashville: Vanderbilt University Press, 2004.

Miller-Bernal, Leslie. *Separate By Degree.* New York: Peter Lang Publishing Inc., 2000, 12.

Miller-Bernal, Leslie and Susan L. Poulson. *Going Coed.* Nashville: Vanderbilt University Press, 2004.

Nash, Margaret. *Women's Education in the United States, 1780–1840.* New York: Palgrave Macmillan, 2005.

Olney, Kent. "The Chicago Mission for the Deaf." In *The Deaf History Reader.* Edited by John Vickrey Van Cleve. Washington, D.C.: Gallaudet University Press, 2007, 174–208.

Robinson, Sara. "The Extended Family." In *Women and Deafness: Double Visions.* Edited by Brenda Jo Brueggemann and Susan Burch. Washington, D.C.: Gallaudet University Press, 2006, 40–56.

"The Early History of Harvard University." Harvard University Web site, http://www.har vard.edu.

Van Cleve, John Vickrey and Barry A. Crouch. *A Place of Their Own.* Washington, D.C: Gallaudet University Press, 1989.

"Women at Harvard University." Harvard University Web site, http://www.harvard.edu.

Zschoche, Sue. "Preserving Eden: Higher Education, Women's Sphere and The First Generation of College Women, 1870–1910." PhD diss., University of Maryland, 1984.

Gallaudet University Archives Primary Sources Papers and Biographical Files

Agatha Tiegal Hanson
Alumni Cards
Edward Miner Gallaudet Presidential Papers and Correspondences
Faculty Minutes
May Martin

Newspapers/Periodicals

American Annals of the Deaf
Buff and Blue, 1892–1900
Columbia Institution for the Deaf Annual Reports
Convention of American Instructors of the Deaf Proceedings
Silent Worker
Silent World
The National Exponent

8

The Struggle to Educate Black Deaf Schoolchildren in Washington, D.C.

Sandra Jowers-Barber

Editors' Introduction

Sandra Jowers-Barber's study adds significantly to what is known about Gallaudet University and issues related to race and education. She reviews the history of African American deaf students in the precollege programs on Kendall Green and then focuses specifically on attempts by black parents Louise and Luther Miller to enroll their deaf son, Kenneth, in Kendall School. After several years of frustration with Gallaudet's administrators and with the Washington, D.C., Board of Education, in 1952 the Millers triumphed. In a decision known as Miller v. D.C. Board of Education, *the U.S. District court ruled that Kendall School had to accept black students from the District of Columbia. Kendall School responded by creating separate facilities, called Division II, for African American deaf students, actively resisting integration until the Supreme Court's 1954 decision in* Brown vs. Board of Education. *Jowers-Barber concludes that Gallaudet, although a unique national institution, funded largely by the federal government to serve all deaf Americans, nevertheless followed the trends of the time and did not challenge prevailing racial policies.*

FOR MANY AMERICANS the chance to obtain an education has been a struggle. Frederick Douglass recounts how during his enslavement his owner's wife started teaching him to read only to stop after her husband forbade the lessons. At the risk of severe physical punishment he used every opportunity he could find to continue his education.[1] For a great many African Americans, hearing and deaf, the struggle to obtain an

113

integrated education lasted well into the twentieth century and ended with the historic *Brown v. Board of Education* decision in 1954.[2]

African American deaf children of school age in the District of Columbia began that struggle after an early, but brief, promise of educational integration. The Columbia Institution for the Instruction of the Deaf and Dumb and Blind was established by Amos Kendall in the district in 1856. A year later, it was incorporated by an act of Congress.[3] On February 16, 1857, Kendall secured the passage of another act that granted an allowance of one hundred and fifty dollars a year for the maintenance and tuition of each child received in the institution from the district.[4]

That same year Kendall offered Edward Miner Gallaudet, by letter, the position of superintendent of the Columbia Institution.[5] Gallaudet's background was above reproach. His father, Thomas Hopkins Gallaudet, co-founded the first American school for the deaf in Hartford, Connecticut, in 1817. His deaf mother, Sophia, was one of his father's first students. Gallaudet and his mother came to Washington together. She took the position of housemother to the students.

When the school opened, an estimated twenty deaf and ten blind students were expected from the district and an unknown number from Maryland.[6] Among the students that Gallaudet was preparing to direct were a few who were Black. This was an unusual situation for this period. Before the Civil War, Black people, both deaf and hearing, struggled to obtain a formal education. Because it was a criminal offense in some states to educate enslaved people, those enslaved persons who learned to read, like Frederick Douglass, concealed that fact. However, the pre–Civil War Columbia Institution accepted Black students, but their numbers were always small. Many came because of the intervention of wealthy white patrons. Gallaudet received numerous requests for assistance and generally responded positively to them by accepting the youth at the Kendall School. Gallaudet clearly saw the school's mission as providing education for all deaf students when he initially accepted both races. He noted in the *History of the College for the Deaf* that there had been "colored pupils since the early days of the school." Although Black and white students had separate sleeping and eating accommodations, all of them were taught together in the classroom.[7]

Gallaudet continued to receive letters in the late 1800s regarding orphaned Black students found abandoned in alleys, sponsored by church groups and other social agencies. He continued to respond positively to these requests for assistance for poor, Black deaf youth in need of training and accepted all who were sent. One such request came in a letter from R. Y. Maussma, dated March 3, 1879.

Wm. N. Catlett, mulatto, 6 years old, residing on Wilson St. County, D.C., was born deaf and dumb. His father, a laborer in the Treasury Dept. wishes him to enter into your institute. What conditions have to be observed to gain admission for him. Please inform.[8]

In another letter dated Nov. 21, 1889, Jenine W. Scudder, asked,

Would you please inform me whether colored deaf mute children are received at Kendall Green? I have discovered a poor deaf mute colored boy, living in an alley and would like to try to help him to "better things" but before anything can be done I must know whether you can receive him or not. May I hear from you as soon as convenient?[9]

The integration of the races in the classroom had been established from the early years of the school. In 1898, Kendall School had fourteen Black deaf students enrolled. However, two years earlier Gallaudet had begun to receive complaints from the white parents about the intermixing of students, and by 1901 white parents had begun to object strenuously to the presence of these students. Soon after the parental objections began, the relationship between the students, which had been cordial, quickly deteriorated. When the white students began harassing the Black students it became obvious to Gallaudet that the ability of the students to coexist had eroded.[10] Contributing to this hostile environment was the conclusion of the 1896 *Plessy v. Ferguson* case, the Supreme Court decision that established the doctrine of "separate but equal" as the law of the land.[11] Gallaudet, feeling compelled to take some action, approached Senator Francis Cockrell (D) from Missouri. The senator offered assistance by obtaining Congressional legislation, approved on March 3, 1905, that provided for the transfer of the African American students to the Maryland School for Colored Deaf-Mutes in Overlea, Maryland.[12]

The Maryland School for the Colored Blind and Deaf was founded in 1872 by Frederick Douglas Morrison, director of the Maryland School for the Blind. The School for the Colored Deaf was located within the physical structure of Maryland's School for the Blind.[13] The legislation sponsored by Cockrell further authorized the education of deaf Black district pupils at the Maryland facility.

For the maintenance and tuition of colored deaf-mutes of teachable age belonging to the District of Columbia in the Maryland School for Colored Deaf-Mutes, as authorized in an Act of Congress approved March third, nineteen hundred and five, and under a contract to be entered into by the

Commissioners of the District of Columbia, five thousand dollars, or such thereof as may be necessary.[14]

The Congressional action eliminated the presence of African Americans at Kendall. The fourteen students in attendance were transferred in September 1905 to the Maryland School for Colored Deaf-Mutes. The resulting policy of educating deaf Blacks outside of the district stayed in place for the next fifty years.

In 1946 Louise B. Miller, a district resident with a deaf child, began her challenge to this policy, a journey that would not end until 1952. On May 21, 1946, Miller met with A. K. Savoy, associate superintendent of the district's schools. At that meeting, she requested that her deaf five-year-old son, Kenneth, be allowed to attend the district's deaf facility, Kendall School.[15] When her request was denied, she asked that he be educated, at the expense of the district, in the Pennsylvania School for the Deaf (PSD) in Mount Airy, Pennsylvania.[16] Founded on May 15, 1821, PSD was an integrated institution that from its beginning accepted out-of-state students.

The Congressional Appropriation Act of March 3, 1905, allowed for support of district students at facilities other than the Maryland school, but Miller was not able to secure this support. The district would not send children to the Pennsylvania school unless they had some special needs that could not be met at the Maryland school. Miller was informed that her son would have to undergo a required preliminary examination before any placement could take place. Following the results of the examination, she was advised that he did not have special needs. The admission committee that reviewed student applications for admission to the school thought that Miller's son was too young for acceptance. Additionally, there were no vacancies at the Maryland institution.[17] To compound the matter there were other students ahead of him on the admission list. Francis Andrews, superintendent of the Maryland School for the Blind commented, "I would prefer that he wait another year, for there are certainly Washington children of school age, who probably should be with us."[18] On October 3, 1946, six months after she first met with Savoy, Miller received a letter from the District of Columbia School Board formally notifying her of their decision. Because of limited space and his young age, the board decided that Kenneth would have to wait until the next school year to be placed with the Maryland facility.[19]

Although the language in the March 3, 1905, Congressional Appropriation Act for the district provided for instruction and maintenance of "colored deaf-mutes," Miller encountered several obstacles in trying to obtain both instruction and maintenance for her child. Kenneth could not be educated at Kendall School because of his race. He was unable to start his education at the Maryland school because of his age and lack of space. Furthermore, his education would not be sponsored by the district at the PSD because he did not have any special needs. Refusing to be deterred, in April of 1947 Miller wrote to G. C. Wilkinson, one of the commissioners of the District of Columbia. She restated her request for immediate admittance of her son to the Pennsylvania School for the Deaf at the district's expense. Wilkinson, responding to the correspondence, contacted Assistant Superintendent Savoy on April 14, 1947, seeking clarification of the situation.[20]

Savoy's memorandum of April 15, 1947, explained the circumstances of the Miller case. He stated that he was acting in accordance with the conclusion of Francis Andrews, superintendent of the Maryland School for the Blind and the Maryland School for the Colored Deaf. Andrews, in a September 7, 1946, letter, reported that the Maryland facility could accommodate Kenneth if

> The District has the funds and if he has been trained to take care of his personal wants, such as toilet habits, Etc. Of course he is younger than we generally take them but we can make exceptions, especially if the child seems most promising. I think when you and I discussed the Washington pupils this boy was one whom we thought we would accept if there was room in the district group.[21]

However, three days later, another letter arrived from Andrews. He had changed his position and explained, "Concerning Kenneth Miller, of whom you wrote; I would prefer that he wait another year, for there are certainly Washington children of school age, who probably should be with us. We certainly will be glad to consider Kenneth in the fall of 1947."[22]

Since Miller's appeal to Wilkinson to have the district support her son's education at PSD also was unsuccessful, she realized that her son's education would have to come without assistance from the District of Columbia, where she and her husband both worked and lived. Miller was employed as a statistical clerk at the Census Department, and her husband, Luther Miller, was a district police officer. They were determined to provide the best educational opportunities for their son. The Millers believed that an early educational start was necessary for deaf children to excel. From 1947 to 1948, the Millers engaged private tutors for Kenneth and paid them $5 an hour to provide the educational foundation they believed Kenneth needed. They decided in 1949, when their son turned eight, to place him in PSD at their own expense. Kenneth's tuition for the first year was $1,350; it rose to $1,650 during the second year.[23] He was educated there for the next two years. Because the institution was a residential facility, Kenneth boarded there. He was away from his family from September until the end of the school year in May. The Millers believed the expense of the tuition, the absence of their son, and the lack of parental guidance for him to be unfair and unnecessary burdens on their family.

Lack of parental guidance and the absence of family support for children boarding at school have historically been complaints of parents with children educated away from home.[24] Ernest Hairston, a Black and deaf scholar and author, addressed the issues of Black hearing families with deaf children in his 1983 book. He acknowledged the value of having deaf children stay in the home environment whenever possible and noted the importance of including the children in all of the family's activities.

> Some Black parents have two or three jobs just so their children will have a better life than themselves. They want to achieve educationally and economically. They have strong spiritual values. Black deaf children when exposed to these things come to feel a part of the family. They learn family values, goals, and expectations. This is a form of communication at its best and the Black deaf child should be part of this sharing in the joy and sorrow of everyday family life.... Parents should be there to share their moments of happiness and defeat, to lend words of encouragement, to say "no" when necessary, and to recognize the frustration many Black deaf children experience.[25]

Sending children away to school at such an early age deprives both parents and the child of the many benefits that Hairston addressed.

Before the Millers made the decision to enroll their son in PSD, however, they had visited the Overlea facility and found that the condition of the school was unacceptable. "I was shocked at the rundown physical plant and the poor system and I could not leave him there," Miller said. More importantly, she stated that at the Maryland facility "children can only communicate by sign language or by writing."[26] In contrast, students at PSD were instructed using the oral method, which was considered a more advanced method of instruction during that period. The decision to send Kenneth to school in Pennsylvania, even though it was a greater distance from the district, was based on the Millers' belief that he would receive a better education there. That outweighed that fact that he would be further from home.[27]

Miller's complaints about the state of the Maryland facility were not unusual. The problems of inadequate facilities and quality education for handicapped and special-needs Black students were pressing issues. The lack of resources for deaf Black students in rural towns in the South was the subject of an article in *The Journal of Negro Education* in 1932. In 1937, James A. Scott, a Black educator, noted the lack of adequate funding made available by states and federal government for the facilities. Howard Hale Long, writing in 1947, looked at the lack of special educational services for Black youth. He included a table that showed enrollment in Southern residential public and private schools of both white and Black students. The District of Columbia provided for 234 white, deaf students and no Black students.[28] It would remain this way until a successful legal challenge in 1952.

Some individuals and organizations in the district were concerned with advocating for equality for all citizens. Paul Cooke, a member of the Greater Washington Area Council of the American Veterans Committee (AVC), took up the cause of the district's deaf Black children. He became, along with his organization, one of their staunchest advocates.[29] Cooke's involvement began when he read in the Congress Appropriation Act of 1950 that Congress had allocated funds for the instruction of the district's white deaf children within the district, but not for Black children. The act provided funding for the education of deaf Black children at an institution outside of the district. Cooke had previously been unaware of this situation. He found it disturbing that such an unfair and discriminatory practice was going on and immediately took the matter to Florence Nierman, the chair of the Washington chapter of the AVC. She called for immediate action. The AVC board declared that the practice of racial discrimination was a denial of the children's rights under the Fourteenth Amendment of the Constitution of the United States, and AVC embarked on a campaign to end this injustice.[30]

Cooke's responsibilities were to research the Congressional acts, interview the parents of the children, determine the contact persons in the responsible district agencies, and prepare communications to them. His research indicated that the major figures in the educational decisions for the deaf children were the Board of Education, the superintendent of schools, the Board of Commissioners, the Federal Security Agency, and the Board of Directors of Gallaudet College, of which Kendall School was a part. Through conversations with churches, charitable agencies, and school officials, he found and contacted parents of deaf children.[31]

Nierman, in her capacity as chair of the AVC, began writing to the agencies and directors identified by Cooke to apprise them of the organization's support of the parents and to try to see if there was an administrative remedy to the exclusion of the Black deaf students. She wrote to Albert Atwood, president of the Board of Directors of Gallaudet, in April 1951. The letter, which was forwarded to Leonard Elstad, Gallaudet's president, expressed the concerns of the AVC at the inequality of the educational situation for the district's Black deaf children.

Elstad's response to Nierman addressed several issues. He acknowledged that white deaf children from the district were educated at Kendall School. He further informed her that the education of "colored deaf children" was provided for in statutes dating back to the founding of the institution. He stated that the collegiate department of the institution had a Black student. According to Elstad there would be more, but "the difficulty has been that the education of the colored deaf is so far behind that of the white deaf that they have not been able to reach college entrance level in their education."[32] He noted that Kendall School had a different situation because of legal segregation and that

> As long as all the white deaf children of the District of Columbia are educated here, we are compelled to refuse entrance to colored deaf children in that department. It would seem, therefore, that if colored deaf children were to be educated here it would have to be on a segregated basis.[33]

Hobart Corning, superintendent of the District of Columbia Public Schools, wrote to Nierman on May 14, 1951. He outlined the policy for educating Black deaf children and explained that the responsibility for that policy was not with the office of the superintendent of public schools. Joseph Donohue, commissioner, District of Columbia, wrote to Nierman on July 23, 1951, and related part of a conference with Elstad.

> As you probably know, under Section 1011 of Title 31 of the D.C. Code, the directors of the Columbia Institution for the Deaf are authorized to provide for the education of colored deaf mute children properly belonging to the District of Columbia in Maryland School. I take it that the authorization contained in that section of the Code is tantamount to a direction ... that the solution of the problem requires an authorization from Congress to establish facilities for teaching the deaf colored mutes of the District of Columbia within the District of Columbia.[34]

Donohue also made a statement about this matter in the *Washington Post* on July 24, 1951. It spoke to the effect of the AVC's advocacy for the deaf children of the district. The *Post* reported,

District Commissioner F. Joseph Donohue said yesterday he plans to study the possibility of having deaf Negro children educated here. They now go to a school at Overlea, Md., near Baltimore. Deaf white children are sent to Kendall School, which is part of the Federally-subsidized Columbian [sic] Institution for the Deaf here which also includes Gallaudet College . . . Donohue announced his plans after hearing requests for local education of the handicapped Negro children from the Greater Washington Council of American Veterans Committee. . . . Because of the shortage of the Negro teachers trained for work with the deaf, Elstad told Donohue, the board of education might have difficulty in staffing the school, but Gallaudet could furnish teachers. Meanwhile, school officials have been studying the entire program of education for the deaf children. A report and recommendations will probably be given the board this fall."[35]

John L. Thurston, the acting administrator of the Federal Security Agency, wrote to Nierman on August 15, 1951. His letter replied to the AVC's inquiry about education for the deaf Black children of the district.

In specific answer to your question, then, it would appear that the matter is not within the control of the Federal Security Agency. In fact, it appears to be inseparably connected with the problem of educational segregation in the schools of the District of Columbia, a matter entirely outside the responsibility or authority of this Agency.[36]

The correspondence with the agencies involved in the process did not bring any immediate change to the children's situation. Cooke and the AVC Board believed that the parents should join together and fight for an end to the policy of educational segregation that had for so long affected their families.[37] The strategy set an example that was used later in the *Brown v. Board of Education* suit filed in 1954. Cooke assembled Miller, Minnie Mayfield, David Hood and his wife, Clyde Howard, Marvin Brown, Grace Jones, and Luke Richardson, all parents of district African American deaf children who attended either the Maryland or Pennsylvania institutions. They gathered at the AVC Clubhouse located in the Northwest section of the district, and there they met representatives from the law firm of Cobb, Howard, and Hayes, which would take legal action on their behalf.

The next step in the AVC strategy was a letter-writing campaign. Parents were encouraged to state their concerns in writing. They agreed to start documenting their requests for a change in the policy of sending their children to another state for education. The letters were sent to the Board of Education. Minnie Mayfield's August 1951 letter to the Board of Education stressed the importance of having a child remain with his or her family, and it became the model for all of the other letters.

> I am the mother of Donald Mayfield, who is living in Washington and attending the Maryland School for the Blind at Overlea, MD. My child is 8 years of age and it works an extreme hardship on the child and me to have the child attending school outside of the District of Columbia. I understand that it is the responsibility of the Board of Education to provide for the education of all children within the District of Columbia. I therefore respectfully request the Board of Education to provide education for my child within the District of Columbia beginning with the September 1951 term.[38]

By December 1951, the AVC had spent more than eight months corresponding with the agencies responsible for the oversight of the education of the district's deaf children. They prepared, wrote, and delivered a six-page statement to the Board of Education on December 26, 1951. The statement, with a cover letter from Cooke, outlined the unequal situation of the students. It set forth the current legislation regarding the education of the deaf students. Additionally, it supported the requests of the Black parents who also wrote the agencies. Their letters requested admission for their deaf children to the Kendall School in the District of Columbia. This statement marked the end of the AVC's first phase of a two-prong strategy to challenge educational policy.[39]

On February 2, 1952, the law firm of Cobb, Hayes, and Howard filed *Miller et al. v. Board of Education of District of Columbia et al. Civil No. 515–52* in the United States District Court for the District of Columbia. Louise B. Miller and her son Kenneth, who was now eleven and on whose behalf she had begun her advocacy in 1946, were the lead plaintiffs. They were joined by Marvin Brown and his daughter, Irene Brown; Mattie Hood and her son Robert Jones; Grace Jones and her son William Matthews; Minnie Mayfield and her son Donald Mayfield; and Luke Richardson and his daughter Doris Richardson. John D. Fauntleroy and Phineas Indritz, respectively, argued the case for the plaintiffs and prepared the plaintiffs' briefs.

The defendants in the suit were the Board of Education of the District of Columbia, the Board of Commissioners of the District of Columbia, and the Board of Directors of Gallaudet College. They were represented by two legal teams: Vernon E. West, corporation counsel, and Milton D. Korman, assistant corporation counsel,[40] and Roger Robb for Gallaudet. The judge in the nonjury hearing was David Pine. An article in the *Washington Afro-American*, on February 8, 1952, summarized the initial filing as follows, "A suit [w]as filed in District Court last Friday to force the Columbia Institution for the Deaf, the District Board of Education and the District Board of Commissioners to educate colored deaf children within the District of Columbia."[41]

The *Washington Pittsburgh Courier* ran an article on the filing on February 9, citing the policy of sending the deaf students out of the city.[42] An article in the *Washington Post* on February 21, 1952, reported on discussions centered on changing the residential program at Kendall to a day school.[43] But it was an article in the *Washington Daily News* on February 21, 1952, that drew the most attention. Written almost three weeks after the filing of *Miller*, it reported on an overture by the District School Board that was prophetic. The article stated that, "School Supt. Hobart M. Corning today has orders from the District School Board to study the possibility of 'integrating' white and Negro schools here, and to report within 30 days."[44]

Judge Pine's decision in finding for the plaintiffs in the nonjury hearing immediately changed the almost fifty-year-old educational policy for deaf Black district children. The judge's decision was based on the ruling in the 1938 *Missouri ex. Rel Gaines v. Canada*, 305 U.S. 337 case. In this case, Lloyd L. Gaines, an African American, was denied admission to the University of Missouri law school because of his race. As a practice, the state paid the tuition of African Americans at out-of-state schools rather than admit them to the University of Missouri. This way the state avoided the expense of having to construct separate-but-equal facilities. The court ruled for the plaintiff and held that Missouri provided no equal access to higher education for both races within its borders. The court found Missouri's policy to be state-practiced racial discrimination, and therefore in violation of the Fourteenth Amendment. Missouri then built and staffed a Black law school within the University of Missouri. Judge Pine, in basing his ruling on that precedent, stated,

> As I see it, the practice involved in this case offends against the Gaines decision; and therefore, to maintain the legality of the separation of the races, it is the duty of the District to provide equal educational facilities within the District for the deaf children of both races, if it provides for any therein.[45]

In the fall of 1952, Black students were again attending Kendall School. Cooke felt that "the victory for the families and students was one of the more significant undertakings of the AVC." Challenging the type of injustice that was inflicted upon the deaf community was one of the reasons he had become a member of the AVC. Cooke believed that a tremendous injustice had been righted.[46]

This victory proved bittersweet for the students as they joined their hearing peers in the district's segregated school system. The policy of segregation mandated that in the aftermath of the court decision the Kendall School had to set up a separate area for Black students. The result was Kendall's creation of Division I for the white students and Division II for the Black students.

A positive and significant change brought about by *Miller v. D.C. Board of Education* was the hiring of Black teachers. This became a necessity after the hostile response of the white teaching staff to the return of Black students. Some were quite vocal in their refusal to teach Black students. A few wore black armbands after the decision and the return of the students to show that they were in mourning for the passing of the institution's policy of segregation.[47]

Finding Black teachers was not an easy matter, for Black teachers of the deaf and deaf Black teachers historically had been in short supply.[48] In 1914, Thomas Flowers, a Black deaf educator from the North Carolina School for the Colored Deaf expressed concern about the specific challenges that Black deaf and hearing teachers faced. Low pay, poor facilities, and large classes kept a significant number of Black teachers from entering the field, he said.[49] At the 1939 Conference of Executives of American Schools for the Deaf, Clarence J. Settles stated that the major reason for the shortage of teachers of color was the absence of special teacher-training schools for Blacks. He also believed that the lack of summer-school classes was a factor.[50]

To determine the current number of Black teachers of deaf Black students and, therefore, the need for more Black teachers, Settles sent a survey to the sixteen schools in the country that had schools or departments for Black deaf students. The educators analyzed the survey data and concluded that a training center for Black teachers should be established at some institution in the South. The survey responses revealed a general consensus that more African American teachers needed to be trained, but when, how, and where varied between schools that had departments and those that had separate schools for Black students. Howard University and Hampton Institute were recommended as good places to set up a summer training program. The never-ending debate regarding whether the training should be oral or manual was also mentioned. The surveyors also noted the issue of financial need, especially for poor teachers who did not have funds to travel.[51]

Surprisingly, the questionnaire did not ask about the race of the teachers. The only question regarding race referred to the principal or supervising teacher of the "colored school." Some institutions, like the Maryland School for the Black Colored Deaf, employed white instructors. James Bledsoe, superintendent of the school, responded that

> Our department for the colored deaf in the Maryland School for the Blind is, I think, one of the oldest in the country. It started in 1872. Since that time our teachers have all been white persons. We have never had any colored people as teachers or officers in that school. So far we have not had any great difficulty in securing teachers. . . . So far as we are concerned, we don't feel that we need any such training as that spoken of by Mr. Settles, but I think that probably, for the majority of the schools in the south, they do need that training.[52]

The 1947 directory issue of the *American Annals of the Deaf* included a list of the 105 Black teachers (71 were women) who were teaching at twelve residential schools in the country. The journal also mentioned that there were 1,160 Black deaf students in residential schools across the country.[53]

In 1953, the *American Annals of the Deaf* published information on the number of teachers and pupils in public residential schools for the deaf as of October 31, 1952, the same year that Kendall School hired its first Black instructors. The journal included the new Division II at the school. The data showed that among five Black schools for the deaf—Alabama, Arkansas, Florida, Maryland, and Mississippi—there were seventeen deaf academic instructors. Three of the institutions (Alabama, Maryland, and Mississippi) collectively had eight deaf teachers for vocational classes. Four of the deaf academic teachers and one deaf vocational instructor taught at the Maryland school. There is no indication, however, that the deaf instructors at the Black schools were Black. The white institutions employed a significantly higher number of deaf instructors. The 61 schools included in the *Annals* reported having a total of 216 deaf academic instructors and 165 vocational instructors.[54]

Although Black deaf teachers had always been a small minority, they had a long history of teaching in the South. North Carolina, which established the first state school for Black deaf children in 1869 in Raleigh, provided two of the earliest known teachers. In 1877, Julius Garrett and Amanda Johnson, both graduates of the North Carolina program, along with H. L. Johns, who had attended the Maryland school for Black deaf children in Baltimore, were hired as teachers at the Texas Institute for Deaf, Dumb, and Blind Colored Youth.[55]

The Texas institution had been established through the efforts of William Holland, a former slave who had become a soldier, legislator, and teacher. His proposal to the Texas legislature resulted in the opening of the school on April 5, 1887, and he was named the first superintendent on August 15, 1887. Holland hired Garrett, Johnson, and Johns that same year.[56] He also hired a Black hearing teacher and artist, Mattie B. Haywood White, in 1900. For over forty years White taught at the school using innovative and creative techniques. Deaf and blind students were not usually instructed in extensive art courses, but White used sign language and written instructions to teach deaf students to paint, draw, crochet, knit, embroider, and make rugs. Her blind students learned how to crochet and weave baskets and rugs.[57]

Kendall School's first Black instructors, Rubye Frye, Bessie Thornton, Mary E. Phillips, and Robert Robinson, were also hearing. They all had training in special education and held advanced degrees. One was an ardent oralist; the other three knew and used sign language in the classroom.

Frye had been educated at Howard University in Washington, where she received her BA degree. She moved to New York and attended Hunter College in New York, where she earned an MA degree in special education. Frye learned the oral method of instruction and believed that it was superior to the manual method.[58]

Thornton received her MA degree in special education from Hampton Institute, in Hampton, Virginia. Before coming to Kendall School, she taught at the Virginia State School at Hampton and the day school for colored deaf in Atlanta, Georgia. She had participated in summer classes taught by Gallaudet instructors at Hampton starting in 1946. Thornton was trained in both the oral and manual methods; however, she believed that the manual method allowed for more effective teaching.[59]

Phillips attended Hampton Institute with Thornton. She also received her MA degree in special education. She had four years of teaching experience in the department for the deaf at the North Carolina School for the Blind and Deaf in Raleigh. Like Thornton, Phillips had taken summer classes on deaf education taught by Gallaudet instructors. She shared Thornton's philosophy on teaching with sign language. Phillips thought that oralism could be used with certain students, especially those who were late-deafened.[60]

Robinson was the only male instructor. The number of male instructors lagged considerably behind female instructors.[61] He received his BS degree from Virginia State College in Petersburg, Virginia, and then Robinson taught at the Virginia State School for the Deaf and Blind in Peters-

Students at Kendall School

burg. He had taken courses in education of the deaf at Hampton Institute.[62] When he was hired at Kendall, Robinson was in the process of
writing his master's thesis. He completed the thesis and received his MA
degree before the start of school. Robinson taught using sign and was a
proponent of the combined method. He used sign language, writing,
speech, and speechreading.[63]

These four hearing Black teachers were charged with instructing the
first class of Black students in almost fifty years at Kendall School. The
class had twenty-four students, sixteen of whom had transferred from
the Maryland School for the Colored Deaf.[64] Because there were no dormitory facilities for them, the Black students arrived at and departed
from the campus in Yellow Cabs.[65] Although Gallaudet College paid for
the students' transportation, this process served to further remind them
that they were a separate part of the school. Former student Robert Milburn remarked that initially the cab rides were fun, but they quickly lost
their appeal. He said that he soon began to think "they wanted to get us
in and out as fast as they could."[66]

Construction began on the dorms for Black students in the fall of 1952
and was completed in spring of 1953. This allowed the students to stay

on campus, although in a segregated environment. That environment prevented the Black students from obtaining education equal to that received by white students. There was a vast difference in the quality of the curriculum offered to the students in Division I and Division II. The curriculum given to the Black teachers consisted of a list of words, a list of prepositions, color words, and number words. The Division I curriculum was similar, but the students had textbooks and they took economics. There were no textbooks for Division II students or any vocational courses for them. The advantages for the Division I students were obvious.[67]

The 1952 *Miller* decision is significant because it made possible the education of Black deaf school-age residents of the district within the boundaries of the city. These children no longer had to leave their families and be without their guidance, support, and interaction. What the decision did not do, and could not do, was overturn the district's policy of educational segregation. Neither could it erase the prejudice and racism of white teachers who refused to instruct Black students. The hiring of Black teachers who were dedicated to providing the best possible education to the students was another positive result of *Miller*. But the dream of educational equality would not be realized until the historic 1954 *Brown v. Board of Education* decision. At the beginning of the academic year after the *Brown* decision, for the first time in almost fifty

Students in an oral class at Kendall School

years, Black and white deaf students took their places in Kendall School classrooms together.

Notes

1. Frederick Douglass, *Narrative of the Life of Frederick Douglass, An American Slave, Written by Himself* (New Haven: Yale University Press; 2001).

2. For more information on *Brown* see Waldo E. Martin, *Brown v. Board of Education: A Brief History with Documents* (New York: Macmillan, 1998); Derrick Bell, *Silent Covenants: Brown v. Board of Education and the Unfulfilled Hopes for Radical Reform* (New York: Oxford University Press, 2004); and Richard Kluger, *Simple Justice: The History of Brown v. Board of Education and Black America's Struggle for Equality* (New York: Vintage, 2004).

3. Edward Miner Gallaudet, *History of the College for the Deaf: 1857–1907* (Washington, D.C.: Gallaudet University Press, 1983), 20.

4. Ibid., 6. In 1901 Congress provided for the free education of all deaf district residents in the act of March 1, 1901.

5. Ibid., 280.

6. The Maryland School for the Colored Blind and Deaf was established in 1872.

7. Gallaudet, *History of the College*, 201–2.

8. Papers of Edward Miner Gallaudet, MS 118, Box 1, File 4, Gallaudet University Archives.

9. Ibid., MS 118, Box 2, File 2. For a discussion of alley dwelling, see James Borchert's *Alley Life in Washington: Family, Community, Religion, and Folklife in the City, 1850–1970* (Champaign: University of Illinois Press, 1982).

10. Gallaudet, 50, 201.

11. *Plessy v. Ferguson*, 163 U.S. 483, 493. For more discussion of *Plessy* and its impact, see Brook Thomas's *Plessy v. Ferguson: A Brief History with Documents* (Boston: Bedford Books, 1997); Charles A. Lofgren's *The Plessy Case: A Legal-Historical Interpretation* (New York: Oxford University Press, 1987); Henry Julian Abraham's *Freedom and the Court: Civil Rights and Liberties in the United States* (New York: Oxford University Press, 1988); Keith Medley, *We as Freemen: Plessy v. Ferguson* (Gretna, La.: Pelican Publishing Co., 2003): and Leon A. Higginbotham's *Shades of Freedom: Racial Politics and Presumptions of the American Legal Process* (New York: Oxford University Press, 1996).

12. Gallaudet, *History*, 202–3.

13. Sandy White's Papers for Black Deaf Project, MSS 118, Box 3, File 1, Gallaudet University Archives.

14. Act of March 3, 1905, Section 31–1011.

15. Constance McLaughlin Green, *Secret City: A History of Race Relations in the Nation's Capital* (Princeton: Princeton University Press, 1967), 305.

16. MSS 118, Box 1, File 2, Gallaudet University Archives.

17. Papers of Paul P. Cooke, Box 813, File 2, Moorland-Spingarn Research Center.

18. MSS 118, Box 1, File 2, Gallaudet University Archives.

19. Papers of Paul P. Cooke, Box 813, File 2, Moorland-Spingarn Research Center.

20. Ibid.

21. Ibid.

22. Ibid.

23. School Board Minutes, 76, 19 September 1951, 258, Sumner Museum and Archives.

24. Mary Herring Wright, *Sounds Like Home: Growing Up Black and Deaf in the South* (Washington, D.C.: Gallaudet University Press, 2002), 85.

25. Ernest Hairston and Linwood Smith, *Black and Deaf in America: Are We that Different?* (Silver Spring, Md.: T.J. Publishers, Inc., 1983), 7–8.

26. "School Board Is Urged to End District Deaf Training Jim Crow," *Washington Pittsburgh Courier*, August 25, 1951.

27. The Maryland School was approximately an hour and a half away. PSD was more than two hours away.

28. Eva T. Honesty, "The Handicapped Child," *The Journal of Negro Education* 1, no. 2 (July 1932): 304–24; James A. Scott, "Educational Facilities Available for Physically Handicapped Negro Children," *The Journal of Negro Education* 6, no. 3 (July 1937): 455–67; Howard Hale Long, "The Availability of Special Educational Services to Negroes," *The Journal of Negro Education* 16, no. 3 (Summer 1947): 474–79. See also Harry Best, *Deafness and the Deaf in the United States* (New York: Macmillan, 1943); and Harry J. Baker, *Introduction to Exceptional Children* (New York: Macmillan, 1944).

29. See, Moorland-Spingarn Research Center, Washington, D.C., Papers of the American Veterans Committee. The American Veterans Committee was unique in that it was an integrated organization of veterans with an agenda that included addressing problems of all Americans.

30. Paul Cooke, interview with author, January 12, 2005.

31. Ibid.

32. Papers of American Veterans Committee, Moorland Spingarn Research Center.

33. Ibid.

34. Paul Phillips Cooke and Ravella G. Beresford, "Discrimination Against Colored Deaf Children," (unpublished manuscript, Papers of Paul P. Cooke, Moorland-Spingarn Research Center, 1951).

35. "Donohue to Study Plan to Educate Negro Children Here," *Washington Post*, July 24, 1951, sec. A, 7.

36. Ibid.

37. Cooke, interview with author, 2005.

38. Papers of Paul P. Cooke, Box 813, File 2, Moorland-Spingarn Research Center.

39. Cooke, interview with author, 2005.

40. Korman represented the district in the *Bolling v. Sharpe* case that was part of the 1954 *Brown v. Board of Education* legal challenge that ended educational segregation. He was later appointed to the D.C. Superior Court.

41. "Parents Sue Board of Education," *Washington Afro-American*, February 8, 1952.

42. "Claim Deaf Children Are Sent Outside Capital to School," *Washington Pittsburgh Courier*, February 9, 1952.

43. "Regular Day Classes Are Urged for Deaf," *Washington Post*, February 21, 1952, sec. B, 8.

44. "School Board Orders 'Integration' Study," *Washington Daily News*, February 21, 1952.

45. *Miller v. Board of Education of the District of Columbia*, 106 F. Supp. 988. Case in the United States District Court, District of Columbia, July 3, 1952. Case heard and decided by Judge David Pine.

46. Ibid.

47. Rubye Frye, interview with David de Lorenzo, October 13, 1981.

48. J. Woodward, "Black Deaf Teacher—Short Supply," *Perspectives for Teachers of the Hearing Impaired* 4, (1985): 18–19.

49. Douglas C. Baynton, *Forbidden Signs: American Culture and the Campaign Against Sign Language* (Chicago: University of Chicago Press, 1996), 46.

50. Clarence J. Settles, "Normal Training for Colored Teachers," *American Annals of the Deaf* 85 (March 1940): 210.

51. Ibid., 210–11.

52. Ibid., 216.

53. *American Annals of the Deaf* 92 (1947): 36, 39.

54. *American Annals of the Deaf* 98 (1953): 182, 186.

55. Jamie Berke, "When Skin Color Separated Black and White Deaf Kids," About.com, http://deafness.about.com/cs/featurearticles/a/segregated.htm (accessed June 22, 2008).

56. *Handbook of Texas Online,* s.v. "Holland, William H," http://www.tsha.utexas.edu/handbook/online/articles/HH/fh030.html (accessed April 4, 2005).

57. *Handbook of Texas Online,* s.v. "White, Mattie B. Haywood," http://www.tsha.utexas.edu/handbook/online/articles/view/WW/fwh78.html (accessed March 16, 2005).

58. Frye, interview with David de Lorenzo.

59. Sandy White, *"Class of '52."* DVD, Gallaudet University Department of Film and Television, 1981.

60. Mary Phillips, undated interview with David de Lorenzo, Sandy White's Papers for Black Deaf Project, Box 2, Folder 2, Gallaudet University Archives. For further discussion on the limits of oralism in children born without hearing see Marc Marschark, *Raising and Educating A Deaf Child* (New York: Oxford University Press, 1998).

61. *American Annals of the Deaf* 92 (1947): 39.

62. For discussion on the training program for Black teachers at Hampton Institute see Nancy Hutchinson, "Teacher Training for Negroes at Hampton Institute," *Buff and Blue,* no. 2 (1951): 1.; and Powrie V. Doctor, "Deaf Negroes Get a Break in Education," *The Silent Worker* (1948): 45–50.

63. Papers of Sandy White's Black Deaf Project, MSS 118, Box 1, Folder 2, Gallaudet University Archives.

64. *American Annals of the Deaf* 98 (1953): 182.

65. Sandy White, "Class of '52."

66. Robert Milburn, interview with author, March 12, 2002.

67. Frye, interview with David de Lorenzo.

9

George Detmold, The Reformer

Ronald E. Sutcliffe

Editors' Introduction

Ronald E. Sutcliffe's article is especially timely and relevant to today's issues. Sutcliffe recounts the period in the 1950s during which Gallaudet, led by George Detmold, an administrator brought in from Cornell University, sought accreditation by the Middle States Association of Colleges and Schools as a fully qualified institution of higher education. Fifty years later, Gallaudet went through another time of self-examination and intense scrutiny by Middle States. Sutcliffe points out the steps taken to achieve accreditation and suggests that they were important in throwing off the yoke of paternalism and low academic expectations that had marked the institution's previous history.

GEORGE DETMOLD BECAME the dean of instruction at Gallaudet College in 1952. He was hired with the primary charge of revamping the college program so that it could be accredited within five years. Detmold was able to enact multiple reforms and carry out many changes in the face of controversy and dissension from (mostly hearing) educators at schools for deaf students throughout the United States. His persistence in implementing his vision amid discord and conflict earned him the title of "reformer," even as these adaptations transformed deaf America. Without the transformations he enacted, the deaf community in which we live, and even how we live, might have been very different.

Until the 1960s, deaf people were not able to live as independently as they do today. Most depended on hearing people for help in carrying out basic life functions, such as applying for jobs or calling the doctor. Hearing people who could sign offered interpreting services, usually

George Detmold

gratis, but often with strings attached in the form of "advice" for the deaf person. During this period, the administrators of state schools for the deaf, all of whom were hearing, were often officially recognized as the voice for deaf people. Networks of hearing people in deaf education were so powerful that most deaf individuals perceived themselves as vulnerable in the face of the influence these hearing people could wield. Deaf people protected themselves in part by avoiding going against the administrators, many of whom were their supervisors in their places of employment. While there were some national organizations comprised of and serving deaf people, the officers tended to be teachers at state deaf schools who had little or no desire to agitate for deaf people's rights, particularly if this meant challenging their hearing supervisors. All in all, "the deaf community accepted the general community's view of deafness as a pathological condition."[1]

Such paternalistic and subservient attitudes might be incomprehensible to many today, but it is worth noting that even Percival Hall, president of Gallaudet College from 1910 until 1945, commented to a young deaf man who wanted to earn a doctorate degree, "Oh, you cannot. It is hard enough to earn a bachelor's degree."[2] Despite these beliefs, attitudes, and barriers, many Gallaudet graduates had successful careers, which at that time were limited mostly to teaching, serving as dormitory house parents, and printing. The latter two did not require college training, although printing offered better pay than the other professions. Few deaf Gallaudet graduates worked in the scientific or business arena, as a consequence of their low expectations for success and their limited career prospects.

When Leonard Elstad became the president of Gallaudet College in 1945, succeeding Hall, the school's facilities were in poor shape and far from adequate.[3] Elstad requested that the Federal Security Agency of the Office of Education hire a consultant to carry out a study of the college's future prospects in order to justify the existence of the school and support his petition for funding to upgrade Gallaudet's facilities. The consultant hired, Buell Gallagher, was also charged with determining the extent to which the federal government was responsible for the education of deaf students.[4] While Gallaudet's enrollment was then 220 students, Gallagher determined that it could increase to 5,600 if deaf people attended college in the same proportions as hearing people.

Gallagher's report noted further that fifteen of Gallaudet's twenty faculty members had earned their master's degrees from Gallaudet, suggesting too much "inbreeding" in the professorship.[5] The college justified hiring so many alumni by stating that they were trained to teach deaf students, emphasizing their knowledge of deafness rather than the subject matter they taught. Their actual knowledge of deafness, however, is questionable. Many people graduating from Gallaudet's teacher training program assumed that deaf students could not think in the abstract. As a result, professors and hearing graduates of the college who became administrators and teachers of deaf children across the country lowered the academic rigor of the curriculum to make it easier for the deaf to read.

Among the long list of Gallagher's recommendations was that Gallaudet should hire faculty with expertise in the subject matter area in which they taught, rather than simply focusing on good sign skills.[6] He also emphasized the need for new and improved facilities to meet expanded student enrollment, which in turn would aid Gallaudet's quest for accreditation. Congress agreed to provide $10 million for this expansion.[7]

In 1952, the Middle States Association of Colleges and Schools, the accrediting agency responsible for colleges in the geographical area in which Gallaudet is located, issued a discouraging report. Middle States said that the college's chances of accreditation were slight because of the paucity of library and laboratory facilities, the dearth of equipment, and the inadequacy of faculty members with expertise in the areas in which they were assigned to teach.[8] In response to this report, Gallaudet hired George Detmold from Cornell University, where he had been assistant dean of the College of Arts and Sciences. He was recruited from a post-doctoral program at Columbia's Teacher College because of his vision of what a college should be. Detmold had no experience or knowledge of the deaf community and no ties with any schools for deaf students when he was hired. He was given five years to get the college accredited; otherwise, support from Congress would be compromised.

Detmold faced many obstacles to securing accreditation. Most Gallaudet professors believed that deaf students were not as intelligent as their hearing counterparts. One even told him that the deaf students had "frozen minds" and that they could not think in the abstract. Another professor thought that abstract ideas could not be taught in sign language. In the course of his evaluation of the college's needs, Detmold found that most course offerings were at the high school level. An example was the use of *Life*, a weekly pictorial magazine that used simple and uncomplicated words, as the required reading for the Social Science course.[9] The professor ordered *Life* because he believed that "the deaf couldn't read but liked to look at pictures."[10]

Ignoring the prevailing orthodoxy, Detmold determined that the deaf students he encountered were bright and that he needed to change the attitudes held by their professors. Superintendents of schools for deaf students, friends of Elstad, criticized him, telling him that Detmold was deluded to think that deaf students could ever be "liberally educated."[11] However, Detmold plowed ahead and redesigned the general education curriculum to bring courses up to college level.[12] He also reassigned the faculty so that they taught in the areas in which they had expertise. Going against the way in which Gallaudet had generally hired faculty, he recruited sixteen people with doctorate degrees. These new faculty members included his good friend from Cornell, William C. Stokoe, who was hired to teach Chaucer. Detmold encouraged Stokoe to examine how deaf people could think in manual code (sign language), and this eventually led to Stokoe's great discovery—the recognition of American Sign Language as a valid language, separate from English.[13]

Detmold's changes received significant resistance from the faculty, and the students also objected vociferously when they realized that they would be required to take more advanced and demanding courses. Irving Fusfeld, the dean of the college who had hired Detmold, also advised against accreditation because the college was too "special."[14] However, President Elstad held firm, reassigned Fusfeld to be a vice president for research, and replaced him with Detmold as dean of the college.[15] The clamor eventually died down when both faculty members and students realized that the changes were for the better, and that upon graduating, students were being offered better jobs with more prospects for advancement.

Gallaudet was able to attain initial accreditation in April 1957 because of the changes that Detmold initiated and carried out, and it has maintained its accreditation ever since. At the same time, the college increased its enrollment and constructed more buildings. The increasing enrollment resulted in accusations of lowered academic and admissions standards from some of the superintendents of the schools for the deaf, who could not believe that their graduates who were accepted at Gallaudet were actually college material. Many educators of deaf students also questioned the students' capacity to complete college-level courses, including such literature classes as on the works of Chaucer and Shakespeare.

To quell the controversy, all school superintendents and selected alumni were invited to a two-day meeting with the college's Board of Directors (now known as the Board of Trustees) to air their criticisms of the college in the fall of 1962.[16] Twenty-one people appeared to testify. Most objected to the points raised in the Gallagher Report that recommended the upgrades in the academic programs for deaf students. The school superintendents also questioned the hiring of faculty with doctorates who were not specifically trained to teach deaf students, wondering if these new professors could communicate at all and how they could teach deaf students in their subjects. They also criticized the college for establishing research offices that were headed by people without backgrounds in deafness. They were disappointed with Detmold for not having people with knowledge of sign language working to develop a sign language dictionary, but rather that he took the completely opposite approach by having Stokoe, who had no background in ASL, do the research on the language. After hearing the complaints and allegations that the college had been lowering its admission and academic standards in

English class

recent years, two consultants from the Middle States Association were hired to review the accusations. They reported that the entrance scores of the recently admitted students were not significantly different from the scores of those admitted twenty years before. The consultants also determined that Gallaudet was now educating and graduating students who had received a creditable college education, and that the college, while not perfect, was performing competently.[17]

Since that time, Gallaudet College has become a university and has produced many graduates who have gone on to graduate school, a rare accomplishment before the arrival of Detmold. Many Gallaudet graduates have earned their doctorates, and a sizeable number have gone into a wide range of professions, including in the medical, legal, political, and business worlds. Even more importantly, most of those schools whose superintendents were so vocal in criticizing Detmold's reforms in the college are now headed by deaf individuals, many of them Gallaudet graduates.

George Detmold had faith in the ability of deaf individuals to think for themselves, live their own lives, and not depend on others. He was the reformer who enabled the changes in Gallaudet, and subsequently in the wider deaf community, that allowed us to live on our own terms now, as independent and self-sufficient individuals who can be professionally and gainfully employed in all manner of occupations.

During his tenure as the dean, he encouraged deaf people to seek and pursue doctorate degrees, and the first Gallaudet graduate in modern times to earn a doctorate, Richard M. Phillips, did so in 1969. Detmold resigned from the deanship and became a drama professor in 1970. He began directing Shakespearean plays at Gallaudet in 1957, which eventually opened doors for deaf actors to enter into acting professions. Detmold retired from Gallaudet in 1974 and moved to Florida in 1976. As time passed, the deaf community, including those who had previously criticized him, began to appreciate Detmold's exemplary work, which had made such a difference in the community. In 1992, the Gallaudet University Alumni Association presented him with a special citation of recognition and honor. The university also bestowed an honorary degree on him in 1996. He died on August 12, 2005, at 88. He was buried in Arlington National Cemetery for his service in the Army during World War II.[18]

Notes

1. Jerome D. Schein, *At Home Among Strangers* (Washington, D.C.: Gallaudet University Press, 1989), 142.

2. Thomas Mayes, personal communication to author.

3. Albert W. Atwood, *Gallaudet College: Its First One Hundred Years* (Washington, D.C.: Gallaudet College, 1964), 59.

4. Ibid., 60.

5. Buell G. Gallagher and G. E. Van Dyke, *The Federal Government and the Higher Education of the Deaf* (Washington, D.C.: Federal Security Agency, 1949).

6. Gallagher, 45–77.

7. Atwood, *Gallaudet College,* 71.

8. "Report of the Evaluation of Gallaudet College," Middle States Association of Colleges and Secondary Schools (Washington, D.C.: 1952), Gallaudet University Archives.

9. Jane Maher, *Seeing Language in Sign: The Work of William C. Stokoe* (Washington, D.C.: Gallaudet University Press, 1996), 49.

10. Ibid., 32.

11. Ibid., 31.

12. George Detmold, "It's Tougher in Classroom Now, But Final Results Are Worth It," *Gallaudet Alumni Bulletin* (Spring 1955): 1, 6–7.

13. Maher, *Seeing Language in Sign,* 33–34, 37.

14. Ibid., 31.

15. Irving S. Fusfeld, "A Critique on the Question of College Enrollment for Deaf Persons in the United States," *American Annals of the Deaf* (March 1963): 220–35.

16. Proceedings of the Board of Directors Meeting with 21 Superintendents and Deaf Leaders Presenting Their Criticism of the College, November 15–16, 1962, Gallaudet University Archives.

17. Report, "Criticism of Gallaudet College, November 1962," 4–5, Gallaudet University Archives.

18. George Detmold, "Obituary," *New York Times*, August 14, 2005.

10

Building Kendall Green: Alumni Support for Gallaudet University

Noah D. Drezner

Editors' Introduction

Noah D. Drezner provides a historical overview of the financial evolution of Gallaudet University and its relationship with the federal government. He compares Gallaudet's fund raising with that of historically black colleges and universities, and he concludes that throughout most of its past Gallaudet, like its counterparts in the African American higher education community, has had low alumni donor participation rates and low endowment levels. The changing nature and priorities of the federal government in the 1980s and afterward, however, forced Gallaudet to put more emphasis on private fund raising during a period when the university faced increasing competition for students, due to the enactment of the Americans with Disabilities Act in 1990. Drezner concludes that Gallaudet should look to historically black colleges and universities to identify a successful fund raising model for the future.

PHILANTHROPIC SCHOLARS, nonprofit organizations, and foundations recently began looking at traditions of giving outside of majority communities. One study stated that philanthropy in the United States was connected to "a relatively small number of White [hearing] families and individuals who enjoyed access to education, owned major businesses, held leadership positions in government, dominated the professions and inherited wealth."[1] Reports and studies such as this, however, have neglected to look at the uniqueness of the American Deaf community, its role in giving, and its own culture of philanthropy.[2] In an era of de-

---

A previous version of this chapter was published as Noah D. Drezner, "Advancing Gallaudet: Alumni Support for the Nation's University for the Deaf and Hard-of-Hearing and Its Similarities to Black Colleges and Universities," *International Journal of Educational Advancement*, 5 (August 2005): 301–16.

creased federal support of higher education and higher costs, Gallaudet University recently has turned for the first time to its graduates, its deaf and hearing alumni, to cover the institution's budget differential. Gallaudet's first formal capital campaign began in 1997 and successfully completed in 2002.

While this is a contemporary issue, it is informative to look at Gallaudet's financial support from a historical perspective. Residential schools for deaf pupils opened throughout the United States in the nineteenth century. In early 1857 Amos Kendall and others convinced the U.S. Congress to incorporate the Columbia Institution for the Instruction of the Deaf and Dumb, and Blind, which eventually became Gallaudet University.[3] Congress began its financial connection to the education of deaf students at Gallaudet University from the institution's inception. Initially it appropriated $150 per year per child for local children attending the school, in order to cover their maintenance and tuition costs.[4] The Columbia Institution's founder gave additional support to the newly established school. Kendall donated a house and two acres of land, finances to cover the start-up costs, and the salary of the superintendent.[5] Kendall's wealth and influence—arguably two separate forms of philanthropy—undoubtedly helped the Columbia Institution gain favor in the Congress and within multiple administrations.[6]

Kendall was a political powerhouse of sorts. For six years he had served as the fourth auditor of the United States Treasury and was postmaster general for five years. This influence was captured in an 1860 report in the *Washington Evening Star*: "At that time, next to [President Andrew] Jackson, [Kendall's] mind was the controlling one in the Government, stamping the impress of its patriotism and will more indelibly upon the future of the United States than those of all the rest of Jackson's advisors."[7] Kendall's influence remained high even after the Jackson presidency.

It was this influence that led to the inception of the National Deaf-Mute College on the grounds of the Columbia Institution in 1864. The college was later renamed for Thomas Hopkins Gallaudet, the founder, along with Laurent Clerc and Mason Fitch Cogswell, of the first permanent school for deaf children in the United States. Subsequently, the college has received the vast majority of its operating budget from the federal government.[8] Government funding, which supported the Columbia Institution since 1858, increased as the institution was given collegial powers, including the ability to confer degrees, by an act of Congress. The act passed unanimously after some debate by the Senate and was signed by President Lincoln on April 8, 1864.[9] Upon passing the authorization, Congress allocated $26,000 to cover the cost of purchasing an additional thirteen acres of land.[10]

Edward Miner Gallaudet, reflecting on the government's involvement, pointed out in a speech given to the Columbia Historical Society in 1911 that it was a unique show of support and investment to deaf education that Congress acted "in providing for a national college for the Deaf . . . at a time when the burdens of [the Civil W]ar were pressing heavily upon the Government." Gallaudet continued by pointing out that the very day that the $26,000 of support was "drawn from the Treasury, all communication, either by rail or telegraph, between the Capitol and the country was cut off by the operations of the Civil War."[11] While congressional action to fund the college was indeed significant, it is important to note that because of the secession of eleven states from the Union, the complete voice of the nation was not part of this decision.[12]

Upon Kendall's death in 1869, only a few months after the college held its first graduation, his estate sold the adjoining eighty-one acres of land to the institution for $85,000; the campus was now a full one hundred acres.[13] The larger campus allowed for expansion and construction. At the January 29, 1871, dedication of Chapel Hall, U.S. President Ulysses S. Grant and then General James A. Garfield spoke about the "courage of the government" to fund the institution while the country was at war with itself.[14] Gallaudet quoted Garfield as saying, "Congress took half a million dollars from the public Treasury and devoted it to this work—I hailed it as a nobler expression of the faith and virtue of the American people, and of the statesmanship of their representatives, than I ever before witnessed."[15]

Garfield continued this "noble[ ] expression" himself. The future U.S. president maintained an interest in the college and its progress for the last fifteen years of his life. One of Garfield's greatest accomplishments on behalf of the institution was securing the funds for the purchase of the remaining portion of the Kendall estate. Garfield helped raise $10,000 from private subscriptions and successfully lobbied Congress for another $70,000.[16]

As a result of its relationship to the federal government, Gallaudet, throughout its history and to some extent still today, has resembled a service academy.[17] In addition to federal funding of the operating budget, students have received congressional appointments for study, diplomas hold the signature of the President of the United States in the position of patron of the university, and the Federal General Services Administration was, in the past, given the task of building the campus.[18]

Federal support of the college was not always as strong as it was under Kendall and Gallaudet, however. During the tenure of the college's second president (Percival Hall, 1910–45), increases in federal support amid two world wars and the Great Depression were minimal. Congress had supported the college fairly generously during the Civil War but was hesitant to support new construction and, at times, even debated whether or not to continue funding the school during Hall's presidency.[19] This decreased funding made it difficult to expand the enrollment, faculty, curriculum, and physical plant. As a result, President Hall considered approaching others for private funding. Nina Van Oss reported this contemplation in the *Gallaudet Alumni Bulletin*.

He [President Hall] felt that *if the alumni could in some way interest* the Ford, Rockefeller, Carnegie or such foundations in the College and obtain grants to the College funds for expanding the curriculum, research, and the like, as is done for other noteworthy and deserving institutions, then much progress could be made."[20] (emphasis mine)

That alumni were thought of first as a means of connecting the institution to foundations, rather than as a source of direct financial support, is evidence of the administration's acknowledgement that their Deaf alumni were not in a real position to support the institution. When Gallaudet pursued private fund raising in earnest years later, reliance on corporations and foundations was obvious. Alumni contributions only made up 7.27 percent of the total income from private support in fiscal year 2004, for example, while corporation and foundation gifts accounted for 5.7 percent and 30.7 percent, respectively.[21]

While President Hall never saw Gallaudet successfully connected to foundations, his successor, Leonard Elstad, helped reconnect the institution with Congress. Soon after entering the presidency in 1945, Elstad was told that Gallaudet needed to become accredited by the Middle States Association of Colleges and Schools. A report on the school's suitability for accreditation commended its faculty, students, and strategic plans, but found that the college had inadequate facilities.[22] Additionally, in 1949, the United States Office of Education and the Federal Security Agency (FSA), the division of the government that the college reported to at the time, decided to review the college as well. The resulting report, *The Federal Government and the Higher Education of the Deaf: A progress report on the Columbia Institution for the Deaf, with proposals for action*, was very positive.

The study found that the federal government had an obligation to continue the financing of postsecondary education for deaf people simply because it was not economically possible for states to fund this obligation. The report continued that in order for Gallaudet to become a first-rate institution, a stronger relationship between the government and the institution would be necessary.[23] In response to the two reports, FSA acting administrator John L. Thurston recommended that Congress and the Bureau of the Budget increase their funding and involvement in the college.[24] At a May 5, 1954, congressional hearing, President Elstad used the results of each report to lobby for increased support.

The result of these studies and Elstad's efforts was a new relationship between the federal government and the college, made explicit in the passage of Public Law 420. Through this law, Congress funded increased faculty positions, curricular development, and improvements to the physical plant. Additionally, the law officially changed the name of the institution to Gallaudet College.[25]

The federal government's increased involvement in Gallaudet can be seen by examining the annual funding appropriated to the college. In Elstad's first year, 1945, Congress appropriated $270,000 for the school's support. By 1969, when Elstad left office, the federal appropriation was $6,900,000.[26] This amounted to a 1,192 percent increase after accounting for inflation, but changes in federal support for higher education would soon affect Gallaudet.[27]

The golden age in American higher education, when federal money was abundant, enrollments were on the rise, and large sums of money were spent on institutions' physical plants, lasted for several decades following World War II.[28] However, this golden age ended in the 1970s and 1980s when federal funds were not as readily available as they once were due to the increases in federal deficits and changes in federal priorities. As a result, many small, private liberal arts institutions began to engage in professionally conducted advancement efforts.[29]

In this new environment, the federal government, which has been either the primary or sole source of financial support for only a small number of institutions of higher education, including the military academies, Howard University, and Gallaudet, eventually began to reduce the percentage of its contribution to Gallaudet's total revenue (fig. 1). The fiscal year 2000 budget appropriation from Congress, for instance, only covered 70 percent of the institution's expenditures.[30] Beginning in the late twentieth century, then, the Department of Education asked Gallaudet to be more self-sufficient and suggested that it increase its tuition to the seventy-fifth percentile of United States land grant colleges and universities. Gallaudet agreed and began to raise tuition. Later, however, the department suggested that Gallaudet limit its annual tuition increase

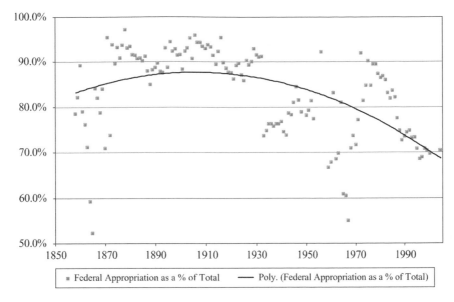

Figure 1. Federal Appropriation to Gallaudet as a Percentage of the Total Budget

Source: Gallaudet University Office of Budget, Administration and Finance. Annual Reports of Columbia Institution, Gallaudet College, and Congressional budget data. *Note:* The costs associated with the Model Secondary School for the Deaf and the Kendall Demonstration Elementary School are included in the federal appropriations. These institutions receive full funding from Congress.

to no more than 10 percent.[31] This hindered Gallaudet's ability to increase revenues through tuition.

Gallaudet's Fund Raising

As federal and state subventions have declined, more and more public and private two- and four-year colleges and universities have started asking for gifts from individual donors. Administrators are searching for all possible nontax revenue sources to help meet budget requirements. Supplemental private dollars "often provide[ ] the bulk of discretionary income for publicly supported institutions, and hence has been referred to as their margin of excellence," one study claimed.[32]

Gallaudet is no different. In order to fill the gap in funding, the university has moved to development. In the past private fund raising was not as central to the institution as it was to many other private universities around the United States. Now, though, Gallaudet uses private fund raising to maintain its level of expenditures. The first Deaf leader of the institution, I. King Jordan, was appointed in 1988 when the University's endowment was only $5 million. He was well-aware of this fact upon his selection and knew it was time to plan Gallaudet's first formal capital campaign.

However, the capital campaign Jordan launched was not the institution's first formal campaign; alumni support for Gallaudet began long before Jordan's efforts. In 1907, to mark President Gallaudet's fiftieth anniversary as the institution's chief executive and his seventieth birthday, alumni, without solicitation, announced that they would establish the Edward Miner Gallaudet Fund. The former students left the purpose of the fund open to their honoree's choice. Gallaudet later decided that the fund should be used to finance the library that would bear his name. Later, in 1919, alumni raised a total of $10,000 in memory of their first president. The money was pledged toward the building of the Edward Miner Gallaudet Library.[33]

In the early 1960s a self-motivated alumnus, David Peikoff, began a centennial campaign with his wife that funded the renovation and endowment of the alumni house—now bearing his name—and the establishment of two additional permanent endowments: the Laurent Clerc Cultural Fund and Graduate Fellowship Fund. Peikoff raised $1 million from fellow alumni by traveling the nation and asking for their support for Gallaudet in honor of the anniversary of the collegiate program's founding.[34]

Although historically Gallaudet did not use private funds for operating or endowment support, there were development discussions on campus prior to the 1988 "Deaf President Now" protests that brought Jordan to the presidency. These deliberations focused on what the fund raising message of the college should be. One segment of the administration thought that the message should be one of charity—that giving to Gallaudet was an act of social justice. Another view, and the one that is currently in place, was that giving to Gallaudet was a philanthropic act of supporting higher education, just as it was at any other institution.[35]

Within higher education generally, this debate over fund raising approaches ended about a hundred years ago. Early colleges with religious backgrounds focused their appeal from a prospective of charity—donors should give to help disadvantaged people. However, around the turn of the century, institutions began to appeal to donors using a philanthropic approach.[36] Gallaudet did not truly contemplate asking for alumni support for over another three-quarters of a century, however. Even though discussions took place in the 1980s, the institution did not formalize its development activities until 1990, shortly after Jordan assumed the Gallaudet presidency.[37]

Where has this neglect of alumni fund raising left Gallaudet? The answer is akin to the situation at historically Black colleges and universities. Gallaudet alumni, like many alumni from historically Black colleges and universities, have believed that their alma mater was strongly funded by the federal government and supplemented by corporations and foundations, and therefore, was not in need of alumni support.[38] Another barrier to increased alumni support and participation, as identified by the Gallaudet Office of Institutional Advancement, has been the culture of giving within the Deaf community.[39]

Philanthropy in the United States has historically been viewed through the lens of wealthy, white, hearing men.[40] Marybeth Gasman and Sibby Anderson Thompkins, who studied fund raising at historical Black colleges and universities, suggested that when looking at the culture of giving in the African American community, the traditional definition of philanthropy was too narrow.[41] This also has been the case when looking at giving in the Deaf community. Former Gallaudet Director of Development Lynne Murray contends that alumni participation and dollars received are both low for several reasons. The first is that, historically, deaf adults do not have access to well-paying jobs and, therefore, do not have the disposable income to donate. The second is that members of the Deaf community are "used to receiving instead of giving."[42] The third reason is that the idea of giving is not passed down within families. Ninety percent of the members of the Deaf community have hearing parents.[43] Finally, before the mid-1980s, most deaf elementary and secondary students attended residential schools.[44] Cathy Sweet-Windham, former executive director of development at Gallaudet, believes that communication barriers between hearing parents and deaf children, as well as the fact that generations of deaf children who went to residential schools did not see their parents give donations, affects the ability for a culture of philanthropy to flourish in the Deaf community.[45]

Much like historically Black colleges and universities, Gallaudet was established to serve an aspect of the population that was excluded from traditional American higher education. Deaf students were almost fully relegated to deaf-serving institutions, such as Gallaudet and the National Technical Institute for the Deaf (NTID) at the Rochester Institute of Technology, until the passage of the Americans with Disabilities Act (ADA) of 1990. The ADA opened the door for deaf students to attend any insti-

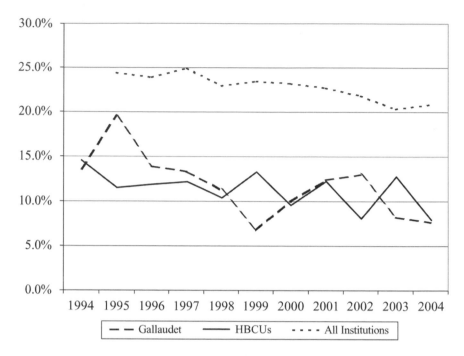

Figure 2. Alumni Donors as Percentage of Solicited

Source: Voluntary Support of Education Survey Council for Aid to Education, New York, NY. *Note:* Reliable data for 1994 is not available.

tution of higher education in the country, requiring the institutions to provide interpreters and other needed accommodations for deaf students should they attend.[46]

While more research needs to been done to fully explore these similarities from a historic perspective, looking at the past decade might shed light on future philanthropic trends. The similarities between Gallaudet and historically Black schools go well beyond those of their origin and necessity; they are peers with respect to development and fund raising as well. For example, alumni participation in fiscal year (FY) 2004 at historically Black colleges and universities averaged 7.8 percent, while Gallaudet alumni participation in the same year reached 7.6 percent, both well below that national average in FY 2004 of 21.2 percent.[47] Gallaudet has closely resembled historically Black colleges and universities' alumni participation for at least the past ten years—consistently being between five and ten percentage points below the national average (fig. 2).[48] Additionally, the average alumni gift (fig. 3) and alumni support

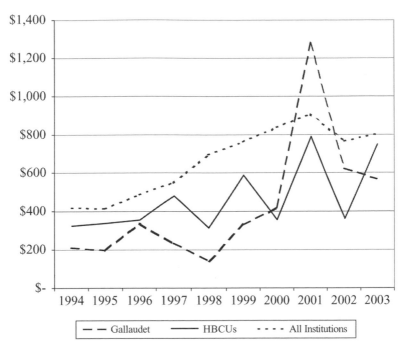

Figure 3. Average Alumni Gift

Source: Voluntary Support of Education Survey, Council for Aid to Education, New York, NY.

per student (fig. 4) were comparable over the same ten-year period as well, with each also below the national average.

Foundation support as a proportion of total giving also was equivalent for Gallaudet and historically Black colleges and universities in the same ten-year period, save fiscal year 1997, when Gallaudet's foundation support reached 68.8 percent, while the Black schools' equivalent was 19.7 percent (fig. 5).[49] The 1997 spike could be explained by the fact that this was the first year of Gallaudet's capital campaign, and foundation support increased for that reason. It is interesting to note that, for both Gallaudet and historically Black colleges and universities, foundation support as a percentage of total dollars raised was higher than that of the national average. This variance in foundation support can be attributed in two ways. First, with a lower proportion of alumni giving, other sources of funds account for a larger percentage of overall giving. Second, foundation giving to both historically Black colleges and Gallaudet was greater than their contributions to the rest of higher education. The

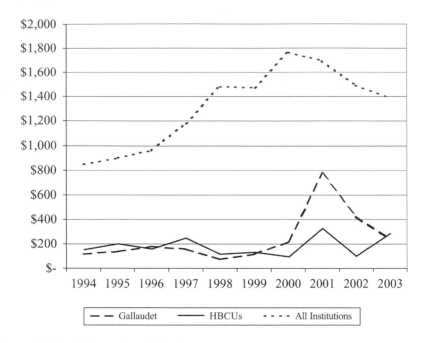

Figure 4. Alumni Support per Student

Source: Voluntary Support of Education Survey, Council for Aid to Education, New York, NY.

greater foundation presence may be cause for concern, since the data indicate that FY 2002 and 2003 marked a point where foundation giving toward Gallaudet and historically Black colleges and universities was on a decline and was about to level out or even dip beneath the national average.

Gallaudet has a strong and unique history within American higher education, one with great federal support. As Congressional funding begins to decrease, calls for self-sufficiency are on the horizon. As corporations and foundations change their funding priorities, it is important for Gallaudet to begin to look more closely at its alumni as prospective donors to the nation's university for Deaf people.

Since Gallaudet is relatively new in the advancement arena and shares many similarities to historically Black colleges and universities, it is important for members of the university community to embrace their past and to look to their colleagues at the historically Black colleges and universities who are successful at fund raising to share ideas. The Deaf community, like the African American community and other cultural groups,

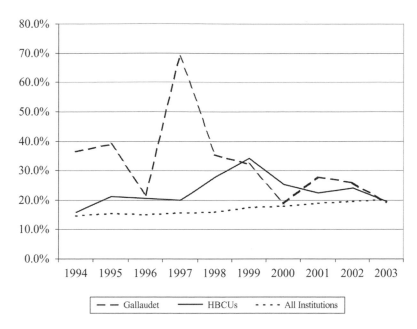

Figure 5. Foundation Giving as a Percentage of Total

Source: Voluntary Support of Education Survey, Council for Aid to Education, New York, NY.

has its own culture of giving. Gallaudet has the opportunity to educate its alumni and students and become a more successful part of this culture.

Notes

1. Council on Foundations, *Cultures of Caring: Philanthropy in Diverse American Communities* (Washington, D.C.: Council on Foundations, 1999), 7.

2. Paddy Ladd, *Understanding Deaf Culture: In Search of Deafhood* (Tonawanda, N.Y.: Multilingual Matters LTD, 2003).

3. Albert W. Atwood, *Gallaudet College: Its First One Hundred Years* (Washington, D.C.: Gallaudet College, 1964); *Statutes at Large of the United States of America, 1789–1873* 11 (1857): 161.

4. H. O. Bishop, "Where the Deaf and Mute Overcome Their Handicaps," *The National Republican*, June 17, 1922.

5. Atwood, *Gallaudet College*, 3.

6. Atwood, 4, quoting *The Washington Evening Star*, 1860; Nancy Bowen Tadie, "A History of Drama at Gallaudet College: 1864 to 1969" (PhD diss., New York University, 1979).

7. Atwood, 4, quoting *The Washington Evening Star*, 1860; Tadie, "A History of Drama at Gallaudet College."

8. Atwood; Edward Miner Gallaudet, *History of the College for the Deaf: 1857–1907* (Washington, D.C.: Gallaudet College Press, 1983); John L. Pulley, "The Sign Language of Fund Raising: Gallaudet University, an Institution Founded for the Deaf, Aims for Donors' Hearts," *The Chronicle on Higher Education,* (July 11, 2003).

9. *An Act to Authorize the Columbia Institute for the Deaf and Dumb and the Blind to Confer Degrees, Stats at Large of USA, 1789–1873* (1864): 45; Atwood, *Gallaudet College*; Tadie, "A History of Drama at Gallaudet College."

10. Edward M. Gallaudet, "A History of the Columbia Institution for the Deaf and Dumb," (speech to the Columbia Historical Society, January 17, 1911), *Records of the Columbia Historical Society* 15; $26,000 was nearly 400 percent of the institution's total receipts for its first year of operation ($6,513.25; $5,263.25 from Congress and $1,250 from private subscriptions); Atwood, *Gallaudet College*.

11. Gallaudet, "A History," (speech), 6.

12. There were only twenty-four states left in the Union and represented in Congress at the time of these decisions. Congress took other actions with respect to higher education under the same circumstances, including the *Morrill Act of 1862, Stats at Large of USA, 1789–1873* 12 (1863): 503.

13. Elizabeth Peet, "The Building of Gallaudet," *Gallaudet Alumni Bulletin,* July 1949, 3.

14. Tadie, "A History"; "Interesting Dedicatory Exercises at the Columbia Institution," *Daily Patriot,* July 30, 1871, 1.

15. Gallaudet, "A History," 12.

16. Edward M. Gallaudet, *President Garfield's Connection with the Deaf-Mute College* (Washington, D.C.: Gibson Brothers, Printers, 1882), 7–11.

17. U.S. service academies include: Air Force (Colorado Springs, CO), Coast Guard (New London, CT), Merchant Marine (Kings Point, NY), Military (West Point, NY), and Naval (Annapolis, MD). In 2002, West Point completed a $218 million campaign (the original goal was $150 million). This was the first campaign by a service academy. The funds are going to be used to fund programs not covered by the Pentagon (e.g., foreign immersion programs).

18. Jack Gannon, ed., *Gallaudet Almanac* (Washington, D.C.: Gallaudet Press, 1994); Gallaudet College Catalogues, 1975–1976, Gallaudet University Archives; Pulley, "The Sign Language of Fund Raising."

19. Tadie, "A History"; Nina B. Van Oss, "On Dr. Hall's Long Range Plans," *Gallaudet Alumni Bulletin*, November 1953.

20. Van Oss, "On Dr. Hall's Long Range Plans," 12.

21. Board of Associates Briefing Book, Gallaudet University, Office of Institutional Advancement, 4 November 2004.

22. Atwood, *Gallaudet College*.

23. *The Federal Government and the Higher Education of the Deaf: A Progress Report on the Columbia Institution for the Deaf, with Proposals for Action* (Washington, D.C.: United States Office of Education, 1949).

24. Atwood, *Gallaudet College*.

25. *A Bill to Amend the Charter of the Columbia Institution for the Deaf, Change its Name, Define its Corporate Powers, and Provide for its Organization and Administration, and for Other Purposes*, Public Law 420, *U.S. Statutes at Large* 68 (1954): 265.

26. Rosita N. Pacto, "Reminiscences of Dr. Leonard M. Elstad," *Buff and Blue* May 8, 1969.

27. *Historical Statistics of the United States* (Washington, D.C.: Government Printing Office, 1975), www.westegg.com/inflation. This Web site calculates U.S. dollars in real values through use of the Consumer Price Index (CPI) statistics.

28. Nathan Marsh Pusey, *American Higher Education, 1945–1970: A Personal Report* (Cambridge: Harvard University Press, 1978); John R. Thelin, *A History of American Higher Education* (Baltimore: Johns Hopkins University Press, 2004); W. Bruce Cook, "Fund Raising and the College Presidency in an Era of Uncertainty: From 1975 to the Present," *Journal of Higher Education* 68, no. 1 (Jan.–Feb., 1997): 53–86.

29. D. W. Breneman, *Liberal Arts Colleges: Thriving, Surviving, or Endangered?* (Washington, D.C.: The Brookings Institution, 1994).

30. Gallaudet University Budget Office.

31. Pulley, "The Sign Language of Fund Raising"; Cathy Sweet-Windham, interview by author, tape recording, November 3, 2004.

32. C. C. Garvin Jr., *Corporate Philanthropy: The Third Aspect of Social Responsibility* (New York: Council for Financial Aid to Education, 1978).

33. Atwood, *Gallaudet College*, 38, 44, 45.

34. Sweet-Windham, interview; Plaque on Peikoff Alumni House, Gallaudet University, Washington, D.C.

35. David Armstrong, interview by author, tape recording, November 3, 2004.

36. B. E. Brittingham and T. R. Pezzullo, *The Campus Green: Fund Raising in Higher Education: ASHE-ERIC Higher Education Report No. 1* (Washington, D.C.: The George Washington University, School of Education and Human Development, 1990).

37. Sweet-Windham, interview.

38. Lynne Murray, interview by author, tape recording, November 3, 2004; Marybeth Gasman and Sibby Anderson-Thompkins, *Fund Raising from Black-College Alumni: Successful Strategies for Supporting Alma Mater* (Washington, D.C.: Council for the Advancement and Support of Education, 2003).

39. Murray, interview.

40. Council on Foundations, *Cultures of Caring: Philanthropy in Diverse American Communities* (Washington, D.C.: Council on Foundations, 1999).

41. Gasman and Anderson-Thompkins, *Fund Raising from Black-College Alumni*.

42. Murray, interview.

43. Ladd, *Understanding Deaf Culture*.

44. Ladd, *Understanding Deaf Culture*; Murray, interview.

45. Sweet-Windham, interview.

46. *Education of the Deaf Act of 1986*, U.S. *Statutes at Large* 100 (1987): 781; *Americans with Disabilities Act of 1990*,*U.S. Statutes at Large* 104 (1991): 327.

47. Council for the Aid to Education, "Voluntary Support of Education Survey—Data Miner," http://vse.cae.org.

48. Only data from FY1994—FY2004 is available.

49. Ibid.

11

The Power of Place: The Evolution
of Kendall Green

Benjamin Bahan and Hansel Bauman

Editors' Introduction

Benjamin Bahan and Hansel Bauman apply the concepts of "Deaf architecture" and "Deaf space" as they trace the architectural history of Gallaudet University's Kendall Green campus. They argue that Edward Miner Gallaudet envisioned the college to be like other institutions of higher learning, retaining famous architects and builders and emulating the designs of other schools. By projecting the physical features of the institution as those of a college, Gallaudet sought to normalize deafness and place deaf students on intellectual parity with hearing students. Bahan and Bauman contend that Gallaudet and subsequent presidents, however, overlooked the "collectivist ways of the Deaf community" in their desire to have a campus that would be physically indistinguishable from others. Finally, they discuss the Sorenson Language and Communication Center as an example of "Deaf architecture" that reaffirms the community's collectivist identity and offers a model for the future.

The concepts and observations put forth in this paper are formulated from student research developed over two semesters in the Deaf Space course offered through the Gallaudet University Department of ASL and Deaf Studies. The Deaf Space class is an important part of the university's new, inclusive, campus-planning initiative known as the Deaf Space Project, in which Gallaudet students, faculty, and administrators are working with design professionals to create Deaf design principles that will guide the future development of the campus.

Deaf people inhabit a highly visual world; they have a visual and spatial language, a visually centered way of orienting themselves within the world, and a strong cultural bond built around their shared experiences. It should follow, then, that the places they build be completely responsive to and expressive of the unique physical, cognitive, and cultural aspects of Deaf experiences. From its inception, Gallaudet University has been both an academic institution and an important cultural center for the Deaf community. Its leaders and designers have endeavored to build a prestigious campus setting with landscape and architectural styles on a par with other institutions, while secondarily attempting to meet the specific needs of Deaf people. The manner in which the campus and its surroundings have evolved reveals the ways that Gallaudet's campus—exemplary of traditional North American campus planning over the past one hundred fifty years—has influenced Deaf identity and the quality of life on campus.

Identity and Place: The Origins of Deaf Architecture

As humans, our identity is deeply connected to the places we inhabit. We feel *at home*—at ease, affirmed, empowered—when we live in places with which we identify and are most familiar. In these places, spatial orientation is easy and memorable and reminds us of who we are—our history, values, social norms, and aesthetic sensibilities. Place not only holds meaning for its inhabitants but also communicates their identity to others in a rich and complex medium that builds a sense of presence in the world, be it at the level of the individual or an entire culture.

The link between place and identity is deeply embedded in Deaf culture. The often-told story of Abbe de l'Epée, for example, is rich with architectural metaphors.[1] However, the best example of the close relationship between Deaf people and their space is the traditional act of rearranging furniture in public places to accommodate group gatherings. These examples point to ephemeral but powerful architectural manifestations of Deaf experiences built around visual and tactile sensibilities, a visual and spatial language, and the deep interpersonal connection that binds the community within a collectivist culture.

Deaf architecture appeals to the senses; it is an architecture of openness and transparency that enables the visuocentric reading of space and activities. Natural and artificial light is modulated to illuminate sign language, heighten spatial awareness, and enrich aesthetic experience. Similarly, building vibration is modulated to heighten spatial awareness and enrich sensory experience. Deaf architecture is at once practical, straight-forward, and expressive. Language and culture influence how we per-ceive and imagine space. The flowing, kinesthetic nature of sign language provides the inspiration for an architecture of soft, free-flowing spaces without physical or visual barriers, one where building forms, surface texture, light, and color are utilized in such a way as to create spaces that are memorable, clearly understood, and easy to move through, espe-cially when Deaf people are focused on a signed conversation instead of the space ahead.

Deaf architecture fosters social interaction. The Deaf community is relatively small but has a strong cultural bond formed by shared cogni-tive sensibilities, language, and life experiences. In many ways Deaf cul-ture is a collectivist culture with traditions of shared activities, decision-making, and caring for one another. Through careful planning of space usage, density, and proper adjacencies, buildings can bring people to-gether and encourage them to linger and socialize.

The designers of the Gallaudet University campus have had a spotty awareness of the Deaf culture/Deaf place relationship outlined here. For example, the *Gallaudet College Facilities Master Plan* prepared in 1975 de-voted only a single page to the architectural and site considerations re-lated to educating Deaf people. It stated,

> Overriding the specific space requirements related to user needs and pro-gram activities for each of the College's buildings there are general consid-erations pertaining to the development of an environment which responds to the physical, sociological, and psychological concerns of deaf persons.[2]

Ironically, during this era major changes were made to the campus that made the facilities less responsive to Deaf ways of being.

Fredrick Law Olmsted, the world-renowned landscape architect and designer of the original college campus, offered a more insightful view in his 1866 master plan for the National Deaf-Mute College. He argued that additional landscaped campus space "should be set apart for orna-mental ground in the vicinity of college buildings; the [students] of your establishment being unable to hear . . . must depend on the development of other faculties. In a well-regulated garden the senses of sight and smell are gratified in a most complete and innocent way."[3] Olmsted ac-knowledged a more complete sensory dimension of Deaf experience and its relationship to the physical world. Yet neither Olmsted's words nor those of later master plans demonstrated a deep understanding of the interpersonal connection deaf people have between one another or of physical place as a manifestation of Deaf culture. These designers, most of whom were hearing, fixated on vision—the one way they could understand how deaf people "compensated" for their lack of hearing.

By overlooking the collectivist ways of the Deaf community, designers of the campus inadvertently have built a campus that offers few comfortable gathering places, which tends to foster a sense of social isolation rather than connection. In short, Gallaudet is a center for a collectivist culture that has no place to collect.

Isolation and Connection in the Early Years

Gallaudet University began as a small school for deaf and blind students on the southwest quadrant of Kendall Green, a two-hundred-acre estate on the northeastern edge of Washington, D.C., owned by Amos Kendall. The school was a collection of drafty wooden houses with a mix of classrooms, living quarters, and support facilities where students and faculty lived, worked, and studied together in an environment more akin to a home for an extended family than a state-run residential school.[4] The social bonds—the sense of belonging and connection—formed in this more home-like setting must have provided a sanctuary for students who were afforded the opportunity to be with others with whom they could easily communicate.

Under Edward Miner Gallaudet's direction this small school, known at the time as the Columbia Institution for the Instruction of the Deaf, Dumb, and Blind, grew into the National Deaf-Mute College, which was chartered by President Lincoln in 1864. Gallaudet understood the importance that a prestigious campus setting would have for building a reputable institution, so he brought some of the very best architects of the time to the school to design a host of new campus buildings. The world-renowned architects Vaux and Withers of New York City were selected to design Chapel Hall, College Hall, the president's house, and the houses along Faculty Row, all in the Victorian Gothic style, which at the time was considered to be the cutting edge in architectural design (figs. 1 and 2).[5] Needless to say, such "progressive designs" did not respond directly to the physical, cognitive, or cultural sensibilities of the institution's Deaf community. However, much like the earlier wooden buildings of Kendall's institution, many of the first college buildings housed a wide mix of uses in close proximity—a spatial pattern that tends to foster social interaction conducive to the collectivist ways of Deaf culture. College Hall, for example, provided classrooms, administrative offices on lower levels, and the boy's dormitory on the top floor. Other

Figure 1. Chapel Hall, Gallaudet University

activities, such as dining and worship, took place in the adjacent Chapel
Hall. Over the years Faculty Row provided multifamily housing for both
faculty and students. In these early days it was possible to stay in visual
contact with one's peers throughout the day—a continual reminder of
belonging to a community.

Fredrick Law Olmsted, designer of Central Park in New York City,
the Boston Common, and the Capitol grounds in Washington, D.C., developed the college's first formal master plan in 1866 (fig. 3). Olmsted's
design for the campus organized the college and Kendall School buildings so that they backed onto a shared service yard with spaces for the
kitchen yard, boys' playground, and the mechanic shop. Kendall School
faculty housing faced the service yard as well, making this area a lively
outdoor space on the campus. The formal entry to the academic buildings in this cluster faced outward to the campus grounds bounded to
the west by Faculty Row, a line of five brick houses for faculty and the
president's house. These campus grounds were designed as a parklike
"naturalistic" setting where pathways meandered through groves of
shade trees and open fields offered a variety of spatial and sensory experiences. Within the informal campus quad between College Hall and Faculty Row, students and faculty alike had many choices of places to either

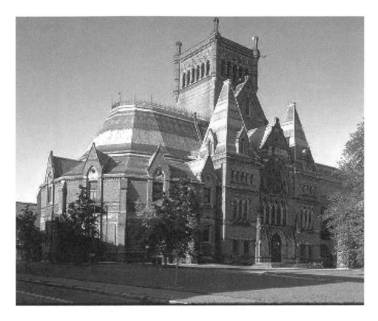

Figure 2. Harvard University and Gallaudet University share a similar appearance. Both are fine examples of Gothic architecture, a popular style for colleges and universities of their time.

seek social interaction or solitude along the paths, where one could linger within the shaded groves and gaze across the open fields. One can still experience this sublime campus experience by walking along the original pathways that surround the historic Olmsted Green.

Much like other college campuses, residential schools, and asylums of the 1800s, the college's physical setting was away from the city center. The spatial separation of these institutions from the main activities of the city carried a powerful political message of marginalization in the case of asylums. In the case of colleges, the spatial separation was meant to reinforce the elite status of higher education.[6] Gallaudet College was in a unique position in that its spatial separation from the city marked its status as both marginalized and as an elite institution of higher education. The Du Bois Tourist Guide Map of 1892 shown in figure 4 provides an interesting view on this double reading. On the one hand, the institution's historic campus is rendered in the same three-dimensional fashion assigned to other important landmarks, such as the Capitol, the White House, and national monuments. Yet the campus, located north of

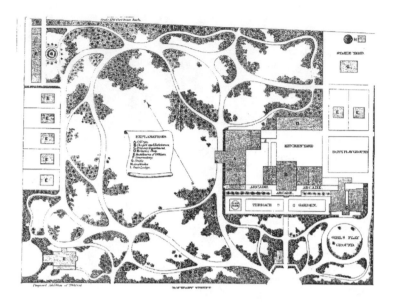

Figure 3. The 1866 Campus Master Plan

Boundary Street (now Florida Avenue), is floating outside of the city's
stark boundary with no apparent means to blend with the city's urban
fabric.

This early disconnect from the city has continued to this day. By vir-
tue of its location on the edge of the urban fabric, the campus has become
surrounded by wide, fast-moving thoroughfares rather than smaller-
scale, walkable city streets. Together the wide streets and the campus
fence create a strong barrier between the life of the campus and that of
the city. Perhaps even more importantly, the run-down conditions of
Gallaudet's surrounding neighborhood separate the campus from the
city. By being built on the edge of the city, where there has been little
control over land use, Gallaudet's surrounding neighborhood has never
had a coherent, pedestrian scale feel that enables easy connection to
places to shop, live, work, or enjoy an evening on the town. As with
other colleges, this kind of separation is a significant problem that tends
to hamper an institution's ability to attract and retain good students who
value a rich life beyond the classroom.

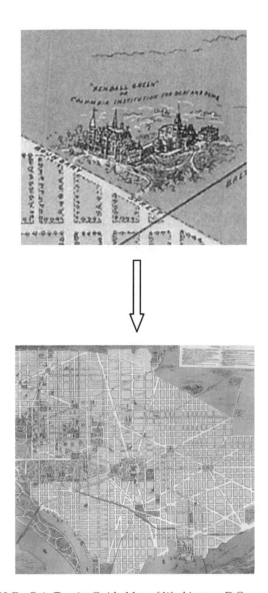

Figure 4. The 1892 Du Bois Tourist Guide Map of Washington, D.C.

Figure 5. Map of Kendall Green showing the orchards, pastures, and access road that the institution acquired in 1870.

Greater Gallaudet: The Mall Campus

Edward Miner Gallaudet must have had a sense of the potential problems with development on the lands that surrounded the campus. In 1870 he invested a great deal of effort to raise the funds necessary to purchase an additional 80 acres of Kendall's land to the east and north of the campus, not for the expansion of the institution, but to provide a buffer to undesirable neighbors, such as slaughter houses and breweries that he feared would one day move to the area.[7] With this purchase the campus land area grew to one hundred acres (fig. 5). Even though the college did not build on this land until the 1940s, the direction of the campus's growth was set by the placement of existing buildings and the farm roads acquired in the 1870 purchase, rather than by a deliberate long-range plan for the campus. From 1945 through the early 1970s, the campus more than doubled in size with new classrooms, dormitories, a new library, a student center, and a gymnasium organized around a campus mall north of Chapel Hall. This new portion of the campus was situated entirely within the confines of an existing access road that looped through the original pastures and orchards of the site. Lincoln Circle is now the long-since-improved version of this original roadway that separated the mall portion of the campus, now known as Olmsted

Green, from the main quad in Olmsted's plan. This split is perhaps one of the first of many spatial separations that would affect the campus in the years to come.

The mall plan, a North American campus tradition, provided a rational means to organize the many different uses on the site in a way that seemed to support Deaf architectural principles. The plan separated the pedestrian realm of the landscaped mall from vehicular access located on the opposite side of the campus buildings. The mall provided excellent visual/physical connectivity, and it provided a common gathering place that fostered interaction and a sense of community. From most all points in the mall one could have clear visual access to all the activities taking place within it and to all the buildings surrounding it. A zigzag pattern of walkways crossed the open mall and led pedestrians directly to building entries across the space.

Given the variety of all the uses placed around the mall, the new expansion was essentially a new campus unto itself. Students could live on the mall in dorms, such as Peet or Ely Hall, walk across the mall to the student center for a meal or to socialize, then go for a swim in the gymnasium next to the main academic building, Hall Memorial Building, or perhaps study in the Edward Miner Gallaudet Memorial Library located next to College Hall. The concentration of such a wide variety of uses around the mall enabled all of campus life to take place around a single space, allowing for many impromptu interactions between students, faculty, and staff—a model setting for a collectivist culture.

With the exception of the library, all of the new buildings and campus improvements of this era were funded, designed, and constructed by the federal government's General Services Administration (GSA). At that time, architects and planners at the GSA, like so many others in the profession, embraced modernism, the popular design trend of the day.[8] It was characterized by clean geometric façades with large expanses of glass without ornament, flat rooflines, and open floor plans. To some degree this was fortuitous, as many of the modernist principles that promote a sense of light and openness are at the core of Deaf architectural design principles. The four-story open lobbies in the Ballard Halls and the central open space of the library building are examples of the early application of visuocentric design principles in these modernist buildings.

The very best example of Deaf architecture on campus was the Student Union Building as it existed during the time. The building served as the social heart of the campus. The fond memories and feelings of belonging that alumni from this era shared in interviews most frequently

Figure 6. *(Top left)* view to the Student Union Building (circa 1965); *(top right)* view to the Student Academic Center (2007); *(bottom left)* the Rathskellar (student lounge), circa 1965, shows a strong visual connection between the student lounge area and the campus mall through large windows; *(bottom right)* the Rathskellar (2007) demonstrates the impact of recent renovations. The student lounge that once faced toward the mall has been replaced by offices with smaller windows, which creates a disconnect between the interior collective spaces and the campus, leaving them underutilized and without the lively social quality the lounge once had.

took place in this building. Here, students would meet for meals, socialize in the Rathskellar lounge or the bowling ally located in the basement, or gather for a lecture or group study session in the student lounge. The facility rounded out its offerings with a chapel for worship, a bookstore, and office space for student groups. All of these spaces were organized around a two-story courtyard allowing diffused natural light to pass through the building both at ground level and the basement level. Large expanses of glass in the student lounge area faced the mall, allowing a generous visual connection between indoor and outdoor activities unprecedented on the campus today (fig. 6). And an outdoor gathering area between the building and Ely Hall provided an inviting outdoor gathering space.

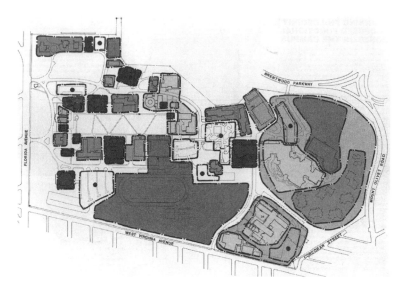

Figure 7.1. Campus Functional-Use Zones map prior to the plan to consolidate similar uses.

Late Twentieth-Century Master Planning:
Seeds of Separation

From the late 1970s through the 1990s, the patterns of student life changed significantly as a result of continued expansion and the decision to consolidate functional uses, such as student housing, academic activities, and administrative services to achieve greater operational efficiency. During this era, student housing, with the exception of Peet Hall, was concentrated around Hanson Plaza on the north side of Lincoln Circle, yet the Student Union Building remained in its place on the mall. Foster Auditorium was added to Ely Hall, effectively eliminating the outdoor gathering area to the south of the Student Union Building that was once one of the liveliest collective spaces on campus. A new field house was constructed on the east side of Lincoln Circle. The Merrill Learning Center was built within the landscaped area of the mall, and administrative offices were consolidated within the historic portion of the campus, far from the majority of academic spaces and student housing.

From a planner's view, these changes achieved the objective of consolidating uses, as one can see when comparing the existing and proposed functional-use maps from the 1975 master plan in figures 7.1 and 7.2.

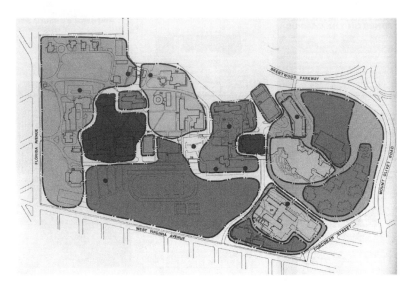

Figure 7.2. Proposed Campus Functional-Use Zone map showing the consolidated uses. The green area indicates housing, and the red zones indicate student-services areas. Note how these areas have been separated across the campus.

But in terms of the experience of student life, the changes dispersed daily activities across the campus, thus weakening the lively social fabric. With wide distances to travel between daily activities, individuals naturally tend to limit their trips across campus only to those that are essential. In the past, by contrast, it was only a few steps to the Student Union Building where one could go for a chance meeting with friends. The fact that spaces for student activities were so remote from student residences only served to discourage some students from participating in student organizations.

As Gallaudet's enrollment expanded in the 1970s and 1980s, it was necessary to construct new facilities at the outer reaches of Lincoln Circle, and they drew a stark dividing line between these buildings and the rest of the campus. Hanson Plaza, the campus residential zone, was the most extreme example of the sense of separation this situation created. Located on the north side of Lincoln Circle and north of—or with respect to the rest of the campus, "behind"—Hall Memorial Building, the plaza and the dormitory buildings surrounding it were separated from the rest of the campus. They became a world of their own. Furthermore the area lacked a cohesive architectural or landscape theme to give it a distinctive sense of place or even a connection with the fine architectural heritage of the older portions of the campus, adding to the sense of isolation and disorientation experienced at Hanson Plaza.

Also during this era, the Student Union Building underwent several renovations and was expanded to include the Student Academic Center. Architects and planners making these changes attempted to design a facility that it would encourage social interaction, but with the broader deployment of campus activities they could only meet with limited success. Combined, the new Student Academic Center and the Student Union Building are the heart of campus life today, with a wide mix of uses, such as classrooms, assembly halls, and a computer lab, in close proximity with a host of other collective uses, such as the popular lunch spot, the Marketplace; the Rathskellar lounge; the post office; and the book store (refer to fig. 6). But these are mostly daytime uses, making the complex a lively place and popular gathering spot during the day, with levels of activity dissipating late in the afternoon. The once active outdoor plaza now has no direct access into the Student Union Building, leaving it underutilized even in good weather. The Gallaudet campus today is a place to look at and move through rather than to be *in* as, perhaps, it once was.

Deaf Space: Building a New Campus of Connection

We can learn from the past, although there are so many variables in the complex relationship between human behavior and the environment that it can be difficult to predict the exact outcome of what is conceived on the drawing board. For this reason, it is critical that architects and planners engage the community early in any design process, particularly when designing spaces for those of a different culture, as is case at Gallaudet.

The new Sorenson Language and Communication Center, which began to be designed in the spring of 2005, reflects a Gallaudet University commitment to an inclusive process that stands to significantly change the way new campus facilities are conceived. Drawing upon the wisdom and insights of Deaf people and the future Deaf inhabitants of the building, this approach aims to create an aesthetic that emerges out of the unique ways Deaf people inhabit the world (fig. 8). With this shift the university hopes to realize its vision to make the Gallaudet campus a truly Deaf place. The university also plans to renovate the Clerc Hall dormitory. Both projects will showcase Deaf architectural principles and, taken together, will constitute an important step toward reconnecting

Figure 8. Architect's sketch of the proposed campus gathering area between the new Sorenson Language and Communication Center and the Student Academic Center.

the residential and academic portions of the campus. In so doing, they will recreate the social heart of the campus.

Beyond these projects, developers are planning to revitalize the local neighborhood, beginning with the redevelopment of the Capital City Market to the west of the campus. By providing design input, the Gallaudet community can be a leading force for smart growth and planning of the area—bringing new opportunities, greater visibility, and an increased presence to Gallaudet.

The university can become a model Deaf place where students' Deaf identity is affirmed. It can become a place where the Deaf community will feel at home and at the same time demonstrate to the larger society a new way of seeing space and of designing a more sensitive environment that is all about openness, light, and fostering a deep connection to others.

Notes

1. Benjamin Bahan, "Memoir Upon the Formation of a Visual Variety of the Human Race," *Deaf Studies Today* 1 (2004): 26.

2. O. R. George and Associates, *The Gallaudet College Facilities Master Plan* (Washington, D.C.: O. R. George and Associates, 1972), 16.

3. Olmsted, Vaux & Co., *Columbia Institution for the Deaf and Dumb, Plan of the Buildings and Grounds* (New York: Olmsted, Vaux & Co, 1866), 3.

4. Edward Miner Gallaudet, *History of the College for the Deaf 1857–1907* (Washington, D.C.: Gallaudet College Press, 1983), 19.

5. United States National Park Service, *National Register of Historic Places* (Washington, D.C.: Government Printing Office, 2000); Robert Harmon, *Victorian Gothic Style in American Architecture: A Brief Style Guide* (New York: Vance Bibliographies, 1983), 10.

6. Nancy Tomes, *The Art of Asylum-Keeping: Thomas Story Kirkbride and the Origins of American Psychiatry* (Philadelphia: University of Pennsylvania Press, 1994), 35.

7. Jack Gannon, *The Gallaudet Almanac: 1974* (Washington, D.C.: Gallaudet College Alumni Association, 1974), 26.

8. Marian Moffett, Lawrence Wodehouse, and Michael Fazio, *A World History of Architecture* (Columbus: McGraw-Hill, 2003), 521.

12

DPN and the Evolution
of the Gallaudet Presidency

I. King Jordan

Editors' Introduction

I. King Jordan was Gallaudet University's first deaf president and the first person whose presidency resulted from political actions by Gallaudet's constituencies. In the spring of 1988, campuswide protests and days of public demonstrations involving students, faculty, staff, alumni, and others caused the newly named president to resign one week after her appointment was announced. The Board of Trustees then elected Jordan, a previous finalist for the position, to succeed her.

The article below is Jordan's personal account of his presidency of Gallaudet from 1988 through 2006. He discusses the usual concerns of college presidents, such as academic quality, fund raising, and construction, but he also emphasizes how the protest, called Deaf President Now, changed the Gallaudet presidency. In particular, he argues that after 1988 the Gallaudet president came to be seen as a representative of both the university itself and the wider deaf community in the United States and throughout the world. Jordan concludes by discussing his vision of what Gallaudet should be and the steps he took to bring his vision to fruition, and he comments briefly on the 2006 protests surrounding the selection of Jane K. Fernandes as president-elect.

I AM NOT A HISTORIAN. I think of history as "stories" of what happened in the past. What we know today about the past depends a lot on who told the stories. Johnnetta Cole, when she was president at Spelman College, reminded us that his-story is probably very different from what it

Edward Miner Gallaudet, 1883

would be if it were her-story. Much of what I will say here is obviously my-story.

During the first 120 years of its existence, Gallaudet University was led by only four presidents. In the next four years, there were four more. The eighth president was named by the Gallaudet Board of Trustees after an historic protest known as Deaf President Now or DPN. Reading about Gallaudet's presidents while preparing this chapter was a fascinating journey into the university's history. I cannot possibly do justice to Gallaudet's presidents in this brief chapter, but I can introduce them and share some stories.

Edward Miner Gallaudet: 1864–1910

Edward Miner Gallaudet, the first president, was the son of Thomas Hopkins Gallaudet, founder of the American School for the Deaf. In 1857 Amos Kendall hired Edward Miner Gallaudet to head his small school in Washington, D.C., the Columbia Institution for the Instruction of the Deaf and Dumb and Blind. He was just twenty years old, with fewer than two years teaching experience at the American School. Some people were skeptical because of his youth, so Kendall told him to bring his mother with him. Thus, Sophia Fowler Gallaudet, who was deaf and fluent in ASL, came to Washington with her son, to serve as matron of the school.

Gallaudet shared his father's dream of opening a college for deaf students and proposed a bill to the U.S. Congress that would authorize the Columbia Institution to grant college degrees. Some members of Congress did not think deaf people were capable of a college education; Amos Kendall had doubts too. But President Abraham Lincoln supported the bill, and when Congress passed it in 1964, he signed the bill into law. Kendall then appointed Gallaudet, then just twenty-seven years old, as the college's first president. In 1864 Gallaudet overcame doubts about whether deaf people could or should receive a college education; 124 years later, in 1988, DPN overcame doubts about whether a deaf person could or should lead the university.

As president, Gallaudet faced the same challenges that all the college presidents have dealt with since: academic standards and communication. Throughout his presidency, he insisted that all classes meet appropriate college-level standards. Despite the decision at the Milan Congress in 1880 that the best way to teach deaf children was through exclusive use of speech and lipreading, Gallaudet believed that deaf people should also be able to use sign language. Consequently, the college community continued to use both sign language and spoken language. It was during Gallaudet's tenure that the Board of Trustees voted to name the college in honor of his father.

Percival Hall: 1910–1945

Percival Hall, the second president of Gallaudet College, graduated from Harvard at the age of nineteen and intended to become an engineer. A visit to Kendall Green with a Harvard roommate triggered an interest in teaching deaf children, and he enrolled in the Gallaudet "normal class" (as teacher education programs in the United States were called at that time). After teaching at the New York School for the Deaf, he returned to the college as Edward Miner Gallaudet's secretary, a position with responsibilities much like a chief of staff today. He also taught Latin and math, and later became director of the Normal Training Department. When Gallaudet decided to retire, he selected Hall as his successor.

During Hall's presidency, the college developed a liberal arts curriculum with a strong focus on scientific and cultural studies. Hall also estab-

Percival Hall

lished a research department that studied the deaf population. He led Gallaudet successfully through World War I, the Great Depression, and World War II. It is fair to say that no president faced greater budgetary challenges than Hall, particularly during the Depression, when Gallaudet's appropriations were drastically reduced.

Leonard M. Elstad: 1945–1969

Leonard M. Elstad, the third president, enrolled in Gallaudet's normal program knowing nothing about deaf people, just as Percival Hall had done. After completing his studies, he taught English and history at Gallaudet and, within a year, became principal of Kendall School. He left

Leonard Elstad

Gallaudet in 1925 to become assistant principal of the Wright Oral School in New York City. Twenty years later he returned to Gallaudet College as president.

Like Edward Miner Gallaudet, Elstad had a strong commitment to high academic standards. He recruited George Detmold from a postdoctoral program at Columbia Teachers College and appointed him dean. Detmold led Gallaudet through curriculum reform that made possible initial accreditation by the Middle States Association of Colleges and Schools (MSA) in 1957.

During the 1950s, a substantial increase in government funding supported an ambitious multimillion-dollar building program and an increase in enrollment from approximately two hundred to seven hundred students, including more international students. Elstad's interest in international deaf students continued in his retirement. Working with Rotary International, he established the International Deaf Educational Assistance Fund so that deaf students from other countries could come to

Edward Merrill

Gallaudet to obtain a college education. This is now among Gallaudet's largest endowed scholarship funds.

Edward C. Merrill: 1969–1983

Edward C. Merrill, the fourth president, began his college teaching career as an English instructor at Asheville Biltmore College in North Carolina. Later, he moved to a number of other teaching and administrative positions and was Dean of the College of Education at the University of Tennessee when he was appointed Gallaudet president in 1969.

During Merrill's presidency, the Model Secondary School for the Deaf

W. Lloyd Johns

(MSSD) was established. MSSD soon received accreditation by MSA and also by what is now the Conference of Educational Administrators of Schools and Programs for the Deaf (CEASD). Legislation authorizing Kendall Demonstration Elementary School (KDES) was also enacted during Merrill's tenure, and both schools moved into new buildings.

Merrill inaugurated numerous public service programs during his presidency, including the International Center on Deafness, the National Center for Law and the Deaf, and four Gallaudet regional centers. The Gallaudet Research Institute was established, and new graduate programs were added. Plans were also made to accommodate an increase in the deaf student population because of the rubella epidemic of the mid-1960s.

During the search for Merrill's successor, some members of the deaf community expressed the view that it was time for a deaf president at Gallaudet. Merrill also promoted this perspective, but there was limited support for the idea at that time, even among deaf people.

W. Lloyd Johns: 1983–1984

Before becoming the fifth president of Gallaudet, W. Lloyd Johns had more than 30 years' experience in education and educational administration. At the time of his appointment, he had been president of California State University, Sacramento, for five years. He resigned the Gallaudet presidency after several months, before he had been inaugurated.

Jerry C. Lee: 1984–1987

When Johns resigned, the Board of Trustees appointed Jerry C. Lee, Gallaudet's vice president of administration and business, as interim president. A national search for a new president was initiated, but within months the board canceled the search and appointed Lee as Gallaudet's sixth president. During Lee's tenure, Gallaudet College was granted university status by an act of Congress in October 1986. The same year, the School of Management and a master's degree in mental health counseling were established, and a fifth regional center opened.

When Lee announced his plans to resign as president in 1987, the desire for a deaf president gained strength. There were more deaf people with Ph.D.'s and many in the deaf community expressed the view that it was definitely time for Gallaudet to have a deaf president. Still, others—even some in the deaf community—questioned whether deaf people were capable of leading a university. The Board of Trustees established a presidential search committee, chaired by a deaf person, and comprised of board members, faculty, staff, and students. The job description contained language encouraging deaf people to apply, and many did. Of the six semifinalists, three were deaf and three were hearing. Of the three finalists, two were deaf and one was hearing. Expectations were very high that the board would select one of the deaf candidates. Instead, the board appointed Elisabeth Zinser, who was assistant chancellor at the University of North Carolina, Greensboro.

Jerry Lee

Elisabeth Zinser: 1988

Elisabeth Zinser was the seventh president of Gallaudet from shortly after her selection by the Board of Trustees on March 6, 1988, until her resignation on March 11, 1988. During that time she was unable to enter the Gallaudet campus, because students—with support from alumni, faculty, staff, advocacy organizations, and friends of the university— protested the board's decision to appoint a hearing person who had never worked with deaf people and could not sign, when there were qualified deaf finalists.

DPN (Deaf President Now), as the movement to block Zinser's appointment was called, was much more than a protest. It was a powerful and effective social movement; in fact, a social revolution for the civil rights of deaf people. Within a few days Zinser recognized this, and in her resignation statement she said, "I am resigning because of this extraordinary social movement of deaf people, not to the demands of

Elisabeth Ann Zinser

the protesters." She stated that she made her decision "to pave the way for the civil rights movement to progress."

After Zinser's resignation the Board of Trustees met again and appointed me, one of the two deaf finalists, as Gallaudet's eighth president. Jane Bassett Spilman, chair of the board, resigned, and Phil Bravin, a deaf member of the board, was elected chair. DPN's success in achieving the appointment of Gallaudet's first deaf president and first deaf board chair, along with the board's decision that going forward 51 percent of the board must be deaf, was strong testimony to the abilities of deaf people. Empowerment of deaf people achieved new heights—and that was just the beginning of dramatic changes.

I. King Jordan: 1988–2006

Appointing a deaf president to lead the university in 1988 was the beginning of a transformation of the Gallaudet presidency. Social movements need symbols. A deaf president at Gallaudet University symbolized to

I. King Jordan

deaf children and adults everywhere that their dreams and aspirations could be achieved.

I have a story from very early in my presidency that illustrates this point. I had been president for a few weeks when I was invited to the Rhode Island School for the Deaf. Because I was so recently in the news, and with DPN being fresh in everyone's memory, a lot of newspaper reporters, TV reporters, and cameras were there—it was quite a show. During a tour of the school, I visited a preschool classroom where all the children had been carefully arranged in a semicircle on the floor. There was an empty, preschool-sized chair in front for me to sit down and talk to them. As I began signing to the group, a little boy got up, walked over to me, looked closely at my hearing aid, and put his elbow on my shoulder. He stayed there the whole time I was sitting down. I'll never forget that day.

He was about five. He almost surely did not know what it meant to be a deaf president, but he knew that the superintendent was treating me with respect and the reporters were busy taking pictures. Most important, he knew I was deaf. He knew I was like him. I do not know what goes on in the heads of little children, but I am willing to bet that he recognized that I was like him, that I was important, and that some day he would be too.

Because I became president of Gallaudet in a very public way, I also became a national and international spokesperson for people who are deaf and hard of hearing and for people with disabilities. It is no coincidence that Congress passed and the president signed the Americans with Disabilities Act (ADA) shortly after DPN. The highly publicized demand for a deaf president gave me the credibility to testify as a lead witness before Congress in support of ADA. Key Congressional leaders, including Steny Hoyer of Maryland in the House of Representatives and Tom Harkin of Iowa in the Senate, and former president George H. W. Bush recognized the key role of DPN in passing ADA.

Clearly, DPN had a huge impact both inside and outside the gates of Gallaudet. During DPN, deaf people throughout the world watched and celebrated, but they often watched from afar. In 1989, Gallaudet hosted Deaf Way, the first international conference that celebrated the history, language, art, culture, and empowerment of deaf people. Registration was in the thousands, far exceeding expectations. Deaf people came to Washington, D.C., from all over the world; they learned, were empowered, and returned to their home communities and countries to make changes to improve the lives of deaf people. In 2002, Gallaudet did it again, with about ten thousand people attending Deaf Way II.

Since DPN, the deaf community and its organizations have been more involved with the university. Many see Gallaudet as the center of the deaf community and deaf culture. Gallaudet does have a large role in this regard, but that is not its primary role. Gallaudet must also maintain and strengthen its focus on its educational mission, the mission mandated by Congress. The growing interest, involvement, and sense of ownership that the deaf community has for Gallaudet must be balanced with the recognition that the university's primary mission is to provide an exemplary education for its students. In my inaugural address in 1988, titled "Let Us Begin . . . Together," I said, "excellence has always been at the heart of our mission." My vision as president was to ensure that everything the university did supported that mission.

Academic excellence and student success were among our highest priorities. In an address to the Gallaudet community in November 2005, I stressed that, together, we at Gallaudet were changing the world for deaf people. The work we did together to ensure student success was essential because it was our students who were the future for deaf people. Did we achieve academic excellence? Did we achieve student success? We certainly made great strides toward these goals. In my 2005 address I reflected on some of the university's achievements during my presidency. We graduated students who are now attorneys, financial advisors and analysts, business owners, corporate leaders, scientists, faculty members at Gallaudet and elsewhere, Hollywood actors, and elected members of parliament. Truly, the list is almost endless.

A few highlights of achievements during the "DPN presidency" demonstrate its intentions and success. When I became president, about one-third of new freshmen qualified for credit-bearing English courses. That number grew to two-thirds of new freshmen. For the 2004–2005 academic year, the persistence rate for returning first year students was 75 percent, compared with 60 percent ten years earlier. Fall semester 2005, 351 new degree-seeking undergraduate students enrolled, the largest number since the rubella period in the early 1980s. The honors program strengthened and grew. There was a significant increase in the number of students who wrote honors capstone theses and graduated with departmental and university honors.

Gallaudet became a leader in the use of technology to support its educational programs. When I left office, Gallaudet's technology use was approximately double the national average, with 75 percent of courses using "Gallaudet Dynamic Online Collaboration" (GDOC) and Blackboard. A "new president's" grant from the Mellon Foundation allowed for training that led to a core group of faculty savvy in the use of technology. Not only did these faculty then train others, but they created an environment in which the use of technology in teaching became the norm.

Gallaudet engaged in extensive scholarly activities during the DPN presidency. One example is a multimillion-dollar grant the university received in 2006 from the National Science Foundation (NSF) for a visual language and visual learning center (VL2). VL2 is one of six Science of Learning Centers (SLC) funded by NSF. VL2 brings together deaf and hearing researchers and educators from a variety of disciplines and institutions to study how language and literacy develop in deaf individuals. Major research universities were among the competitors for these funds, so this was an outstanding achievement for Gallaudet. Imagine the implications of the VL2 research for the education of deaf children.

A successful university also must have an informed and involved board of trustees. After DPN, the Gallaudet board also evolved. A strong relationship developed between the board and the campus, characterized by open and honest communication. Board members worked with the Association of Governing Boards to ensure that the board's role and function were consistent with best practices in higher education and supported strategic planning efforts. Board members became more visible on campus and participated in a number of shared governance workshops that involved the campus community.

Exemplary education requires highly qualified faculty and staff and that requires competitive salaries. When I became president, salaries lagged significantly behind those at comparable colleges and universities. During my tenure, Gallaudet's faculty salaries reached parity with those institutions.

In addition, a new compensation system was developed for staff that improved wages and benefits. Gallaudet established a unique program, the president's fellows program, to encourage deaf individuals to pursue terminal degrees and to provide them with support to help them do so. The president's fellows program has been successful in "growing our own" deaf faculty and surely will lead to a significant increase in the number of deaf faculty members holding terminal degrees.

A review of staff characteristics shows a much more diverse workforce at Gallaudet since DPN. The percentage of employees from traditionally underrepresented groups increased from 30 percent to 38 percent, and the percentage of deaf and hard of hearing employees from 25 percent to 41 percent. More striking, the percentage of deaf and hard of hearing faculty/teachers increased from 14 percent to 44 percent, and the percentage of deaf and hard of hearing administrators increased from 19 percent to 40 percent.

The university president also has responsibility for the financial resources needed to support the university's mission and to carry out its strategic goals. Looking back, it is ironic that those who thought the university was not ready for a deaf president focused mainly on concerns about Congressional and donor relations. As president, I developed strong relationships with Congress for our annual appropriations and with corporations, foundations, and individual donors to secure other significant gifts. Reflecting on my presidency, I consider that to be one of my strengths. During my presidency, the endowment grew from less than $10 million to more than $175 million. Gallaudet's first capital campaign raised $40 million to fund scholarships, programs, and construction costs for the student academic center. All of these efforts have been essential to maintaining a balanced budget and keeping Gallaudet debt free.

The university's facilities must support its mission. The Student Academic Center was designed so that academic and student life programs were housed in the same building, fostering integration of these aspects of the students' college experiences. At the time of its design and construction, it was so unusual to combine student support and academic programs that the architects won a significant award for the innovation.

The Sorenson Language and Communication Center (SLCC) will be a world-class teaching, research, and service center on deaf people's language, culture, and community. The building and the programs located within it will foster communication and collaboration among disciplines that traditionally work independently. The building is intended to be "visucentric," designed with input from and for deaf people, who process language and other information with their eyes. Corporate and foundation funding from the Sorenson Corporation and the Sorenson Legacy Foundation, as well as from other corporations, foundations, and individuals is providing the financial support to make this building possible.

The Kellogg Conference Hotel (KCH) at Gallaudet was made possible by a $12 million grant from the Kellogg Foundation. Many Gallaudet sponsored conferences and meetings take place at KCH, as do conferences and meetings by outside groups. The Gallaudet Board meets there and the mental health center is located there. The Bistro, an informal restaurant on the main floor, provides a place for people to eat and socialize. KCH is on the site of the former Kendall Division II School, the segregated elementary school for black deaf children. The building was erected shortly after the 1952 court ruling that ordered Kendall to enroll black deaf children from the District of Columbia who previously had been transported to a school in Maryland. A plaque recognizing this hangs on the back of the hotel sign, opposite the Bistro's glass windows. Visitors often comment on the sign. Kendall School became integrated soon after the U.S. Supreme Court ruled against segregated schools in 1954.

I am not proud that Kendall school was once segregated. I am not proud that it took a Supreme Court decision for Kendall to educate all deaf children in the same classrooms. I am proud that fifteen years before the Tuskegee airmen were awarded the Congressional gold medal, one of them was the invited speaker at a president's scholar's dinner on Gallaudet's campus.

When I announced in September of 2005 that I would step down as president, I spoke of the unique spirit at Gallaudet, the spirit that has made Gallaudet successful. I recalled a comment made by the MSA evaluation team in their report in 2001.

> Many American universities these days spend a great deal of time fabricating reasons to declare themselves unique. Gallaudet university, the MSA team is convinced, truly is unique . . . every college these days has a mission statement, Gallaudet actually has a mission.

In my 1988 inaugural address, I linked excellence to "reach[ing] out to people of any age, with any degree of hearing loss. People who sign, people who speak, and people who both sign and speak. People who were born deaf and people who became deaf later in life. People who are not deaf but who will contribute to the lives of deaf individuals." In 2004, the planning document, "New Directions for Academic Affairs," reaffirmed the substance of my inaugural statement, stating in direction No. 3: "Gallaudet University is the university of choice for an increasingly diverse pool of potential students who are deaf and hard of hearing, and for hearing students who want to prepare for careers in the deaf community."

"New Directions" represented the voice of the Gallaudet community speaking to what it considered to be important for Gallaudet's future. The Academic Affairs Planning Committee—a committee of diverse faculty, staff, and students established by the provost—spent two years gathering data and listening to the perspectives of the Gallaudet community expressed during focus groups, stakeholder meetings, online discussions, and two enrichment days. A draft document went through many revisions until the committee was satisfied that it represented the perspectives of most of the Gallaudet community. The Board of Trustees endorsed the final document enthusiastically, and in May 2005, approved elevating direction No. 3 and the other four directions to Gallaudet University strategic goals.

The "New Directions" document supported my belief that it is possible to remain true to Gallaudet's valued traditions, to be a welcoming university to an increasingly diverse population of students, and to support students in exploring their identity as deaf people. Gallaudet's rich cultural heritage can be preserved and the study and appreciation of deaf culture, deaf history, and American Sign Language can be supported campuswide. A range of services tailored to the needs of individual students can be provided to make the university's curriculum, programs, and facilities accessible while students with little knowledge of the culture, language, and history are acquiring it.

The Gallaudet spirit I mentioned earlier suffered during the protest over the selection of Jane K. Fernandes as Gallaudet's ninth president. The community was divided and there was a great deal of pain. Healing of the divisions will take time and will require a commitment to good will on the part of everyone and willingness to work cooperatively and respectfully together to restore the strong sense of community which was present before the protest. Gallaudet has a solid foundation on which to build, but it is too soon to assess fully how the protest and decisions now being made will affect the university and its direction.

DPN had a major impact on Gallaudet University and on the presidency. Before DPN, few people outside the deaf community had heard of Gallaudet. Regularly, when I attended a conference away from Washington, D.C., or a social event in the metropolitan area before DPN, I would be asked where I worked. When I responded that I taught at Gallaudet, the response was often "Gall-a-what?" Gallaudet was not an active participant in higher education associations or a full partner in Washington, D.C., higher education groups. Gallaudet was simply not on the radar screens of people outside the deaf community.

After DPN, Gallaudet became a very active member of higher education organizations. As a full member of the Consortium of Universities of the Washington Metropolitan Area and the Washington Research Library Consortium (WRLC), many benefits accrued to Gallaudet students and faculty. Full membership also allowed the president to serve on the policy and decision-making boards of these organizations. I was a respected and influential member of these boards. Twice, I was chair of both the Consortium and the WRLC.

Before DPN, the Gallaudet president was highly regarded by administrators, students, and staff at schools and programs for deaf students, but not well known in higher education. The president served as a spokesman for issues related to deaf education and as an advocate for deaf children and adults. After DPN, the president was catapulted into the role of national and international spokesperson for all people with disabilities. When I became president, it was almost as though I had two jobs. None of the presidents before DPN had the dual role of CEO and spokesperson for people with disabilities. I believe that all of the deaf presidents from now on will—or should. This is a key component of the evolution of the Gallaudet presidency.

Before DPN, the Gallaudet president did virtually no fund raising. After DPN, the president essentially became "fund raiser in chief" and was very successful. One measure of this success is that the interest alone from Gallaudet's current endowment, which is used to support operations and programs, is greater than the total endowment before DPN.

Most people no longer say, "Gall-a-what." Now, almost everyone knows Gallaudet. A search of the Internet will find thousands of citations after 1988, and few before. Nearly all of the citations before the protest in 2006 were positive. There was even a Starbucks coffee mug that included Gallaudet University as one of the important landmarks in Washington, D.C.

DPN had a major impact on the Gallaudet presidency and on Gallaudet. During its first 150 years Gallaudet achieved greatness through the vision and dedication of its presidents and countless other people. I have spent more than half my life at Gallaudet University—as a student, faculty member, department chair, dean, and president. I am, and always will be, passionate about Gallaudet. My hope is that the next generation of leaders will build on the foundation of Gallaudet as an educational institution committed to excellence and inclusiveness, with strategic goals that steer its course into a future where people everywhere continue to see Gallaudet as a beacon of hope.

Contributors

Benjamin Bahan
Ben Bahan is professor of Deaf Studies at Gallaudet University. He has published dozens of articles related to the field of Deaf Studies and ASL linguistics and coauthored such books as *Journey into the DEAF-WORLD* and *The Syntax of American Sign Language*. He prefers to be known as an ASL storyteller and has produced and appeared in several videos.

Hansel Bauman
Hansel Bauman is a San Francisco–based architect and planner currently leading the Deaf Space Project at Gallaudet University. Bauman is teaching a course in Deaf space and architecture at the university while also developing the Gallaudet Deaf Campus Design Guide. He received his master's degree in architecture from the Southern California Institute of Architecture in Los Angles, where he later served as a design studio instructor. Over the past twenty years his work has explored the interrelationship between cultural-identity architecture through work in the United States, Europe, and Asia.

David de Lorenzo
From 1980 to 1988, David de Lorenzo was University archivist and head of special collections at Gallaudet University. From 1988 to 1997, he held the position of curator of manuscripts and archives at Harvard Law School until his appointment as the France-Merrick Library director at the Maryland Historical Society (1997–2001). Since 2001, he has been associate director and head of technical services, the Bancroft Library, University of California, Berkeley, and holds the academic rank of librarian with distinguished status. He is also an adjunct professor at San Jose State University's School of Library and Information Science, where he teaches courses on archives and records management.

Noah D. Drezner

Noah D. Drezner is assistant professor of Higher Education in the Department of Education Leadership, Higher Education, and International Education at the University of Maryland, College Park. He holds a B.A. from the University of Rochester, an M.A. from the University of Pennsylvania, a graduate certificate in nonprofit leadership from Roberts Wesleyan College, and a Ph.D. from the University of Pennsylvania. Drezner's research interests include philanthropy and fund raising as it pertains to higher education. He is an associate editor of the forthcoming book, *Philanthropy, Fundraising, and Volunteerism in Higher Education*.

Brian H. Greenwald

Brian H. Greenwald is associate professor of history at Gallaudet University. He was the chairperson for the conference "150 Years on Kendall Green: Celebrating Deaf History and Gallaudet," from which these articles are drawn. Greenwald's B.A. is from Gallaudet, and he was one of the first two President's Fellows at Gallaudet University. He received his Ph.D. in history from the George Washington University in 2006. His articles have appeared in *The Deaf History Reader* and *Genetics, Disability, and Deafness*.

I. King Jordan

I. King Jordan served as president of Gallaudet University from 1988 until his retirement in 2006. The university's first deaf president, he earned a B.A. in psychology from Gallaudet in 1970. The following year he earned an M.A., and in 1973 a Ph.D., both in psychology and both from the University of Tennessee. A former professor of psychology and dean of the School of Arts and Sciences at Gallaudet, Jordan also has been a research fellow at Donaldson's School for the Deaf in Edinburgh, Scotland; an exchange scholar at Jagiellonian University in Krakow, Poland; and a visiting scholar and lecturer at schools in Paris, Toulouse, and Marseille, France. He holds eleven honorary degrees and is the recipient of numerous awards, including the Presidential Citizen's Medal, the Washingtonian of the Year Award, the James L. Fisher Award from the Council for Advancement and Support of Education (CASE), the Larry Stewart Award from the American Psychological Association, and the Distinguished Leadership Award from the National Association for Community Leadership. Jordan is president emeritus of Gallaudet University.

Sandra Jowers-Barber

Sandra Jowers-Barber is assistant professor of history at the University of the District of Columbia in Washington, D.C. She teaches courses in United States history, African American history, and women's history and directs the Oral History Center. A native of Atlantic City, New Jersey, she holds a doctorate in United States history from Howard University. Her research interest is disability history with a focus on the African American deaf community. She is a member of the American Historical Association, the National Black Deaf Advocates, the Association for the Study of African American Life and History, and the Association of Black Women Historians.

Marieta Joyner

Marieta Joyner holds a B.A. in African American studies/psychology, an M.A. in sociology from the University of Massachusetts at Boston, and a Ph.D. in history from the University of Massachusetts at Amherst. Her area of research focuses on African American studies, culture, and ethnic studies. She has taught at the University of Massachusetts, Boston and Amherst, Roxbury Community College, and Brandeis University. She has several journal publications and is currently working on a book about the education of Deaf African Americans after the Civil War to the 1954 historic *Brown v. Board of Education* decision.

Christopher Krentz

Christopher Krentz is assistant professor of English and American Sign Language and director of the American Sign Language Program at the University of Virginia. He is author of *Writing Deafness: The Hearing Line in Nineteenth-Century American Literature* and editor of *A Mighty Change: An Anthology of Deaf American Writing, 1816–1864*.

Christopher A. N. Kurz

Christopher A. N. Kurz holds a B.S. in mathematics from the Rochester Institute of Technology and both an M.A. in deaf education and a Ph.D. in foundations of education from the University of Kansas. His dissertation concerned mathematics education for deaf students during the nineteenth century. Deaf himself, Kurz is assistant professor in the instructional faculty at the Rochester Institute of Technology, specializing in mathematics education.

James M. McPherson
James M. McPherson is the author of over a dozen books. In 1989, he received the Pulitzer Prize for *Battle Cry of Freedom: The Civil War Era*. In 1998, his book, *For Cause and Comrades: Why Men Fought in the Civil War*, received the Lincoln Prize. McPherson was named the "Jefferson Lecturer in the Humanities" in by the National Endowment of the Humanities in 2000, the highest honor the federal government "bestows for distinguished intellectual achievement in the humanities." McPherson is past president of the American Historical Association. His latest publication is *This Mighty Scourge: Perspectives on the Civil War*. He is the George Henry Davis '86 Professor Emeritus of Princeton University.

Michael J. Olson
Michael J. Olson graduated from Gallaudet University with a B.A. in history in 1979. He did graduate work in library science at the University of Maryland. He began employment in the Gallaudet University Archives in 1981, where he processes many personal papers of Deaf individuals and organizations. He has given numerous lectures about the Gallaudet archives and tours of Gallaudet's archives facilities to students, alumni, individual researchers, and groups. He currently is a Gallaudet University archives technician as well as a member of Deaf History International and the State Historical Society of North Dakota.

Lindsey M. Parker
Lindsey M. Parker is a doctoral student in women's history at the Ohio State University. She received an M.A. in Deaf Studies from Gallaudet University in 2005 and previously earned a B.A. in sign language studies from Madonna University. She has contributed to *The Encyclopedia of American Disability History* and *At the Intersections: Deaf Studies Meets Disability Studies*.

Ronald E. Sutcliffe
Ronald E. Sutcliffe graduated from Gallaudet College in 1959, and he holds a Ph.D. from the University of Maryland. He has served as professor in the Department of Business Administration and dean of the School of Management at Gallaudet. Currently, he is the executive director of the National Deaf Business Institute and dean emeritus at Gallaudet.

John Vickrey Van Cleve
John Vickrey Van Cleve taught history at Gallaudet University for thirty-one years. He also served in various administrative capacities, including

chair of the history department. He was an executive director in Administration and Finance when he retired. Van Cleve is the author of numerous articles about deaf history and culture, coauthor of *A Place of Their Own: Creating the Deaf Community in America*; editor-in-chief of the *Gallaudet Encyclopedia of Deaf People and Deafness*; editor of *Genetics, Disability, and Deafness, Deaf History Unveiled: Interpretations from the New Scholarship*; and *The Deaf History Reader*; and coeditor of *The Study of Signed Languages: Essays in Honor of William C. Stokoe*. He is now professor emeritus at Gallaudet University.

Index

Page numbers in italics denote illustrations or photographs.

accreditation, 132–37, 143
ADA (Americans with Disabilities Act),
    147–48, 181
African Americans: double consciousness,
    13, 16–17; financial support for higher
    education, 147–50; historical parallels to
    Deaf world, 6, 10; oppression, 2, 7, 65–
    66, 80–82, 113–29, 184
alumni donations, 143, 146–49
American Civil War, 1–2, 5–7
American Revolution, 2–3
Ames, Blanche, 103, *104*
Anderson-Thompkins, Sibby, 147
Andrews, Francis, 117
Anglo-conformity, 8
antebellum era, 4
architecture, 154–68, 184
Arms, H. P., 35
ASD (American School for the Deaf), 25, 95
ASL (American Sign Language), 136
assimilation, 7–10
audism: Deaf double consciousness and,
    13–20; in E. M. Gallaudet's leadership,
    33–34, 36–44; historical influences, 7–8;
    low academic expectations and, 134–36

Bahan, Benjamin, 154–69, 189
Ballin, Albert, 40, 42
Bauman, Hansel, 154–69, 189
Black, Ella Florence, 95
Board of Trustees, 172, 177, 178–79, 183
Booth, Edmund, 35

Brown, Thomas, 36
Brown v. Board of Education, 113–14, 121,
    128–29
Buff and Blue, 101–2
Burnet, John, 16, 17

Calvinism, 3–4
campus planning, *160*, 162–68, *166*
Carlin, John, 12–20, *15*, 40, 87
Chapel Hill, *158*
Civil War. *See* American Civil War
Clarke, Edward, 86
Clerc, Laurent, 3, 16, 17
Cockrell, Francis, 115
coeducation, 85–108
Cogswell, Alice, 37. *See also* monument
compensation, 183
conformity, 8
Cooke, Paul, 119, 121, 123–24
Cragin, Aaron Harrison, 65–66, 67–68
Craig, Douglas, 65–82, *73*, *76*, *78*
Crouch, Barry, 88, 100
cultural assimilation, 7–10

Dawes, Henry L., 9
Deaf architecture, 154–68, 184
Deaf community, 100, 154–58, 181
Deaf double consciousness, 12–20
deaf education: historical influences on,
    1–11; pedagogical arguments, 50–61
Deaf President Now (DPN), 170, 172, 178–
    81, 186–87

195

Deaf space, 154, 167–68
Deaf Way conferences, 181
Declaration of Independence, 2–3
de Lorenzo, David, 22–32, 190
Detmold, George, 132–38, *133*, 174
Donohue, Joseph, 120–21
double consciousness, 12–20
Douglass, Frederick, 113
DPN (Deaf President Now), 170, 172, 178–
    81, 186–87
Draper, Amos G., *51*; about, 62n6; pedagog-
    ical arguments, 50–61; role in monu-
    ment commission, 36, 38–39, 43
Drezner, Noah D., 140–53, 190
Du Bois, W.E.B., 13, 17

Elliott, Georgia, 92, 95, 99
Elstad, Leonard, 120–21, 134, 143–44, 173–
    75, *174*

faculty members, 134–36, 183
Faculty Row, 158
Fanon, Frantz, 16
federal government: financial support, 29,
    114, 135, 141–45, 174; historical influ-
    ences on deaf education, 1–11
Fernandes, Jane K., 170, 186
financial support: alumni donations, 143,
    146–49; federal government, 29, 114,
    135, 141–45, 174; foundations, 149–50;
    fund raising, 28–29, 145–46, 183–84,
    186–87; philanthropy, 140–41, 146–47;
    for T. H. Gallaudet monument, 34–36,
    43, 44–46; tuition revenue, 144–45
Flournoy, John Jacobus, 18, 20
Flowers, Thomas, 124
Freedman's Village, 66
Freedmen's Bureau, 6
French, Daniel Chester, 35, 36–46
French Revolution, 3
Froehlich, Theodore A., 34, 35–39, 44
Frye, Rubye, 126
Fuller, Angeline, 92
fund raising. *See* financial support
Fusfeld, Irving, 136

Gallagher, Buell, 134
Gallagher Report, 134, 136
Gallaudet, Edward Miner, *24, 38, 171*; ar-
    chitectural decisions, 157–58; on coedu-
    cation, 88–108; on communication meth-
    ods, 8, 172; historical influences on,
    4–5; land expansion, 162; leadership leg-
    acy, 22–31, 32n23, 171–72; pedagogical
    arguments, 50–61; racial integration pol-
    icy, 114–16; role in monument commis-
    sion, 33–34, 36–44
Gallaudet, Sophia Fowler, 23, 30, 52, 87,
    114, 172
Gallaudet, Thomas Hopkins: about, 23, 52,
    87, 114; at ASD, 25; gratitude towards,
    18; historical influences on, 3–4; monu-
    ment to, 33–46, *41, 45*
Garfield, James A., 142
Gasman, Marybeth, 147
gender discrimination, 85–86, 88–108, *104*
Greenwald, Brian H., 190

Hairston, Ernest, 118
Hall, Percival, 77–79, 81, 134, 143, 172–73,
    173
Hanson, Agatha Tiegel, 96, 98–99, 101–2,
    105
Hanson Plaza, 165, 167
Henry, Joseph, 56–57
Hodgson, Edwin A., 38, 40
Holland, William, 125–26
housing, 88, 158, 165, *166*
Howard University, 6, 10, 144

immigration, 7–8
Indian Emancipation Act, 9
International Deaf Educational Assistance
    Fund, 174–75

Jacksonian democracy, 4–5
Johns, W. Lloyd, *176*, 177
Jordan, I. King, 146–47, 170–87, *180*,
    190–91
Jowers-Barber, Sandra, 113–31, 189
Joyner, Marieta, 65–84, 191

Kellogg Conference Hotel, 184
Kendall, Amos, 5; on Edward Miner Gal-
    laudet, 27, 28–29; as Jacksonian Demo-
    crat, 4–5; philanthropy of, 25, 87, 141
Kennedy, Lydia, 88
Kershner, Emma, 106

Krentz, Christopher, 12–21, 100, 191
Kurtz, Anna Luella, 95
Kurz, Christopher A. N., 50–64, 191

Larson, Lars M., 34
leadership, 23–28. *See also* presidency
Lee, Jerry C., 177, *178*
Leffler, Hattie A., 95–96
Life (magazine), 135
Lincoln, Abraham, 1–3, 5–6
Long, Hale, 119
Lowman, Alto, 95, 97, 99

Martin, May, 99, 101–2, 105–7
Maryland School for the Colored Blind
    and Deaf, 115–19, 125
mathematics education, 50–61
Mayfield, Minnie, 121–22
McDill, Laura, 106
McPherson, James, 1–11, 192
melting pot model, 8
Merrill, Edward C., Jr., 81, *175*, 175–77
Middle States Association of Colleges and
    Schools, 132, 137
Milan Congress (1880), 172
Milburn, Robert, 127
military academies, 144
Miller, Louise B., 116–19, 121
Miller v. D.C. Board of Education, 113, 122–
    24, 128
Missouri ex. Rel Gaines v. Canada, 123
Mitchell, Lydia, 88–89
Model Secondary School for the Deaf,
    175–76
monument (T. H. Gallaudet/A. Cogswell),
    33–46, 41, 45
Morrill Land-Grant College Act, 6
Murray, Lynne, 147
"Mute's Lament, The" (Carlin), 14–18

Nack, James, 14, 17
NAD (National Association of the Deaf),
    12
"New Directions for Academic Affairs"
    document, 185
Nierman, Florence, 119–20

Ole Jim, 91–92, 93
Olmstead, Frederick Law, 156, 158

Olson, Michael J., 33–49, 192
oralism, 7–8
O.W.L.S., 101–2, *103*

Palmer, Lewis A., 35
Parker, Lindsey M., 85–112, 192
paternalism, 33–34, 36–44, 132–36
Patterson, James W., 67–68
Peikoff, David, 146
Phillips, Mary E., 126
Phillips, Richard M., 138
Platter, Amelia, 93–94
Plessy v. Ferguson, 115
pluralism, 8, 10–11
Porter, Samuel, 101
presidency: Deaf President Now, 170, 172,
    178–81, 186–87; Edward Miner Gal-
    laudet's legacy, 22–31, 32n23, 171–72;
    historical overview, 171–87. *See also spe-
    cific presidents*
PSD (Pennsylvania School for the Deaf),
    116

racial integration, 65, 82, 114–15, 184
racial oppression: at Gallaudet University,
    65–66, 80–82, 113–29, 184; historical in-
    fluences, 2, 7
Rathskellar lounge, *164*, 167
Rich, William J., 80–81
Robinson, Robert, 126–27
Rudd, Margaret Ellen, 96, 99

Saint-Gaudens, Augustus, 42
Savoy, A. K., 116–17
Scott, James A., 119
Scott, Moses, 15
Second Great Awakening, 3–4
Settles, Clarence J., 124
Sheridan, Laura, 90–91
slavery, 2, 6
Smith, Adelaide, 88
social conformity, 8
Sorensen Language and Communication
    Center, 167, 168
Sparks, Emma, 88
sports teams, 102
statue. See monument
Stickney, William, 26–27
Stokoe, William C., 12, 135–36

Student Academic Center, *164*, 167, *168*
Student Union Building, 163–65, *164*, 167
Sutcliffe, Ronald, 132–39, 192
Sweet-Windham, Cathy, 147
Swiler, John W., 94
Szymanoskie, Annie, 88

Thornton, Bessie, 126
Tilden, Douglas, 40, 43–44
Tresch, J. F. J., 40, 43
tuition, 144–45
Turner, Job, 42

Van Cleve, John Vickrey, 88, 100, 192–93
VL2 (Visual Language and Visual Learning Center), 182

Weeks, William H., 34, 36
White, Mattie B. Haywood, 126
Wilkinson, G.C., 117
Williams, Job, 94–95
Wilson, William L., 105

Zinser, Elisabeth, 177–79, *179*